Christianity
and World Revolution

Christianity
and World Revolution

Edited by EDWIN H. RIAN

Harper & Row, Publishers

NEW YORK, EVANSTON, AND LONDON

Contents

INTRODUCTION ix
by Edwin H. Rian, *President, The Biblical Seminary*

PART I. *THE POWER STRUGGLE*

1. THE STRUGGLE FOR POWER WITH COMMUNISM   3
by Russell Kirk
   Research Professor, C. W. Post College
   Long Island University

2. VALUES IN A WORLD OF CONFLICT   13
by William R. Kintner
   Associate Director, Foreign Policy Research Institute
   University of Pennsylvania

3. THE POWER STRUGGLE AND THE UNITED NATIONS   24
by Andrew W. Cordier
   Dean, School of International Affairs
   Columbia University

4. THE POWER STRUGGLE AND THE NEW NATIONS   37
by Waldemar A. Nielsen
   President, African-American Institute

PART II. *THE RAPPROCHEMENT*
BETWEEN SCIENCE AND RELIGION

5. THE NEW RAPPROCHEMENT BETWEEN SCIENCE
AND RELIGION   55
by Donald H. Andrews
   Professor of Chemistry
   Johns Hopkins University

6.   CAN SCIENCE AID RELIGION?   73
     by Émile Cailliet
          Professor Emeritus of Christian Philosophy
          Princeton Theological Seminary

PART III. *THE RELATION*
          OF PSYCHIATRY AND RELIGION

7.   PSYCHIATRIC UNDERSTANDINGS OF MAN:
     A THEOLOGICAL APPRAISAL   87
     by Seward Hiltner
          Professor of Theology and Personality
          Princeton Theological Seminary

8.   THE POWER OF THE PERSONAL: A STUDY OF
     THE RELATION BETWEEN RELIGION AND PSYCHIATRY   106
     by Reuel Howe
          Director, Institute for Advanced Pastoral Studies

PART IV. *COMMUNICATION*

9.   COMMUNICATION   119
     by Edgar Dale
          Professor of Education
          Ohio State University

10. THE MASS MEDIA AND THE CHURCHES   130
     by Dallas Smythe
          Research Professor of Communications
          University of Illinois

PART V. *WORLD CHRISTIANITY*

11. WORLD CHRISTIANITY   149
     by Lesslie Newbigin
          Director, Division of World Mission and Evangelism
          World Council of Churches

Contents   vii

12.   CHRISTIANITY AND THE CHALLENGE OF AFRICA TODAY   164
      by Donald M'Timkulu
            General Secretary, Provisional Committee
            of All Africa Conference

13.   THE VOCATION OF THE CHRISTIAN APOLOGIST:
      A STUDY OF SCHLEIERMACHER'S *Reden*   173
      by Jaroslav Pelikan
            Titus Street Professor of Ecclesiastical History
            Yale Divinity School

14.   THE NEW CHALLENGE BEFORE THE YOUNGER CHURCHES   190
      by Richard Shaull
            Professor of Ecumenics
            Princeton Theological Seminary

PART VI. *A THEOLOGY FOR THE NUCLEAR AGE*

15.   A THEOLOGY OF REPENTANCE   209
      by Joseph Haroutunian
            Professor of Theology
            Chicago University Divinity School

16.   THE GOD OF THE BIBLE VERSUS NATURALISM   225
      by Carl F. H. Henry
            Editor, Christianity Today

Introduction

THIS BOOK COMPRISES THE LECTURES OF SIXTEEN DISTINGUISHED authorities given at The Biblical Seminary in New York City. The series on "Christianity and World Revolution" was initiated in order to highlight the vast and basic changes now developing in society, and their resultant challenges to Christianity. Many areas of life are affected, but it seemed wise to limit the discussion to six crucial phases which require immediate attention by the Christian world if Christianity is to remain relevant to the issues of the day. The lectures, which were open to the public and broadcast over FM radio station WRVR, represent varying points of view, not necessarily those of the Seminary. This series has presented an unusually interesting and challenging forum for controversial issues facing Christianity.

The six areas mentioned above contain the power struggle—that is, the major political, social, and economic upheavals of the modern world, with their significance for the gospel.

The greatest conflict today is between two totally different world cultures. One is centered in God, the other in man. The man-centered culture takes two forms: secularism and statism. Both are deadly enemies of Christianity, a God-centered philosophy of life. The conflict is tremendous, the stakes are high, involving the souls of men, and the decision final. These are not academic discussions between friendly opponents, but a life-and-death struggle for supremacy.

The new rapprochement between science and religion is another sphere that demands reappraisal. In this generation science is in the ascendancy and is attracting many of the best minds, especially among young people. Will Christianity meet this claim for pre-eminence by acknowledging what is true, by using what is helpful in the real attainments of science, and also by challenging what is sheer materialism? Or will the Church of Christ settle back into obscurantism and fail to recognize that God is the source of all truth in science as well as religion? Science and religion can be handmaidens to learning more of truth and freedom.

Psychiatry and religion have reached a stage where their co-ordination holds much promise for man's personal ills. Some psychiatrists are skeptical of religion and predicate their findings upon a naturalistic basis. It is equally true that some leaders of religion are wary of psychiatry's answers. On the other hand, there has come an awareness on the part of both psychiatrists and religious leaders that each can contribute toward a better understanding of man himself and his needs.

The tensions and frustrations caused by the tempo of society today demand the pooling of knowledge and wisdom to solve man's inner conflicts. Here is an instance where the revolution is within man. How important, then, to resolve these conflicts!

A tremendous revolution has occurred in communications during the past two decades. Mass media—radio, television, and film—are being heard and seen by millions every day, with consequent effect upon the lives of the listeners. News, events, and ideas are transmitted, often simultaneously with their actual moment of occurrence. Here is an opportunity as well as a threat to religion. Christianity now has within its grasp the chance to reach millions where it once reached mere hundreds or thousands. It, too, has to deal with the mass media in its total impact upon people, morally and spiritually.

In both respects Christianity is fighting a battle that is not yet won. It has not learned how to project its message and values in an effective way. What is more, the number of degrading programs put on far outweighs what might contribute to the intellectual, moral, esthetic, and spiritual life of the nation. The Church has not learned how to use mass media to its advantage.

The challenge to Christianity by other religions, by the rise of new nations, and by other cultures is creating immense problems and crises never before experienced in a single generation. The re-emergence of non-Christian faiths as missionary religions—especially Islam, Buddhism, and even Judaism—has set up a rivalry to Christianity that has not been so vital since the crusades. It is claimed, for example, that Islam is winning twice as many converts in Africa as Christianity.

New nations in many areas of the world bring a resurgence of nationalism as these people struggle for understanding. The missionary enterprise over the last hundred years has preached the gospel of the equality of all men before God. Now these people want the implied freedom and recognition.

This revolution brings a desire for churches of their own, managed and controlled by their people. It raises profound problems for the missionary enterprise, especially the churches in the United States. It involves a restudy of the whole outreach of the Christian Church, and no adoption of new slogans such as "the mission of the Church" instead of "foreign missions" is adequate.

In the light of such a revolution, Christianity must rethink its strategy and concepts. It listens and considers all views, con and pro, often gaining new insights. It should never hesitate to proclaim that God was in Christ reconciling the world unto Himself, for the gospel of Jesus Christ is adequate for the whole world. The answer is not simple, as the diagnosis is not easy. But unless the gospel in all its fullness is the solution, Christianity ceases to have much meaning. Theological concepts alter, approaches must adjust to succeeding generations, strategies will change; but the underlying conviction of faith in God through Christ must undergird the message.

These sixteen lectures represent different points of view, so that a real forum was possible on controversial issues. No pat solutions were offered, nor was there any attempt to create a false uniformity among the lecturers. The questions are faced honestly, answers are given, and the revolution that is upon us is recognized as the gravest Christianity has confronted in more than a hundred years.

It is hoped that these addresses by men of authority in the various areas will stimulate the Christian Church to take whatever measures are necessary to meet the challenge of revolution. Unless the Church of Christ faces these issues squarely, with utmost honesty and heart-searching thought under the guidance of the Holy Spirit, civilization may become even more indifferent to the Word of God.

EDWIN H. RIAN

President
The Biblical Seminary in New York

Part I

THE POWER STRUGGLE

1

The Struggle for Power
with Communism

RUSSELL KIRK

IN THE GREAT GRIM STRUGGLE OF OUR MORAL AND SOCIAL ORDER
against the Soviet Union and its allies, one thing should always form
our policy: the knowledge that we are, in Burke's phrase, "combatting
an armed doctrine." We have to deal, not merely with a national
rival—not simply with a hostile pattern of politics—but with a
fanatic ideology. An ideology of this sort is "political religion," and
its spokesmen promise the terrestrial paradise as a substitute for
heaven. We are confronted, in fine, with a false religion, a caricature
of Christianity, and unless we acknowledge that fact we will misunderstand the nature of our enemies' power and ignore the sources
of our own strength.

As Britain during the age of Pitt gradually came to understand
the nature of the Jacobin and Napoleonic peril, which was quite different from the dynastic struggles of the seventeenth and eighteenth
centuries, so nowadays we Americans and our allies are beginning—
reluctantly and haltingly—to apprehend the character of the totalist
system by which we are menaced. The struggle for power is a contest
between what Dr. Leo Strauss calls the "Great Tradition" of our
civilization and the wholly different view of man, as well as of the
social order, embodied by our Communist adversaries. For all practical purposes it is a struggle between Christian belief, on the one
hand, to which are allied more or less consciously the views of other
religious bodies, and on the other hand the totalist ideology of the
Soviets, with their fellow travelers and subject nations.

"The true dividing line in the contemporary crisis," writes Eric

3

Voegelin, "does not run between liberals and totalitarians, but between the religious and philosophical transcendentalists on the one side, and the liberal and totalitarian immanentist sectarians on the other." Our real power—the power of those who intelligently oppose Communism—has its source in religious conviction, and particularly Christian doctrine, which offers a realistic and enduring understanding of human nature—an understanding of both its greatness and its vices. God has given to the essence of life certain laws, and a politico-economic creed which denies those laws must defile mankind.

THE LINE OF DEMARCATION

If we ignore the great line of demarcation between our order and the terrible order of the modern totalists, we promptly fall into confusion as to the cause of our present discontents, the means for dealing with our time of troubles, and the proper use of power to protect ourselves. If our strength comes from religious understanding and observance, then a national polity predicated merely upon self-interest and reluctant concessions to the enemy must lead us into danger, perhaps to disaster.

When the thoroughgoing secularist and the nominal Christian, for instance, are compelled to say why the fountains of the great deep are dried up in our time, their answers are shallow. They tell us, usually, that the revolutions and international conflicts of the twentieth century have been produced by poverty, desire for democracy, and the decay of superstition. But these arguments will not bear close examination, Historically considered, revolutions have usually occurred, not when a people were abysmally poor, but in periods of increasing general prosperity; if a low standard of living were the real cause of violence we might expect modern Eire—perhaps the poorest land of Western Europe—to be seething with insurrection, when obviously enough it is remarkably tranquil. This is quite as true of most of modern India, where religious differences and national aspirations, not poverty, are the causes of discontent. As for rising democracy, real democracy has not increased at all in our century, and the new nation-states promptly turn, most of them, to some intolerant master, as in Indonesia, Ghana, or Egypt. Decay of superstition? Old creeds indeed have lost their followers; but those beliefs ordinarily have been supplanted, not by an Enlightenment but rather by virulent ideology or recrudescent savage faiths, as in the revival of witchcraft in Africa.

THE CAUSES OF DISORDER

The real causes of the disorders that plague us lie elsewhere. Only in part are these genuine afflictions produced by the decay of religious conviction; yet we cannot set about their remedy without recourse to first principles, which must involve certain theological and philosophical assumptions. We may discern two large sources of confusion in our age: first, the decline of normative understanding and moral imagination; second, the swift pace of change, technological and social, with its consequent internal and external disorder.

Communism, or any other voracious ideology, rushes in to fill a spiritual and intellectual vacuum. The decline of apprehension of norms—of those enduring standards in morals and politics and taste which distinguished the truly human person from the brute—leaves man without a measure; and so a violent and materialistic ideology offers new, though false, principles by which the civil social order may be made to operate, and nations embrace these doctrines in the absence of the Great Tradition. Evelyn Waugh's sardonic little novel, *Scott-King's Modern Europe,* describes in a hundred corrosive pages how the norms of order and justice and freedom, Christian and classical, are forgotten in modern times, and suggests that moral and intellectual disorder, internal anarchy, must produce social anarchy or tyranny. Somewhere there must be a control upon man's passions, Burke wrote at the beginning of our era; and the less of this control there is within, the more of it there must be from without. Communism is one dreadful form of that merciless outer control which must follow upon decay of the inner check, the moral rein upon will and appetite. Enduring order, justice, and freedom cannot be restored until the soul of the human person is ordered once more. Thus, as Irving Babbitt said, economics moves upward into politics, politics upward into ethics—and, one may add, ethics into theology.

Parallel with the decay of normative understanding, our time has experienced a vertiginous degree of change, unsettling customs and usages and prescriptions by which men have lived for many centuries. Wholesale industrialization, the concentrating of population in what Sir Osbert Sitwell calls the "proletarian cosmopolis," the doubling and tripling and quadrupling of populations, the abrupt increase of human mobility, the collapse of venerable communities—all these phenomena and a good many others have swept man away from his roots. The uprooted are necessarily confused and discontented, easy prey to any vigorous idealogue. This is not to say that we can alleviate

these difficulties by mere preaching of Christian doctrines, but that
any attempt at solution undertaken without reference to the first
principles of human nature and society must end in failure. And it is
not possible to attain to such first principles without accepting at least
a part of the Christian understanding of the human situation.

Just so it is with the problem of power. In essence, power is the
ability to do as one likes with other people, with or without their
assent. The intelligent Christian, knowing power to be perilous, endeavors to balance and check and hedge the amount to be wielded by
fallible and sinning men, and he knows that all men are fallible and
sinning. He understands, too, that power in itself, though dangerous,
is neither good nor evil; all depends upon its employment, the devices
for curbing it, and the virtue of those who hold it. Fortified by this
knowledge, he proceeds to examine the resources of power possessed
by the modern totalists and to measure against their force that other
kind of power which has given our society its vigor.

ARMED DOCTRINE

Communism is an armed doctrine; we contend not merely against
the Red army and the Soviet economy, but more importantly against
the pseudo-religion that gives Communists their fortitude and motive.
And it is not possible to restrain the power of a false creed unless
one repairs to a true one. As Soviet power wells up from devotion to
false gods, so our power originates in worship of the living God. T. S.
Eliot writes, "If you will not have God—and He is a jealous god—
then you should pay your respects to Hitler or Stalin." In the final
test, the power of a nation or a civilization will be weighed, not in
missiles or divisions but in faith, whether false or true.

As Orestes Brownson recognized in the year of the Communist
Manifesto, Communism apes and distorts Christian belief, and from
that inversion derives its power over men's minds and bodies. In
recent years this perversion of Christian doctrine into Marxist dogma
has been traced by John Hallowell, Arnold Toynbee, Charles Wesley
Lowry, Martin d'Arcy, and other writers. Communism has all the
characteristics of a powerful heresy, and so draws its strength from
Christian sources. The Marxists make immanent the Christian symbols. Christ came to save sinners, of whom I am the chief—but Communists alter this to read the salvation of the proletariat through
revolution. The Christian idea of charity they pervert to mean com-
pulsory equality of condition. Equality in the sight of God they make

into the classless society. For love they write solidarity. For the millennium they substitute the withering away of the state. Thus runs Communist dogma, appealing to notions of justice and duty and generosity which most men have acquired through Christian teaching, but converting them into a system thoroughly antipersonal. The power of Communism, to be brief, is very like the power of the Antichrist as mystically described by St. John.

Communists teach that by revolution and compulsion the perfect society shall be established here on earth, and thereafter all men shall be wholly happy—free, in Marx's words, to "hunt in the morning, fish in the afternoon, make love in the evening, and criticize at dinner just as they please"—a child's dream of pleasure. But the child's fantasy becomes the man's nightmare; for power unrestrained by moral habits and imagination, power which has denied the source of its own being, in no time at all becomes the *libido dominandi,* most consuming and tormenting of lusts, which ceases not till death.

In order to contend successfully against the power of this secularized heresy, the friends of prescriptive order and justice and freedom must turn to realism as the antidote to traumatic totalist illusion; the nightmare must be ended by waking to the day. And Christian doctrine provides the realistic understanding of human character and of the order to which we are born. It offers an analysis of men derived both from revelation and from many centuries of observation; it presents a concept of true community.

Now it must be emphasized here that Christianity prescribes no especial form of politics and no particular economic system. The Church has endured, and sometimes prospered, during various political dominations: monarchical, aristocratic, republican, democratic. It has coexisted with the most primitive nomadic economies and with the most complex industrial organizations. The Church does not try to assimilate to itself the state. Two there are, said Gelasius, by whom this world is ruled. Christians render unto Caesar that which is Caesar's.

Yet, this said, we must remember that there also exist political dominations with which the Church cannot live in comparative harmony. To employ a word cherished by Ambrose Bierce, Christianity and totalism are "incompossible"; for even if Christians could bring themselves to endure the atheistical total state, that behemoth in turn has no intention of tolerating them; the Marxist knows that Christianity must be extirpated, or at the very least reduced to an impotent remnant, for Christian ideas of human dignity and love and charity and justice would always present a perilous challenge to the power of the total state's oligarchs. The Marxist knows, even if many of us have forgotten, that ideas have immense power. The Church could do its work under Roman persecution because the Roman state was not efficient enough to efface Christianity altogether. But the twentieth-century total state—supposing it to be triumphant universally—might very well destroy the Church, visible and invisible, root and branch.

So Christians, and other religious persons who perceive the real nature of Communist power, have to contend against the Communist system or else perish. If Christianity offers no precise pattern of politics, how can Christians apply their great body of learning, and their devotion to a transcendent order, to the controversies of our age? Not, one would think, by drawing up a manifesto or a specific political program, but rather by recourse to a higher realism which, properly apprehended, has immediate bearing upon nearly every prudential question, and especially upon the problem of power.

THE CHRISTIAN ANSWER

In politics Christian realism commences with the recognition of original sin. Human nature being corrupt, perfection of the individual and of society is impossible; at best we must settle for an order tolerably free and just. This awareness saves the Christian statesman from the follies of what Gordon Chalmers called "disintegrated liberalism." The disintegrated or "ritualistic" liberal assumes with Rousseau—in some sense, with Pelagius—that human nature has no necessary taint of sin or need of divine grace; so, he thinks, we need only alter institutions radically and men can achieve perfect happiness in some brummagem Utopia. Eric Voegelin calls this attitude modern Gnosticism, making immanent the Christian symbol; and it is precisely this, he writes in his *New Science of Politics,* that has put the Soviet Russians on the Elbe. Under such illusions, men mistake their mortal enemies for persons of good will—a little hasty in taste and temper, perhaps, but requiring only gestures of friendship to make them love us. The diabolical power that animates the modern totalists is confounded with a too enthusiastic humanitarianism.

Into this pit the intelligent Christian will not fall. Similarly, he will not be deceived by the specious argument that international peace may be achieved simply by a general increase in the standard of living in underdeveloped countries. Recognizing that man does not live by bread alone, he knows that many appetites are stronger than those of the belly. The appetite of the masters of the Soviet system, for instance, is for naked power; Communist demands for peace and economic equality ordinarily are mere masks upon the face of the *libido dominandi,* or at best subordinate to the fierce desire to assimilate all the world to the Marxist terrestrial paradise. In his inverted way, the zealous commissar is little more likely to be diverted from his chosen path by the offer of a mess of pottage than St. Jerome, say, could have been converted to paganism by the fleshpots of Alexandria. Though they may nowadays wear business suits, commissars are not really to be equated with American businessmen.

And aware that we mortals cannot rest content in an eternal changelessness as if we were angels, without passing through the gates of death, the Christian statesman will view with suspicion all neat schemes founded upon secular expediency for establishing a perfected world order that predicates the assimilation of all peoples to one "modern" or "progressive" mode of existence. Diversity, he knows, is the inclination and the blessing of mankind. With Phyllis McGinley he remembers that even God is said to be three separate Persons:

> Then upright or upon the knee,
> Praise Him that by His courtesy,
> For all our prejudice and pains,
> Diverse His Creature still remains.*

It seems worth while, indeed, to digress upon this point, to the end of illustrating the Christian thinker's way of approaching the struggle for power.

AMERICANISM NOT THE SOLUTION

A few years ago, a spokesman for a great labor organization declared that we Americans are destined to assimilate all the world to our institutions and manners and appetites; some foreigners may not like this, but it's progress, so be damned to them! Not long after, I heard a president of the Chamber of Commerce of the United States express almost identical convictions. Such "liberal" secular evangelism, the Christian realist feels, not only will fail of its object but may disorder still further this time of troubles.

Such gentlemen are convinced that all societies ought to be reconstituted in the American image, and that Americans ought to pay for the process—eventually, perhaps to be repaid. By an American-

* From "In Praise of Diversity," in *Times Three* by Phyllis McGinley, © 1953 by Phillis McGinley. Used by permission of Viking Press, Inc.

sponsored industrialization of underdeveloped regions, under forced draft, they would have us out-materialize the Soviet materialists. Sometimes they sound curiously like Khrushchev—reminiscent, for instance, of his scowling admonition to the Javanese that they ought to abolish their handicrafts and turn to standardized industrial production. The world is to become one immense copy of American society, repeating our campaign phrases, copying American technology, adopting our ways, and presumably inheriting all our problems and afflictions. This brand of 100 per cent Americanism, so the argument runs, may be imposed quite simply, with equal facility, upon the ancient civilizations of India and the primitive peoples of Africa. And this latter-day liberalism may justly claim an intellectual descent from Bentham and James Mill.

But the Christian realist looks differently upon this attempt at unity. He discerns a law governing all life: from the unicellular inanimate forms to man, every living organism endeavors above all else to preserve its identity as a species. Whatever lives, tries to make itself the center of the universe; only the Christian law of love has exerted any restraining influence upon this passion. Whatever lives, resists with the whole of its strength the endeavors of competing forms of life to assimilate it to their substance and mode. Every living thing prefers even death, as an individual, to extinction as a distinct species. Now if the lowliest algae struggle to the death against a threat to their peculiar character, we ought not to be surprised that men and nations resist desperately and even unreasoningly any endeavor to merge their nature with that of some other social body. Extending deep below the level of consciousness, this resistance is the first law of their being. There is one sure way to make a deadly enemy, and that is to propose to anyone in effect, "Submit yourself to me and I will improve your condition by relieving you of the burden of your identity and reconstituting your personality in my image." For men and nations to speak with this arrogance is to usurp the throne of God; and even God does not demand of Christians that they lose personality in His bosom.

Yet just this is what some gentlemen proclaim as a rallying cry for American policy-makers in a revolutionary world. They do not employ precisely these phrases, and seem to be unaware of the vast presumption in their own humanitarian projects; but that does not alter the *hubris* of their demand. If the United States should wish to make American influence detested throughout the world, the surest method, one may imagine, would be to dispatch ideologues of this persuasion globe-trotting, bestowing gratuitous counsel among the nations. Let such emissaries tell every people to submit themselves to a recasting in the American image; let them patronize and cajole and bully in every remote land where order is shaken; let them serve as representatives of the American mind and conscience. "In this Nuclear Age," writes one such energumen, a well-known politician, "without such a vision the people perish." Really? Without such a vision—or because of it?

In the long run, and perhaps the short run, the reaction to our secular proselytizing would be that of the Arab in Cunninghame Graham's story, "Sidi bu Zibbula"—sitting, like Job, upon a great dunghill: "I have seen your Western cities; and the dung is better." Much of our foreign aid program, for example, the Christian politician understands, is vitiated by such fallacies.

Brotherhood in Christ does not exact monolithic political unity and the destruction of diversity. Christian doctrine teaches men to set limits to power and informs us that, power tending to corrupt, absolute authority in our hands can be quite as dangerous as absolute authority in the hands of our adversaries.

Yes, the Christian understanding of man and society cautions us to set limits to power. But it does not provide us with mere negative checks. The Christian faith gives us the will to dare and endure, for the sake of the compact between God—who has set His bow in the heavens—and man; and for the sake of that immortal society which joins the dead, the living, and those yet unborn. Man is made for eternity. If we of the Great Tradition really believe this, we enjoy an enormous advantage over the Communists in the struggle of our times. For the Marxist, death means extinction to the person and the end of hope for a society. But the Christian, as Herbert Butterfield observes, has always known the world is destined to a bad end; he sees that even death by the atomic bomb would be no more significant— and perhaps less painful—than the death on the road that most of us confront daily. For the religious man death is only a beginning, an entrance to the eternity for which he was created. And in this confidence our Christian civilization, so far as it is still really animated by Christian belief, ought to muster that courage for defense which is also the best deterrent of aggression. The power of belief really can exceed the power of Caesar.

To repeat, in this twentieth century of the Christian era the real contest is between the power of transcendent faith and the power of the totalist revolt against order. Not wealth or know-how or even worldly wisdom will bring us victory in the struggle. Decadence, as

C. E. M. Joad defines it, is the loss of an object, and people who rely wholly upon material advantage are decadent, for they have forgotten the end of existence.

The high culture and liberties of the Greek cities fell to their ruin because of such decadence, once the norms of their life were neglected. Some time ago, wandering in Sicily, I came to Girgenti, which in Pindar's time was Akragas, "most beautiful of mortal cities." Its beauty lies in ruin now, for the Carthaginians conquered and burned it, the richest and most powerful state of the West. The golden columns of the temples are still flushed pink by Carthaginian fire. So long as the spirit that created those broken temples lived in Akragas' people, the city stood in its glory; but once piety and veneration had trickled away, all the ingenuity and riches and mercenaries at the command of the Greeks could not keep out the barbarian. Toward the end, at Akragas, there seem to have been few who abided by the old faith or sacrificed willingly for the commonwealth.

"And . . . that house . . . fell; and great was the fall of it." Imagination rules the world, Napoleon said. I think it truer to say that faith rules the world, and even a false faith, like that of the Communists, will triumph over mere material power. In our hour of crisis the key to real power, to the command of reality which the higher imagination gives, remains the fear of God.

2

Values in a World
of Conflict

WILLIAM R. KINTNER

THE CRISIS NOW FACING HUMANITY IS A SPIRITUAL CRISIS MORE THAN
a power struggle. At issue between the free world and the Communist
orbit are two fundamentally different views as to the nature of man.

The spiritual dilemma of the human race can be traced to the first
chapters of Genesis. At the dawn of the human race men living on
earth aspired to be as God, to know good and evil, to mix the finite
limitations of man with the unknowable wisdom of the infinite Creator.
This spiritual wrestling with the unknowable has always been the central problem of the human race. What are we? What are we doing on
this planet? How did we come here? Where are we going?

People living in this modern world are still preoccupied with these
questions. Those who are seduced by their own finite intelligence look
to the imagination of their own minds and finally come to believe, like
Lucifer, that they contain in themselves all the mysteries of the universe. They lose sight of realms far beyond what our finite human
minds can understand. And losing that, fall into spiritual blindness.
They create towers of Babel, imaginary kingdoms of their own on this
earth which they believe will last forever. They search for treasures
that rust cannot corrupt nor moths destroy.

The quest for false Utopias has often led the human race to conflict and misery. Those who see only the material base of life deny
that this wonderful universe was made for some purpose—for the
creation of human beings to live in the image and likeness of God.
The awe and mystery of divine purpose have grown obscure in our
Western world, and nowhere more than in the perversion of Christianity called Communism. The very fundamental principles of religion,

13

with its concept of the transcendental, are obliterated in dialectical materialism. This creed asserts that even our consciousness is an effervescence of the stones, mud, water, and air that surround us. Marx and the many who adhere to his views assert that materialistic forces are the only important forces in the universe, that our consciousness is merely a froth of those forces and has no connection with invisible reality.

The crisis of our times reflects the trend toward secular beliefs, the rejection of any divinity whatsoever. This rejection has occurred throughout history. But since the advent of the modern age, the age of humanism, of scientific materialism, most people with advanced education come to believe that the human mind can eventually understand everything. The epitome of this point of view is developed in the doctrines of Marx, Engels, Stalin, and Khrushchev. One must understand the theological implications of these doctrines to comprehend the crisis facing the human race. Behind the Iron Curtain there exists a positive view of human destiny, the concept of historical materialism, the dialectic of history spinning itself out to create a new paradise on earth.

DEVELOPMENTS IN THE WESTERN WORLD

Contrast that development with what has taken place in the Western world. In the West, since the advent of positive relativism, the idea has taken root that only a fact is worth while. When we refuse credence to anything but facts, universal terms of reference have no meaning, for each individual sensation is significant only as a self-contained experience. This idea—so prevalent in the West—has eventually lead to the discrediting of almost any concept of purpose in human existence beyond what we can smell, see, measure, or touch.

There have been interesting consequences to the spread of positive relativism in the Western world. First, there has arisen a deep confusion of values which is visible all around us. One may see examples of the nebulous character of Western values in the recent articles on goals in *Life* magazine, in the report of the President's Commission on National Goals, and in various debates about purpose and morality. There are no longer any guideposts to define the limits of the finite human mind. Each man swims in an uncharted sea, unable to determine where he is going. Modern man does not know whence he came, nor is he certain what his purpose in life should be. Because they have rejected the transcendental, many intellectuals have turned to the certainties provided by Marxism with its supposedly solid philosophical base. Communism provides a certainty that is generally found lacking in the modern humanism of the West.

The two chief drives that motivate human beings are recorded time and time again in the Bible. They are the lust for power—the power urge—and the desire for things. These are the usual objectives men set store by, the false gods mentioned throughout the Bible and commented on in various ways by Christ. The modern world rejects almost completely the characterization of man in the Old Testament, which in a remarkably candid way exposes the human soul. The authors of the Old Testament described the good and the bad. The Bible contains some very revealing passages about the nature of man and his predilections for evil as well as his aspirations toward good. There is no attempt to gloss over human foibles in the Old Testament.

It is important to understand that there are two concepts of man at issue. One point of view holds that man is a little lower than the angels and has drives toward evil as well as aspirations toward good. The opposite contention, favored by the Soviets, is that man is entirely a creature of his external environment and can be manipulated, engineered, and even recreated. This concept unfortunately has a tremendous appeal to the Western world. There are many who reject the idea of responsibility for moral action; who fix the source of evil on environment. The idea of personal responsibility is dismissed. This is in accordance with pure Marxism: the environment changes, the man changes, and in the process a new society is created. In contradistinction we have the message of Christianity and the spiritual insight revealed in the Bible.

Both of these divergent philosophies concern themselves with human beings. They express themselves through the power of human beings to find fulfillment in a world which is not peaceful and calm but a scene of tension and strife, in which many ideas contest for supremacy. Although much has been said about values, the power of contrary ideas in the conduct of the struggle is important. Regrettably, most Americans feel ill at ease when various aspects of power are discussed. They somehow feel that power is indecent, something we can overlook or ignore. We are used to dealing with power in our domestic lives, but when it comes to power in relation to the international struggle, many Americans would like to close their eyes.

THE COMMUNIST STRATEGY

We live in a world of continual revolution: a world whose standards began falling apart in 1914, a world whose political structure is changing in directions those of us now living cannot know. We are going downstream in rapids—we cannot foresee where we are headed; we cannot even tell whether we are going to stay on top of the water. But we believe that future societies will have a completely different outline from the society we now know. A world in revolution appeals to the Communists because they possess a doctrine of change. As Marx said, "We came not to reform the world but to destroy it altogether." Note the difference between those words and Christ's, "I am not come to destroy, but to fulfill." The Marxian point of view is that the past is wrong. The whole system of society was designed to oppress; consequently it must be overturned and completely destroyed.

The Communist demand for a complete overthrow is addressed to a world already in a state of revolution, itself an amplification of revolutions in communications and technology, the population explosion, and the breakdown of all cultural systems. Because the world is in turmoil the Communists' insistence that they do not want to maintain the status quo, but to break it up, has an obvious appeal to many people. The Communists bring to this struggle a doctrine of revolution and a plan and a strategy for capitalizing on it.

The strategy of protracted conflict has already been described— the scheme whereby a weaker power gains over a period of time the means to displace a stronger power. It implies power accumulation. It operates in the psychological realm. It gradually whittles away confidence of victory in our society and replaces it with defeatism. The struggle has been going on for four decades. In the past several years Communist leadership has grown more and more confident that dialectical materialism, the dynamics of history, will finally bring them the victory; as Khrushchev said in his speech of January 6, 1961: "Comrades we live in a splendid time. Communism has become the invincible force of our century." In another of his speeches we read: "The analysis of the world situation at the beginning of the sixties can only evoke in every member of the great Communist movement, feelings of profound satisfaction and legitimate pride."

The Communists appear to be confident of achieving victory. What do they want from the victory they seek? Some people believe that their idea of dominating the world may be utopian—may never be within their grasp. On the other hand, the logic of their position demands that they displace our system. They argue that the reason the world is in its present shape is because the external environment is false. Human evil exists, they contend, because of the capitalist system, particularly because we have the right to own property. The free exercise of the use of property is, according to them, the root of all evil. Eliminate this and you eliminate those tendencies toward selfishness and aggrandizement which lead to conflict between peoples, between cities, between states, and between nations. Therefore, if their heaven on earth is to be achieved, the brave new socialist order they seek must be established everywhere. Our entire system must be eliminated; this includes everything that we stand for as well. For them, there can be no partial solutions: "One side or the other must perish."

They base their strategy on several heritages. There is the heritage of social conflict that began with the French Revolution. Since that day Communist theorists have analyzed some four hundred revolutions for the operational lessons they contain. They examine them to see how to agitate, how to "smell" revolution in the air, how to manipulate it, how to engineer it; how to support and arm it, and finally, how to determine the moment to strike. This is one aspect of their strategy.

Another is the application of military methodology and organization to the solution of a political problem. The question is how a small group of people can gain and maintain control over a large number of people who may not be sympathetic to their purposes. They have solved this problem by creating a unique organization, the Communist Party, a disciplined group with a definite chain of command, which maintains secrecy and utilizes all the organizational methods that military forces employ in time of war. In this manner a small number of Communists can control and manipulate a large number of people. The Communists are aware also of the material elements of power. Consequently, over the past forty years they have pushed their industrialization program. They apply it primarily to those elements of technical productivity that relate to power, whether in space activity, ICBM's, Red army divisions, economic aid to selected countries, or whatever else may be to their benefit. In the course of time they have gradually achieved a power base which to all intents and purposes is almost equivalent to ours. This is true even though our gross national product is twice as large as theirs. Whereas we give a great deal of attention to consumer goods, they apply proportionately more of their effort to developing the sinews of power.

Finally, they bring to their strategy the force of future orientation. Many of us in our private lives only worry about what happens from day to day. Some of our city officials worry about where they will be living presently. Most national government leaders think, in financial terms, from one budget to the next. But the Communists take the long view—the five-year plan, the seven-year plan, and then a twenty-year plan. This may be Khrushchev's great contribution to Communism. His last plan, which will run until about 1982, is comprehensive enough to include a place for every one in this country. This plan envisages the type of world the Communists want, and they believe that by then circumstances will enable them to establish it almost everywhere. The Communists are revolutionaries who intend to change the existing order. They have a general program for obtaining their goal. They do not have a detailed time schedule stating what will be done in 1963 or 1964, for they do not operate that way. Instead they create the resources, and then, as opportunity arises—as the dialectic of history presents opportunities—use them.

The Communists view the world scene from two angles. They look first at the objective factors: how much steel, how many divisions, how many ICBM's. Then they look at the subjective factors: what do people think about them? At this moment, Khrushchev would probably conclude that objective factors do not yet completely favor him. On the other hand, he has been working very hard on the subjective attitudes of his opponents. Khrushchev believes, whether rightly or wrongly, that time is on his side and that he is winning the struggle. Therefore, if he manipulates his cards carefully he can induce us to give in without much of a fight. This is the gist of his presentations, the heart of his strategy, the concept that underlies peaceful coexistence.

Peaceful coexistence is a rather interesting strategy. If everything is going well, as it has often appeared to be from Khrushchev's standpoint, why does he from time to time say, "Let us have peace, let us compete without war, let us find a basis of understanding"? He does this because we are living in the thermonuclear age—an age in which an ICBM can hit any point on the earth's surface in less than thirty minutes. With a powerful 50-megaton warhead it can destroy most of a city as big as New York. This is a devastating weapon, and Khrushchev has found the ICBM-nuclear combination a useful supplement and support for his world-wide system of Communist organizations. But the thermonuclear weapon is like a two-edged sword—if and when he pushes us too far and too rapidly, we may react violently. Under these circumstances, even if we cannot win, we can always sabotage a total Soviet victory. Khrushchev understands this and has developed a clever method of dealing with it.

He tries to adjust each plunge of the aggression needle so that we do not react in a violent and irrational way. He pushes it in just so far, and when it becomes too painful he pulls it out. Then he talks of co-existence. "Let us get together. Let us find a peaceful basis for negotiations." By the time we have forgotten what caused the irritation, he picks up the needle once more and plunges it into some other area.

This is the strategy which he hopes will enable him gradually to gain an expansion of his power without incurring what he would consider an unreasonable reaction of the capitalist system in its dying days. This is the operational structure of the doctrine of coexistence. It is similar to Pavlov's experiments with dogs. In place of the dinner bell you have negotiations. In place of the electric shock you have a crisis, whether it be Quemoy or Berlin. This strategy has been well defined by Khrushchev, who speaks differently behind the Iron Curtain than when he is on our side. He made this interesting comment in Warsaw in 1956: "We must realize that we cannot coexist eternally or for a long time. One of us must go to his grave. They [meaning us, of course] do not want to go to their grave. So what can be done? We must push them to their grave." Khrushchev is a sincere individual and when he said, as he has many times, that he will bury us, he meant it, for he recognizes the inescapable conflict between Communism and the societies of the free world.

In his famous January 6 (1961) speech, Khrushchev presented positions which somewhat parallel our own point of view. Broadly speaking, there are just wars and unjust wars. Every war fought by the Communists, by definition, is a just war because they are fighting on the side of the higher morality of history, the unfolding of dialectical materialism, the Communist heaven on earth. On the other hand, within this broad category there are several varieties or species of wars. The first type is the general thermonuclear war. This is a bad war, because if it were waged it might destroy all Soviet industrialization achieved since the revolution. The Communist position parallels our own in that this is not a rational choice for either side to make.

Secondly, Khrushchev said he is against local wars because they might escape into general war and bring about unwillingly the type of damage he does not want. By this assertion he hopes to discourage us from developing means of dealing with such wars. If the Soviets are successful in this they can then exploit politically their own great superiority in conventional forces.

In wars of national liberation the Communists combine political and military action and psychological warfare into an ambiguous strategy. Through this combination Khrushchev hopes he can undermine our position piece by piece so as to achieve such preponderant power that we will have to give in. This is a strategy we will probably see much more of in the next few years. Unfortunately, up to now we have not found a good formula for dealing with it, although the government is giving top priority to the discovery of the combination of motivation, political development, economic growth, and other factors required.

Finally, as the last arrow in his quiver, Khrushchev is a great believer in disarmament. He talks about it quite often. He made a major speech about it at the 1960 Assembly of the UN before he took off his shoe and hammered on the table. One of the reasons for his disarmament effort is to derogate the Western and particularly the American military position. A primary condition for progress and disarmament is mobilization of the people—therefore, place pressures on any "imperialistic" government to force it to disarm.

It is noteworthy that Khrushchev talks much about disarmament; but specifically, how can his plan for a universal, general, and complete disarmament be implemented? He has always found ways to evade the concrete issues. It is also noteworthy that he has always avoided talking about demobilization of his political warfare machine. He is manipulating about eighty Communist parties throughout the world. He has people in training at the Lenin School and in various institutes in Africa, Latin America, and elsewhere. They are trained in political warfare. If we ignore his political warfare machine, will we be able to contain it after we disarm?

In his disarmament schemes Khrushchev has found some interesting support in the Western world. For instance, Bertrand Russell's famous line, "I'd rather be Red than dead." This essentially takes the view that the Communists are a much rougher and more cantankerous group than the Western imperialists and will go closer to the brink than the Americans. However, the Americans might possibly stumble into war by miscalculation. For the sake of humanity Russell argues that the best thing to do is to accept Communist domination. Taking a long view of history, in a thousand years the human race will pass through this as they have passed through various other things.

In his 1961 speech before the United Nations, President Kennedy alluded to the fact that, if by chance we should get into a war in which nuclear weapons might be used, the possibility would be very high that this globe of ours might be turned into a silent funeral pyre traveling through the solar system without a single living person on it. If one accepts the Christian thesis that the Lord made this universe, the world, and all that dwell therein, has He given man the possibility of destroying the very foundation of earthly life?

Another point to bear in mind is the formula that bomb zero equals moral zero. There are many people who say that where a certain amount of damage is involved it may be a moral act to oppose evil, but if the damage is widespread, then it cannot be a moral act. When our ancestors worked their way west from the Alleghenies some groups were attacked by Indians and every person killed. Would it have been a moral act to try to defend such a group of people, or would it be a moral act to surrender? The numbers involved in conflict are larger now, but the fundamental question of morality remains the same. When, working toward something worth while, an action has to be taken which might result in some one being hurt or killed, is it less moral if the numbers are multiplied? Some say that the thermonuclear weapon has reduced all morality to the same level because no single action worth fighting for can be opposed, in view of the consequences. And yet, fundamentally morality cannot be transformed by numbers. Pain can only be suffered by one human being, but all can enjoy another's happiness. Death is an individual thing. None of us can share our pain or our death, no matter how hard we try. This being the case, to equate the moral dimensions of a particular act—whether fighting the Communists in Korea or opposing them in Berlin—with the number of people that might be involved is a procedure to be examined very carefully. If there is no moral or spiritual distinction whatsoever between what the Communists offer the world and the heritage we share in the West—if this be the case— if it is only a choice between which ant controls which particular ant heap—what difference does it make, after all? When Molotov met with Ribbentrop in 1939, he said, "Politics is only a matter of taste." Is that the type of cynical world to which we want to return?

THE CHRISTIAN VIEW

If there is, as Christian belief maintains, a purpose in this universe and in our human existence, this divine purpose, whatever it may be, is exercised through men, through their individual choices and by the various nations on the earth. Many times throughout the Old Testament we are told of nations being weighed in the balance and found wanting, and their kingdoms given to someone else. Does not that principle of judgment operate at the present time? Somebody has to represent in one way or another forces that, spiritually speaking, are relatively better or relatively worse than others. The biblical statement is that where there is no vision, the people perish.

One of the prevalent views in the Western world—scientific materialism—offers no basis whatsoever for opposing Communism. This philosophy provides no fundamental moral principles. Unfortunately, there are altogether too many scientific materialists on this side of the Iron Curtain. There is no real conviction among many of our intellectuals that what Christianity represents is very meaningful. Western man, trained in a humanist tradition, seeks to preserve the political values he has found, overlooking the fact that all these values sprang from a theological base—namely, the human soul, made individual and different by a divine Creator. He tends to ignore this, and yet accepts all the attributes that Western political man has come to treasure: the uniqueness of the individual, his rights, his liberties, his aspirations. In other words, he has discarded the old source and wants to keep the end product. The modern intellectual feels that somehow or other we achieve these values, or others will achieve them, without having a spiritual basis. This may not be so. Some people maintain that Christianity is outmoded, outdated, and has nothing to offer the modern world. The concept of human life that we possess in the West has never existed in the Orient in any of its religions, whether Buddhism, Hinduism, Shintoism, or Confucianism. It is only in the Western world, with its inheritance from the Old Testament and its concept of the mercy seat standing over the ark of the covenant, further expressed by Christ when He was on earth, that there is an idea of compassion—an idea that the individual human being is in himself a treasure and should be regarded as such. Yet many modern political scientists and sociologists throw overboard the source of the political freedoms we hold dear. How long can these freedoms survive?

There is a contradiction in the modern world, and this is that the Communists, although their goals are materialistic, seem to be applying much more spiritual dedication to their achievement than we of the materialistic West. Many of us have completely forgotten the spiritual foundation on which our freedoms rest. Thus in the contest between societies and systems we often see, whether it be forced or persuaded, more dedication, purpose, and drive on the part of the Communists. It is also true that in the Western world the social conditions we live in are dynamic, tense, and difficult because they involve freedoms of choice. This Western demand of freedom is often rejected by people who want security. They do not want to live with the challenge, the difficulty of choice, the constant responsibility of having to make up one's mind.

THE ULTIMATE CHOICE

To sum up, the struggle is not primarily a struggle for power. However, power is necessarily the factor by which the ultimate judgment between the Communist-controlled world and the free world will be made.

In ages past a crisis such as we now face would have led to wars, to conflict, to revolution and dramatic upheavals. What is our problem? It is to forestall a catastrophe that seems to be close upon us— a catastrophe evident in our own society, evident in the under-developed areas, evident in the competition that exists throughout the world for power, prestige, and influence.

We must determine under whose order the future world image is to be created. This requires that we have a positive purpose of our own. That purpose should be the promotion and extension of freedom. With all the faults in our society, we have the supreme value—the right of choice. There is nobody telling us what to think: whether we are to be religious or irreligious; whether we are to be collectivists or liberals in the old sense of the word. This is the value under which all freedoms can flourish and true spiritual life develop. Our purpose must be to sustain this value. If need be, we must be willing to defend it by mobilizing all the types of power required. And power is not just the ultimate expression of force. That is a requisite. But power also involves ideological influence, persuasion, information, dynamic culture, and a sense of confidence.

If in the long run we are unable to mobilize the power needed to meet the Communist challenge, then perhaps in the course of history the objective factors which they regard as so convincing and value so highly will give them the victory. Eventually we may have to accommodate to their designs. But if we can follow the mysterious dictates of Providence and search for and live the truths that make us free, we will do what the Lord requires of us. Then the spurious values of Communism will fall.

3

The Power Struggle
and the United Nations

ANDREW W. CORDIER

ON OCTOBER 23, 1961, TWO EVENTS TOOK PLACE SIMULTANEOUSLY which reflect the opposing trends involving issues of war and peace confronting our world today. In Oslo, the Nobel Peace Prize Committee announced the granting of the Nobel Prize to Dag Hammarskjöld posthumously for his service to the cause of peace as Secretary-General of the United Nations. At the same time, ironically, the needle of the seismograph of the observatory at Uppsala, Mr. Hammarskjöld's home town, near the cemetery where his body now rests, registered the explosion somewhere in Arctic Siberia of the largest megaton bomb yet tested.

These two events symbolize the profound contradictions of our times. The awarding of the Nobel Peace Prize to Mr. Hammarskjöld, one of the most extraordinary human beings of our generation, was recognition of the great contribution he had made to peace. When the full story of his deeds on behalf of humanity is recorded it will be seen with what intelligence, courage, and persistence he strove for the realization of a more peaceful world. He was a man of realism, vision, and effective action in great causes in which all mankind had a stake. He was the master interpreter of that instrument of peace, the United Nations Charter, and of the various organs that operate under it—interpretations always aimed at the broadening and deepening of effective means through which gains for peace could be realized.

But while the granting of the Nobel Peace Prize was, in the first instance and basically, a tribute to the life and work of Dag Hammarskjöld, it was in the broader sense a means of voicing mankind's yearning for peace. The pathway to peace is not always clear, and even honest men often differ deeply on the meaning of the guideposts along the way.

Hammarskjöld himself referred to this problem in a speech at the University of Chicago several years ago.

Perhaps a future generation, which knows the outcome of our present efforts, will look at them with some irony. They will see where we fumbled and they will find it difficult to understand why we did not see the direction more clearly and work more consistently towards the target it indicates. So it will always be, but let us hope that they will not find any reason to criticize us because of a lack of that combination of steadfastness of purpose and flexibility of approach which alone can guarantee that the possibilities which we are exploring will have been tested to the full. Working at the edge of the development of human society is to work on the brink of the unknown. Much of what is done will one day prove to have been of little avail. That is no excuse for the failure to act in accordance with our best understanding, in recognition of its limits but with faith in the ultimate result of the creative evolution in which it is our privilege to cooperate.*

Having been privileged to work at a unique vantage point as his close collaborator, I would regard the latter part of Hammarskjöld's statement, if applied to himself, as grossly incorrect, for he was a man of vision, of clarity of view, and never allowed means to be employed to distort or compromise the high ends to be attained.

But in this quotation one may suppose that he is referring to the total action of all of us around the world as we strive for peace. There are fumblings, there is confusion. Sometimes our collective sights are very dim indeed, and the great ends to be attained for humanity are sometimes blurred by the less than satisfactory means employed.

But regardless of the frailty of man, whether in mind or spirit, not only his welfare but his actual survival requires that he dedicate himself and a much larger share of his energies and devotion than is now the case to the attainment of a more stable and peaceful world.

The detonation of the super-megaton bomb was a milestone, indeed a great thunderclap in an ominous chain of events. If there was once an art of warfare, we live in the day of the science of warfare. In the last twenty years the remarkable achievements of science have been fully mobilized for means and methods of war, and each of the

* *Servant of Peace,* a Selection of the Speeches and Statements of Dag Hammarskjöld, Wilder Foote, ed. (New York, 1962), p. 260.

two greatest powers possesses the destructive strength, not only to destroy the other, but to destroy humanity many times over. Mankind has followed this development in helpless anxiety. If this race can last indefinitely without an all-out, cataclysmic thermonuclear war—whether initiated by design, by accident, or by helpless acquiescence in a chain of worsening events—it will be one of the great miracles of all history.

Today the world spends between 125 and 200 billion dollars annually, depending upon the character of the calculation, on military preparedness and defense. The magnitude of this expenditure and the extraordinary scope of effort and energy behind it contrast sharply with the expenditures and efforts for peace and human betterment. If we have watched these developments with anxiety, it has been an anxiety mixed with increasing dullness of reaction. For the human mind, subjected to the impact of endless stories of the capacity of modern weapons for destruction, galvanizes itself against reflection on their implications. If some modern Rip Van Winkle, after slumbering for twenty years, should suddenly awaken to the reality of present-day military developments and tensions, he would no doubt agree with Walter Lippmann as to the insanity of our times, and its corollary: a return to sanity as today's supreme necessity.

The two events of that October 23 represent for humanity a crossroads and a choice. Should world efforts and the cause represented by Dag Hammarskjöld weaken with the years, we would resign the field to the threatening forces represented by the bomb. Is the reverse trend possible? Time alone will provide the answer, but human beings—you and I and millions of others—will play some role in determining it.

Norman Cousins, in his book *In Place of Folly* graphically describes the dilemma in which humanity finds itself in the armament race. A definite advance by one side is not accepted by the other in a mood of defeat. Rather it stirs the determination of the party that is behind to speed its efforts to get ahead.

Says Cousins,

The main flaw in the deterrent theory, however, is that it does not deter. The possession by the Soviet Union of advanced nuclear weapons has not served as a deterrent to the United States in matters involving national interests. The United States has not allowed fear of nuclear weapons to deter it from making clear that it was prepared to fight with everything it had to keep from being pushed out of Berlin. Each has attempted to convince the other that it is prepared to let fly with everything it owns rather than back down.*

This unimaginable nuclear might of the two titans of the world was brought into being by the cold war that began almost immediately after World War II, as well as by concurrent and unprecedented achievements in the fields of atomic energy and thermonuclear science.

Even while the Soviet delegation was participating in the United Nations Conference on the drafting of the Charter at San Francisco, its government was engaging in the building of an extended security cushion in Eastern Europe. The Baltic countries were forcibly integrated into the Soviet Union, while the Eastern European countries, through political and military pressure, came under its firm ideological hegemony. In countries such as Poland and Czechoslovakia, in particular, where democratic institutions and ideas were firmly rooted and well advanced, Soviet intervention gave decisive support to *coups d'état* placing monolithic Communist regimes in power and bringing these countries firmly into the Soviet camp. The Western powers countered with the creation of the North Atlantic Treaty Organization (NATO), while the Soviet group drew up the Warsaw Pact, which, apart from its security provisions, was intended to give to the world the image of the free consent of its signatories.

The cold war has been marked by numerous, indeed almost continuous, diplomatic incidents. The unsteady equilibrium in Berlin flared into a diplomatic crisis in 1950 and again in 1961 and 1962. Apart from the major question of the agreed formula for the presence of the great powers in Berlin, which the Soviet Union challenges at will, the building of the wall by East Berlin to prevent the escape of its citizens into the freedom of the West has greatly envenomed the issue. The cold war, while reflecting high levels of tension, has also paralyzed the attainment of effective results in the protracted conferences on disarmament and nuclear control that have been held over the years.

There is no need for recapitulation of cold war issues. Practically all international issues for more than a decade have been affected directly or indirectly by the cold war. All foreign offices, all governments—whether of the great powers or members of military blocs or those holding to a neutral status—have had to deal in one form or another with cold war issues. Many of the smaller countries, par-

* Norman Cousins, *In Place of Folly* (New York, 1961), p. 94.

ticularly those outside of military blocs, have striven hard to avoid involvement in the struggle and in particular issues have attempted to isolate the cold war aspects from other angles of the issue.

During much of the fifties the United States pursued as the main feature of its strategic policy a program of containment of the Soviet Union. But this policy, involving military pacts, military bases, and the stationing of soldiers abroad, lost something of its effectiveness and usefulness as intercontinental ballistic missiles were brought to a state of perfection and accuracy. The conquest of the sky and outer space—the speed and scope with which destructive power could be brought to bear upon points halfway around the world—led both great powers to a re-examination of their strategic policies, each regarding the other as a threat, each developing deterrent power as a safeguard of its security.

Behind the naked power struggle of these two great nations are deep motivations relating to their contrasting ideologies and ways of life. The extent to which Soviet strength and claims for an extension of influence in the world are derived from Russian character, traditions, and interpretations of national sovereignty—as opposed to the convictions and drive derived from Marxian dialectic—is a subject still widely debated. In any case, Marxian ideology is deeply ingrained in the minds of the ruling class of the Soviet Union. It has the optimism and the scent of victory often associated with youthful movements. Slogans like "the wheel of history" (incapable of being stopped), "the wave of the future," and "the world triumph of Communism" are often used in propaganda efforts to persuade wavering millions to join their cause.

On the other hand, the United States makes no conscious effort to graft its ideology, its way of life, or its order of government upon other governments and peoples. In the long stream of history we are a young nation, but in the present world contest we are relatively old and have lost something of the original fervor and crusading zeal for democratic ideals and ideas. We have made them a part of our system, we have built them into our way of life; others may see and imitate, but there is no revolutionary zeal on the part of the American people or government to transplant them to other parts of the world. Our international goals are in this respect more modest, and therefore possibly more effective. The whole of our national life—its educational institutions, churches, industries, agriculture, and commerce—are laid open for non-Americans to observe and, if they wish, to benefit from. President Kennedy and Secretary of State Rusk have both proclaimed the role of freedom as the central principle controlling the sense of direction and destiny of newly developing states. Our policy is to contribute to the free and unhampered growth of new nations; to stimulate their sound and stable development; to free their peoples from poverty, disease, hunger, and illiteracy; to stimulate the development of their resources; and to enable them to live in dignity, freedom, and peace among the nations of the world.

Which of these two philosophies grips the imagination of men? Not enough time has passed to give the final answer. Certainly some millions, whether for reasons of ideology, of propaganda, or of influence, have joined the Communist camp. But millions of others, deeply rooted in democracy, love the fruits of freedom and are devoted to a way of life that offers great promise for the future. Among them are the millions who have fled from East to West Germany, exchanging unbearable conditions for freedom.

A second power struggle of our time, different in character but just as dramatic and far-reaching as that of the cold war, is bound up with the collapse of empires and the establishment of new nations in the great continents of Africa and Asia. At the time of World War I nearly two-fifths of the human family lived under the control of the metropolitan powers of Europe. The League of Nations, unlike the United Nations, was very largely a European club; the silent masses of Africa and South Asia had no voice in world affairs. Their spokesmen, whether at the League or elsewhere, were representatives of the European colonial powers. The interests of some of them, those living in mandated territories, were safeguarded in some measure by the Mandates Commission of the League.

At the same time a popular movement for the self-government and independence of the great Indian subcontinent began to develop. World War II brought heavy strain on the British Empire and accelerated the steps toward independence. With the unique British capacity for mingling power and persuasion, coercion and courtesy, the peoples of the Indian subcontinent emerged through a relatively peaceful process as new nation-states. This was the first giant stride in the liquidation of colonialism and the achievement of independence. Its magnitude and success caused similar movements for independence to sweep like an uncontrolled forest fire over other parts of Asia and most of Africa. People after people became independent, established new governments, and sought membership in the United Nations.

Of the 104 present members of the United Nations approximately one-half are Afro-Asian. The pace of independence has been much

more rapid than anyone anticipated at the time of the San Francisco
Conference. It was assumed then, as careful attention was given to
provisions of the Charter relating to dependent peoples, that the
process of liquidation of empires would take a generation or more.
The main strength of the movement for independence has come
from the peoples themselves. Its roots have been in Asia and Africa,
where the yearnings for freedom, rightful self-assertion, and strong
tides of nationalism have combined to form a movement destined to
succeed.

During the last few years debates in the United Nations and actions
taken by it have added momentum to the movement. The Charter itself, in its Chapters XI, XII, and XIII, provided a genuine Magna
Carta for dependent peoples. Article 73 of the Charter, its first
part in particular, states clearly the principles of the organization in
support of the interests of dependent peoples. The first clauses read
as follows:

> Members of the United Nations which have or assume responsibilities
> for the administration of territories whose peoples have not yet obtained
> a full measure of self-government recognize the principle that the interests
> of the inhabitants of these territories are paramount, and accept as a
> sacred trust the obligation to promote to the utmost, within the system
> of international peace and security established by the present Charter,
> the well-being of the inhabitants of these territories, and, to this end:
>   a. to ensure, with due respect for the culture of the peoples con-
> cerned, their political, economic, social, and educational advancement,
> their just treatment, and their protection against abuses;
>   b. to develop self-government, to take due account of the political
> aspirations of the peoples, and to assist them in the progressive de-
> velopment of their free political institutions, according to the partic-
> ular circumstances of each territory and its peoples and their various
> stages of advancement; . . .

These and other clauses of the Charter relating to dependent peoples
were regarded at the time and for some years thereafter as most progressive and totally in the interest of the inhabitants.

As years passed, more and more petitioners from colonial or
trust territories presented the cases of their peoples or parties in person before various bodies of the United Nations. They were always
given courteous and, indeed, very extended hearings. Those statements and responses to interrogations became a part of the United
Nations record, and resolutions passed by the Trusteeship Council
and the General Assembly often reflected decisively the political views

presented by the petitioners. Many of these same petitioners subsequently became top leaders of their respective governments and now return to the United Nations as full-fledged representatives of their countries.

The effort of the Soviet Union to initiate and be the champion of anticolonial moves in the fifteenth session of the General Assembly was partially thwarted by the Afro-Asian countries, who regard themselves as the proper, bona fide champions of this cause. During the last three sessions of the Assembly they have in fact carried the initiative and determined the general sense of direction on the issue. The important anticolonial resolution passed in the fifteenth session of the General Assembly contained a radical departure from, or extension of, the progressive features of Article 73 of the Charter. In operative paragraph 3 this resolution stated that the political readiness or economic viability of a territory should not be taken into account in determining the timetable for independence. This seemed to some members of the Assembly sheer rashness and a blind disregard, by those favoring the immediate liquidation of colonial status, of the difficulties that would confront some new nations. But of those who supported this clause of the resolution, some argued that the pace of effort on the part of some metropolitan governments was so slow, so ineffective, and so insincere as to make a prolongation of colonial status in the interest of further progress before the attainment of independence a sheer waste of time. In any case, the resolution reflected the temper of the majority and the powerful sweep of the movement for independence.

In the sixteenth session of the General Assembly a further resolution was passed implementing the previous one by providing for the establishment of a committee of seventeen members with responsibility for facilitating, with the metropolitan governments and the peoples concerned, the independence of trust and colonial territories. This committee has in fact pre-empted the responsibility for dependent peoples from other United Nations bodies—the standing committee on non-self-governing territories and the Trusteeship Council. In any case the latter body, a principal organ of the United Nations, will soon have completed its work, since only one trust territory now remains under its competence.

The strong drives in the power struggle may produce an impression that individual and group initiatives in stopping, changing, or directing their course are totally impossible. But such a surrender to events does not take into account man's faith in man, man's faith in religious values, man's faith in education, or his evaluation of the issues at stake. Individual and group effort does count in the world and must be made to count in blunting the edges of the cold war, in promoting peace and human welfare, and in giving direction and stability to the great political evolution represented by several score of new emergent states.

The United Nations is based upon faith—faith that threatening situations can lose their threat, that disputes can be resolved, that actual conflict can be contained and brought to an end.

A distinguished scholar stated in the middle fifties that the United Nations had become an instrument through which its members were attempting to carry out their national interests. For this reason he doubted its further usefulness, and in particular any service it might perform in the implementation of American foreign policies. But the phrase "national interest" deserves analysis. How has national interest changed in our generation, and to what extent has this been recognized by our government and by other governments? Is it not true that at San Francisco each of the participating countries was helping to define and to reformulate not only collective but national interests in a way corresponding with the realities and risks of the contemporary world? With the destructive and savage war then just coming to a close, it was in the direct national interest of all the participants to join their efforts, "to save succeeding generations from the scourge of war."

The purposes of the United Nations as set forth in Article I constitute a part of our direct national interest as well as that of the other signatories. The maintenance of international peace and security, the development of friendly relations among nations, the achievement of international co-operation in solving international problems of economic, social, cultural, or humanitarian character, and the promotion and encouragement of human rights and fundamental freedoms for all, without distinction as to race, sex, language, or religion —these were agreed upon as collective objectives. But these purposes are nevertheless a part of the total scope of national interest.

A distinguished delegate, on leaving the United Nations after a long period of service, gave a proper interpretation of national interest as expressed through the United Nations when he said his service here with that organization was the most rewarding of his diplomatic career. He served, he said, in two capacities, almost always related and consistent. On the one side, he was a representative of his government and tried to be a faithful and intelligent spokesman of its position in the meetings of various United Nations bodies. While valuing that role, he placed a special premium on the second role, which fell to him because his government as one of the signatories of the Charter had committed itself to the high undertakings of that document. Hence he was a person who could be depended upon as a devoted and capable diplomat to serve with other "disinterested-interested" persons in helping to resolve the innumerable political questions that came before the United Nations. His broadened interpretation of national interest was made possible by the deliberate act of his own government in joining with others in 1945 in spelling out great common objectives to be gained by collective effort, the fruits of which would be in the national interest of each and all. Thus the United Nations may certainly be called an instrument of redefined national interest—redefined in terms of the requirements of our revolutionary times and of the paramount need of preserving peace.

Let us look at some assumptions regarding this body. There were those at the time of the San Francisco Conference who believed the United Nations would guarantee the peace. I personally was not among them. I felt then, as now, that the United Nations provides the nations of the world with a valued and practical instrument through which great international objectives can be gained, if peoples and nations join their efforts in doing so. Benjamin Franklin's wise comment regarding the American Constitution, to the effect that "it is what you make it," is valid also for the United Nations Charter and the organization created under it. Even the United States Government—a federal structure—temporarily broke in 1861 under the strain of great social tension. The United Nations—an association of sovereign powers—has not yet broken, but has been subjected to grievous strain under the tensions and major crises of our time.

The second assumption with regard to the United Nations is that it has accomplished little. This, too, is an error. It has accomplished much in preserving peace, unstable as it is. Iran, Korea, Suez, Lebanon, Jordan, the Congo, and Cuba must be catalogued among countries, and crises, in which the influence of the United Nations has been decisively felt. In many other cases tensions have been reduced and threatening situations brought under control. The full catalogue of the achievements of the United Nations—some, to be sure, less than fully successful—is convincing evidence that the institution is worth its cost and has played a positive role in world life. The question of whether it does or does not function along certain lines, or functions differently from what was intended at the time of the San Francisco

Conference, does not prove its lack of value at the present time. The arrangements then made, the views then expressed, and the course of events within the United Nations since that time, throw light upon its character and capacity to perform its present duties.

For example, responsibility for the maintenance of peace and security was vested in the Security Council, and within that Council in the hoped-for unanimity of the great powers. It was perhaps too much to expect, considering their political interests and motivations, that they should hold together in the implementation of this high purpose. In any case, unity disappeared almost at once. Perhaps the most radical innovation in the evolution of the United Nations that has contributed to its success has been the developing role of the smaller powers in keeping the peace. The smaller powers represent a significant "third force" in international affairs and have often, in co-operation with the Secretary-General, scored significantly in support of peaceful adjustment of disputes.

The small nations attach great value to the United Nations and to their membership in it. This is for no reason of vanity or desire for prestige or special position; it arises out of sheer self-interest. The interlacing character of contemporary life means that they cannot live alone. Furthermore, advances in the science of warfare and the threat of thermonuclear destruction give them a rightful claim to participation in efforts to prevent such conflicts, from which no nation could escape. But apart from convincing grounds for self-interest in active participation in United Nations affairs, they bring to the United Nations a moral purpose of great value to the organization. In the absence of military power, their national interest is more clearly and completely focused upon participation with others in practical support of the principles and aims of the Charter. They might be said to be the "disinterested-interested" parties of the organization, and through their collective activities, especially in times of great crises, have come to be known in United Nations circles as the "fire brigade." This does not mean to imply that they do not have other interests of their own, which they sometimes advance with great energy and persuasiveness; yet they represent an element in the life and structure of the United Nations which has contributed much to its vitality from the early years.

Dag Hammarskjöld encouraged their participation in the peace-making and peace-keeping functions of the organization. They, together with him, created a kind of common law in useful practices in the maintenance of peace.

The division of the great powers and the use of the veto in the Security Council threw the balance for action in the United Nations to the General Assembly. The "uniting for peace" resolution as well as the growing tendency of members to appeal to that body, gave the Assembly significance beyond that contemplated in San Francisco. It is a body intended primarily for discussion, but also for negotiation. And negotiation brings discussion to meaningful ends. Furthermore, it has become more and more a body for action. In its work of negotiation and action the Secretary-General has played a role of deep significance.

As executive head of the organization, Hammerskjöld left a deep impact upon the quasi-legislative functions of the Assembly. Furthermore, the Assembly, which now has more than one hundred members, looked to him increasingly for policy guidance upon matters of implementation, and placed increased burdens upon him for the carrying out of actions under important resolutions. In the two major matters previously mentioned, the cold war and the emerging nations, both were his major preoccupations. He once said, "The Organization in fact exercises the most important, though indirect, influence on the conflicts between the power blocs by preventing the widening of the geographical and political areas covered by these conflicts, and by providing for solutions whenever the interest of all parties in a localization of conflict can be mobilized in favor of its effort." He also referred repeatedly to the need of "blunting the edges of the cold war," and in concrete situations, such as Suez, Lebanon, Laos, and the Congo, he tried as far as possible to isolate cold war issues from those more local in character.

The role of the emerging nations in the United Nations is of central importance both to themselves and to that organization. The United Nations assisted them in the steps leading to independence. Upon achieving it, they immediately sought membership, which has given them a ready-made platform for the focusing of their first national interest, and a responsible outlet for expression. It channels their efforts at a time when divisions can easily develop. It provides them with a sense of belonging which would not otherwise exist. In no part of the world is the United Nations flag held higher than among the new nations. It is to the United Nations that they look for assistance, for they know it has no ax to grind, no ulterior motives to serve. Furthermore, as members of the United Nations they assist through its organization in the formulation of programs to help them and other countries. Technical Assistance is their program; OPEX is their program; the Special Fund is their program; and the Children's Fund belongs to them. Organic and functional relationships with instruments of aid eliminate psychological and political barriers that sometimes reduce their effectiveness.

Membership in the United Nations family also helps to eliminate some of the problems of giving and receiving. Top officials of a number of the receiving countries have told the Secretary-General of the difficulty of receiving because of its humiliation. Yet they have needs, tremendous needs. Millions are underfed, illiteracy should be erased, resources should be developed. The psychological problems of giving and receiving have arisen in part because of the attitudes we associated with giving.

When Jesus said, "It is more blessed to give than to receive," it was a way of opening the purses of the selfish to assist the needy. But giving has come to be associated with pride in the act and with an expectation of gratitude. Pride in giving almost always results in humiliation in receiving. It is important for us to learn the simple lesson that people to whom we give have something to give in return. If they are treated as equals, as human beings who have their own contribution to make—perhaps not in material things, but in matters of the mind and spirit—a wholesome reciprocity will exist. This approach is necessary for effective teamwork and for wholesome collaboration among the nations of the world within the United Nations, in order to bring the most solid and steady advance in the development of new nations, as well as to strengthen the sinews of peace.

4

The Power Struggle and the New Nations

WALDEMAR A. NIELSEN

THE DEMISE OF COLONIALISM

THREE STATISTICS TELL THE STORY. IN THE YEAR 1960, 17 NEW MEM-ber countries were admitted to the United Nations. Since 1945, 40 countries had achieved political independence. The total population of these countries is nearly 900 million. This is the magnitude and the speed of the disintegration of Western colonialism.

The process, though well advanced, is not yet complete. In Africa particularly large areas are still in dependent status, and some long, bloody battles are in prospect before colonialism in the form in which it has been known for the past few centuries is totally eradicated. There is little doubt, however, that it *will* be eradicated, probably by the end of the present decade.

In the demise of colonialism there is profound cause for hope. Although it was not totally without benefit to the subject peoples, the system on the whole was exploitive, degrading, and unjust. It became a crust, restricting mankind's development, and now that it is being cracked off great potentialities for progress are opening up. The attainment of national independence may be the beginning of literacy and enlightenment for hundreds of millions of God's creatures; the beginning of health and better material conditions of life; the beginning of social justice and the removal of racial discrimination; the beginning of freedom, responsibility, and individual dignity.

But not necessarily. Political revolutions, like scientific revolutions, do not inevitably result in human benefit. Every fledgling nation faces

37

the possibility that the results of independence for its people may be catastrophic. For the evidence of centuries suggests that the movement from subjugation to independence is not linear but circular. In too many cases the elimination of foreign political and economic control has resulted merely in the establishment of equally burdensome indigenous control.

One of the great questions of the 1960's, therefore, is: Will the many frail new nations now full of optimism and expectation as a result of independence manage to survive and prosper? Or will they, after a brief and hopeful period of independence, fall quickly back into bondage of some new form? The hazards the new nations face as they begin to make their own way in the world are both internal and external. Let us consider first the former.

THE STRUGGLE FOR NATIONAL DEVELOPMENT

Hard though the struggle for independence typically is, the struggle for national development that succeeds it is harder, more protracted, and more complex. We can understand something of this difficulty by recalling that in Latin America, where independence was secured more than a century ago, internal reform and development have as yet hardly begun.

This problem—namely, of development in the impoverished parts of the world—is one that we in the United States have greatly underestimated. We have also maintained overoptimistic views about the progress so far made and the prospects for the future.

There is a widespread impression, for example, that as a result of foreign aid, scientific progress, and various development programs the gap in living standards between the richer and poorer countries has now begun to narrow. The facts, unhappily, are precisely the contrary. The gap each year steadily widens, because living standards in the developed countries increase much more than the standards in the poor countries. Moreover, with the expected differential impact of future scientific achievements on both developed and less developed countries, the tendency will be for the former to move ahead still more rapidly.

As of today, then, there seems little possibility that the poorer countries can even keep pace with the growth of richer nations, let alone begin to overtake them—unless of course the latter incinerate themselves in a nuclear war.

It can be argued that the comparison of standards between rich and poor countries is far less important to the people of the latter than comparisons of their own present living standards with their situation in the past and their prospective situation in the future. This may well be true. But if so, the facts again provide only a slender basis for optimism.

With hard and intelligent effort, and with considerable outside help, a modest rate of economic growth in most of the poorer countries can be generated and sustained. Marked improvement in levels of nourishment and health, specifically, are attainable. But in many regions the gains will, over time, be largely and literally eaten up by population increase.

Politically, the implications of the situation are ominous. Economic development is not proceeding as fast as it must if calamitous consequences are to be avoided.

We Americans must therefore take an intelligently critical look at the aid programs we have been supporting. This is not to suggest, of course, that there has been any lack of criticism of these programs up to now. There is in fact very widespread unease in the United States about foreign aid programs, and a number of theories about what is wrong with them are in wide circulation.

There are those who, like the authors of *The Ugly American,* attribute the failure to the rudeness, stupidity, and venality of our public servants overseas. Others think it more probably due to the rudeness, stupidity, and venality of some member of Congress. There are those who feel that the failures have been primarily quantitative—either we have given too much aid, thereby deadening foreign initiative; or we have given too little to make serious impact on a problem of monumental proportions. There are those who see the failure in terms of strings—either we attach too many and produce foreign resentment, or we attach too few and thereby permit waste and corruption.

There may be truth in some of these views. But they do not get at the root of the matter. Our failures have not been merely individual, or quantitative, or technical. They have been more fundamental.

As a nation, we have righteously and repeatedly congratulated ourselves for our great generosity in giving aid. But in fact we have lacked conviction about the importance of foreign aid and foreign economic development. We have shown a lack of understanding about major elements of the development problem. We have lacked an effective philosophy for using the instrument of foreign aid to induce self-generating development in the recipient countries.

Most Americans, it seems to this writer, still consider foreign aid a semicharitable activity and foreign economic development a worthy but secondary objective in our foreign policy. We have therefore kept the economic aid agencies and their personnel in a second-class, temporary status in the structure of government. We have kept appropriations for foreign aid on a year-to-year and hand-to-mouth basis. In determining the composition and distribution of our aid, we have not infrequently given greater consideration to domestic pressures and requirements than to the needs of recipient countries. Our aid programs have thus been halfhearted and halfway undertakings.

Second, we have been preoccupied with the physical aspects of economic development—with the building of roads, the installation of machinery, and the irrigation of land. We have tended to disregard the most important potential resources for development in the poor countries—and the most important potential barrier to it: the human beings who live there.

Though we have given some technical assistance and technical training, we have on the whole neglected the problem of foreign educational development. This is particularly curious in a country like the United States, which has long believed in universal education and has so magnificently demonstrated the relationship between education and development. The land-grant college system, celebrating its hundredth anniversary next year, is living proof of the value of investment in education as a means to national, social, political, and economic growth.

Third, we have failed to use our assistance effectively as an instrument to induce necessary institutional changes within the recipient countries. The heart of the development problem is not economics; it is politics. Unless there is reform—in some cases deep and far-reaching reform—the supplies and assistance we send will be nothing more than seed scattered upon barren ground. It should be quite clear by now that antique economic structures can waste more, also that corrupt and selfish interests can steal more, than all the assistance we can ever provide. To turn a venerable piece of wisdom around, they can drink it faster than we can make it.

Yet for much too long we have innocently taken the view that merely pouring materials and technical assistance into any kind of social, political, and economic structure abroad would somehow result in progress. We have been unwilling to try to correct even flagrant cases of misuse of aid, on the ground that to do so would involve intervention in the affairs of sovereign states. And indeed it is much easier to talk about "insisting on needed reforms as a condition for aid" than to impose such a requirement acceptably and effectively.

Nevertheless, a much better answer to this dilemma than we have so far devised must soon be found. President Kennedy's Alliance for Progress in the Western Hemisphere and the executive branch proposals on foreign aid this year reflect a major step forward in correcting some of the basic deficiencies in our aid concepts and programs of the past. But reactions in Congress to these proposals, plus what seems to be a wide and deep disenchantment on the part of the American public about foreign aid programs, lead one to feel that American help in the great world-wide labor of development will continue to be too little, too unpredictable, and too lacking in boldness and imagination to be of decisive value in breaking through the barriers to progress.

I am a pessimist, therefore, about the prospects for sufficiently rapid development in the poorer countries. The great hopes that now prevail in these countries about rapid industrialization and improvement in living conditions are unlikely to be fulfilled. As a result, we can anticipate growing waves of public frustration and desperation in the poorer nations in the years ahead. Such desperation in turn will lead to public disorders, revolutions, and authoritarian regimes of various kinds. In a number of instances, control will come into the hands of elements of a totally corrupt, reactionary, and antidemocratic character. In other cases, military factions may take over and prove to be more progressive, honest, and patriotic than the regimes they displace. But in every case where there is a turning to authoritarianism it will represent the death, in some degree, of both economic and political ideals for which the struggle for independence has been fought.

Military or right-wing dictatorships are two of the dangers; the third is take-over by Communist elements. Such an eventuality would involve not only the destruction of hopes for progress on a democratic basis within the victim country, but also the degeneration of its independence as a nation. Communism in the emergent nations is therefore best treated as an aspect of the external dangers they face. In plainer language, Communist take-over involves not only dictatorship but also recolonization.

A WORD TO NEW NATIONS

In the view of most leaders of underdeveloped countries, the principal external threat facing them is from the West. This shocking fact is not quite so incredible when one attempts to view the world scene from their perspective and in terms of their past experience.

But they are profoundly wrong in their estimate. Their error, if persisted in, will result not only in disadvantage to the United States and the Atlantic Nations but also to the emergent countries themselves.

The reader will be spared any general discourse on the virtues of democracy and the faults of Soviet totalitarianism. We have already been drowned in verbosity concerning the philosophical and ideological aspects of the struggle that is now ripping our planet to shreds. Moreover, the world situation has deteriorated to the point where general discussion of these issues—particularly in underdeveloped parts of the world—has become unpersuasive if not irrelevant. We are all now in a predicament of danger in which we must put aside word games. All of us, in both developed and underdeveloped free world countries, are confronted with brutal and immediate choices. I should like, therefore, to address some plain talk to my friends among the leadership of the less developed nations.

One can understand why you feel passionately about the dangers from the West—Western colonialism, Western imperialism, and capitalistic neocolonialism, in the vocabulary you currently employ. You have as children and adults grown up in colonialism. You have suffered on more than one occasion the humiliation and brutality of Western policies and white colonial administrators. You have in many cases spent time—sometimes years—in colonial prisons, and with deep bitterness and resentment have seen not only yourselves but your families, your friends, and your entire nation subjected to the same conditions.

One can understand the meaning of the bloody and bitter events of Algeria and Angola to you, or why Berlin and the grave human and political tragedy it represents have less impact upon your feelings than, for example, South Africa. One can understand your reactions to Katanga and its confirmation in your eyes of the intentions and power of Western economic interests.

But if we are speaking, not of the imperfections of the West—of which I am sorry to say there are many—but of threat, of naked danger to the very independence of your countries, then one may fairly ask you to weigh carefully the validity of the following minimal propositions.

First, the Western countries despite their overwhelming predominance in military power will not go all-out in their effort to maintain control over their remaining colonial possessions. This is not said in unawareness of the magnitude of the French effort in Algeria or the brutality of Portuguese activity in Angola. Nevertheless, on the whole the Western colonial powers are steadily relinquishing control—sometimes gracefully, sometimes disgracefully—but nevertheless relinquishing it. The battles for independence by feeble and underequipped liberation armies are, one by one, successful. These successes cannot be entirely explained by the heroism and determination of freedom fighters, nor by the existence of tensions between East and West. The Western withdrawal from colonialism is fundamentally explicable only by a much deeper factor—one whose importance for your own future you appear not to have fully grasped, and to which we shall return later.

Second, once a country has achieved independence, the Western powers will not seriously attempt to intervene militarily to reimpose their control. Cuba might appear to be evidence to the contrary. But the Cuban case is quite in point. The United States—with all the military and other power necessary to take control of Cuba—could not mount and follow through on a serious invasion effort even in the face of the most extreme provocation. The deepest reason is to be found in a realm beyond military and strategic considerations.

Third, the West will no longer attempt to defend the position of private economic interests in foreign areas with military force. When the newly independent countries have taken measures—even extreme measures—against Western economic interests, they have been able to do so with impunity. Certainly they have been showered with protests, verbal denunciations, and all the other normal manifestations of national outrage by the injured and aggrieved Western nations. But the fact remains that new governments have on the whole been able decisively to control the power and privileges of Western economic interests within their borders.

The Western nations are going to continue to behave as nations and not as angels. You in the less developed areas are going to continue to receive trouble and annoyance from them, along with a substantial amount of help. But these Western powers because of their character, interests, and responsibilities will not be more than a nuisance. They are not, and will not be, a direct threat to your sovereignty and national existence, assuming you display a reasonable degree of courage and intelligence in running your own affairs.

On the other hand, I submit to you four propositions in support of the view that the real danger to your sovereignty derives from the Communist side.

First, Soviet ideology is clear and specific on the point that genuine independence in the emergent countries is, from the Communist viewpoint, intolerable. And ideology in that system plays a not unimportant role. In their theory, revolutions for national independence are mere stages on the road to a double form of national subordination of the country: internally, to a dictatorship of the Communist party; and externally, to the "socialist camp"—that is to say, to the policies and control of the Soviet Union.

Throughout the world the struggles for national independence since World War II have not been fought under Communist banners, nor led by Communist leaders, nor inspired by Communist ideals. It is necessary therefore for the Soviets to jump on the bandwagon of this great historic movement. They are trying to reinterpret its origins and objectives in order to pave the way for substituting Communist leadership and objectives. For the Soviets, therefore, to describe your victories of national independence as merely preparatory steps to Communism is to degrade and misrepresent them. It is also to reveal their intention to try to take them over.

Second, the Soviet bloc is fully prepared to use military force to establish direct physical control over the weaker independent countries. In the Greek civil war we saw a major military effort against an independent country initiated and nourished by leadership and supplies from the Communist area. The Soviet-Chinese attack against Korea was likewise of major proportions. The action against Tibet, which took place in the shadows and silence of the closed Communist world, was the murder of a heroic but helpless country by military means.

The fact that not all these efforts succeed is not due to any reluctance on the part of Communist invaders to use force. Let that be clear.

Third, the Soviet system is fully prepared, despite repercussions upon world opinion, to suppress with unlimited military force any effort on the part of a once subjugated area to regain its independence. Yugoslavia is, of course, the miraculous case to the contrary. But the examples of East Germany in 1953, Hungary and Poland in 1956, and Berlin and East Germany again in 1962 prove the general point.

Syria may be able to break away from Nasser, but any leader from an underdeveloped country who visits Budapest will quickly understand that secession of an area from the Soviet bloc is a different matter. There, 6,000 tanks were moved into a single city and some 80,000 human beings murdered in the course of a week to break the back of an independence movement.

Many friends in the less developed countries feel that the term *colonialism* is not precisely applicable with respect to the situation in Eastern Europe, largely because the matter of color and racial discrimination is not involved. But consider Yugoslavia, with whose Communist leaders I have talked intimately. For complex reasons of their own, the Yugoslavs still follow a policy of duplicity in their public and official announcements. They are still not willing to say in public what they quite freely express in private. But their description of Soviet policy and action against Yugoslavia prior to the historic break in relations makes it unmistakably clear that this was unmitigated colonialism in its most exploitive sense.

Fourth, I submit that the Soviet system is now actively carrying on large-scale, co-ordinated programs of propaganda, subversion, economic influence, and diplomatic and military pressure to destroy and take over independent governments in the emergent countries wherever it can. By now these activities of the Soviet Union are widely recognized. Soviet tactics and techniques of internal penetration, of systematically destroying the reputation and position of non-Communist leadership, of obstructing all constructive efforts to solve national problems through democratic methods, are increasingly understood.

From a Western viewpoint, the most impressive aspects of these programs are the willingness of the Soviets to invest very large resources over a long period, as well as their brilliant co-ordination and generalship.

But to the leadership of the less developed countries these Soviet techniques and programs have more immediate implications. They are a continuous, deliberate effort aimed at destroying any man and program contrary to Communism. These are not the polite and gentle efforts of the Western countries in the field of information, cultural exchange, and diplomatic intercourse. This is war in a new and subtle form—war against the independence of your countries.

In sum, to return to the question of the locus of the true threat, the evidence I believe adds up to this: for the less developed countries, the Western nations in the future may be a disappointment, a nuisance, and cause of pain, but they will be a source of assistance. However, the Communist system will be not merely a nuisance or painful, but also a direct, implacable threat. It has the power and the will to recolonize the now emergent countries and to absorb them. Moreover, it is now widely engaged in programs to this end.

To have to discuss relations between developed and underdeveloped areas in terms of where the greater threat lies is indeed a commentary on the present state of the world. And yet, despite the grimness of the situation, I am optimistic about political developments in the less developed areas in the years ahead, unless the failure of economic development efforts is complete.

For one thing, Khrushchev is rendering magnificent service in clarifying to people everywhere the real issues involved in the East-West conflict. In this respect, one could say he has been a thumping success.

Moreover, I have great confidence in the character, the realism, and the patriotism of the leadership of the emergent countries. The problems with which they are faced are cruel and complex. Their views on all things do not, and obviously cannot, coincide with ours. Some have made mistakes and have led their countries along dangerous paths. But with few exceptions they are men of humane and independent spirit. Therefore I believe that, in time, they will more and more recognize that their principles and objectives are fundamentally in harmony with those of the West and that their interests lie in friendly association with the West.

For the Western countries, with all their faults and imperfections, are nevertheless those countries in the world in which the ideas of democracy, social justice, and respect for national independence have the greatest hold and the greatest direct influence on national policies. It is the moral and liberal elements in the Western countries that assure the emergent nations of their chances of survival. These forces of liberalism and democracy are subject to challenge and contest within the Western world; but they are already strong, in some cases dominant, and in all cases growing more powerful.

In the Soviet system, however, such forces, if they exist, have no bearing upon policy. It is this absence of democratic control along with the absence of respect for liberal ideas, national independence, or self-determination in Soviet philosophy that makes Communism the threat to the independence of new nations.

We are entering a precarious decade. There are reasons to feel hopeful and causes for discouragement. But in the face of the awesome prospect of the years ahead, a man cannot find his way merely by trying to tote up the evidence. He must look into his own heart to perceive what he truly values and what he is prepared to live, and if necessary die, for. The outcome of this dark, impending decade, like that of all great issues, is not foreordained, but rests upon the human beings involved and upon what they believe and will do.

For all of us, this embraces essentials of our political views as well as our spiritual convictions. What, then, in the words of the title of this series of talks, is the role of Christianity in a period of world revolution?

THE ROLE OF CHRISTIANITY

In the underdeveloped and emergent areas themselves, the influence of Christianity will be on the decline. But before elaborating the reasons for this negative judgment it will be well to recall the fact that the involvement of Christianity in their revolutions and development is deep and wide.

No Western institutions, not even the economic, are more extensively at work in these areas. In a number of the less developed countries Christianity is the dominant faith. In a considerable number, primary and secondary education, in so far as it is available, is largely provided through Christian institutions. In many, health and welfare services, in so far as they are available, are likewise dependent upon Christian organizations.

Christian groups are heavily engaged in the administration of technical assistance and economic development. The principal American foreign aid agency, AID, has only one-fourth as many people working overseas in these activities as do the American Christian churches.

But the involvement of the churches is not merely in the administration of educational, health, and charitable projects. Far more fundamental has been the influence of Christian precepts on the thinking and values of people in these areas. Ideas of the dignity and worth of the individual, of human brotherhood, and of love and freedom have been sparks in the tinder of misery—sparks that have ignited the vast revolutionary conflagration now sweeping the world.

Nonetheless, great though the role of Christianity and of Christian activity has been in the underdeveloped areas, I believe it is destined to diminish in the future.

First, in the emergent areas this is a time of nationalistic spirit, of resurgence of ethnic consciousness, and in some cases of antiforeign feeling. In many countries Christianity is regarded as a foreign element, out of harmony with notions of sovereignty, revolution, and material development. Wherever countries fall victim to Communism, as in China and Cuba, Christianity will be under attack or driven out. Elsewhere, as in India, Egypt, and certain areas of sub-Saharan Africa, its activities have been and will be resisted. Already declining in statistical terms as a world religion, Christianity in the years ahead will find the scale of its activities outside the developed Western nations steadily curtailed.

Second, Christianity has lost a great deal of its moral prestige in these areas in recent decades, a loss which it is not likely to be able to recoup in the decade ahead. The role it has played in the emerging areas prior to and during the process of national liberation has been a checkered one. There are cases in which the churches have stood strongly against the colonial system, economic exploitation, and racial discrimination. But there are as many instances in which they have been implicated in, and beneficiaries of, exploitative and discriminatory arrangements.

There are cases where the Christian influence has been applied directly and forcefully in bringing about decolonialization, and in which indigenous leadership has been Christian in outlook. But there are more cases in which the churches have played an equivocal or negative role in relation to movements for national independence.

It is not surprising, therefore, that in far too many places the Christian churches are regarded by the indigenous populations as essentially a white man's religion, a religion associated with the establishment and maintenance of colonialism and more commonly to be found on the side of the preservation of the status quo than on the side of national independence and reform.

Equally important, though less directly, is the fact that Christianity in the eyes of much of the world is now associated with mass warfare and destruction. In recent times at least, it is the Christian nations that have been mainly involved in the great wars.

Nor can the consequences of the colossal failure of Christian precepts in the case of Hitler Germany be overlooked. Here in this Western country, a cradle of Protestantism and a stronghold of Catholicism, was committed one of the ugliest and most massive crimes in all history against every decent human principle and ideal. We may be able to find ample reasons or rationalizations to explain away such failures, but it should not astonish us to find that people in the non-Christian areas do not.

Third, the Christian approach in much of its economic and welfare activity in the less developed areas is of secondary importance in efforts toward national development and reform. In hundreds of places overseas sincere, devoted Christian men and women are teaching children, ministering to the sick, and providing training in basic skills. But the poor countries seek and require not only better basket-making but large-scale industrialization. They need not only demonstration plots for teaching better methods to the local farmer, but also far-reaching land reform. They require not only instruction in concepts of tolerance and brotherhood, but basic overhauling of economic, political, and legal systems.

Christian charitable activity in the nineteenth century was earnest and well-meaning, but it largely failed to grasp the broader needs for institutional reform created by the industrial revolution. Consequently secular leaders, not Church leaders, were principally responsible for the major advances made in human welfare and social justice at that time.

Today, also, Christian efforts seem admirable and well-intentioned, but largely on the periphery. One sees no convincing evidence that Christian leadership has yet grasped the fact that the village handicraft project, the mission school, and the jungle hospital, however decent and deserving of praise, do not suffice and are not in some cases even relevant to the great undertakings required for economic and social reform, industrialization, and democratic political development.

THE NEED FOR CHRISTIAN ACTION

To summarize this gloomy assessment, Christian agencies have already had their period of maximum opportunity in the less developed areas, and to a substantial degree they have failed. In the coming phase they will be a fringe factor. History in these areas will be made by secular and, on the whole, non-Christian leaders. The revolutionary world, for better or worse, is not looking to Christian leadership.

What then is to be done? First, let me emphasize that the good work now being carried on by Christian agencies overseas should be continued and strengthened, not abandoned. For it is better to be a fringe factor than no factor at all. Moreover, in a turbulent period which will be characterized by great human suffering, violence, the widespread disruption of traditional institutions, and preoccupation with material aspects of national development, the need for Christian ministration and Christian teaching is even greater than in the past.

However, the main opportunity, in my judgment, and the main need for Christian action in the present revolutionary period, lies here in the United States. Quite obviously, American power will play the decisive role in the defense of Western principles and positions in the continuing struggle against Communist imperialism and colonialism. Moreover, ours is a country deeply infused with Christian influence, in which popular opinion directly controls the general direction of national policy. Thus the actions and beliefs of Christians as citizens are translated without blocking or deformation into the guidance of our national conduct.

Too many of us, for far too long, have been bemused by the needs and possibilities of contributing to peace and human welfare by activities abroad. But this can be a dangerous kind of escapism. It is all too easy to be a good Christian a long way from home. The heart of the battle is here in the United States. Head-cracking problems of American policy abound which will require the attention and ideas of all of us, including the questions of American policy in Angola, of protecting freedom in Berlin, of nuclear testing, of support for foreign aid, and a long list of others.

In calling for greater Christian influence and activity in national affairs, one is aware that there are those who believe our foreign policy should be shaped exclusively by considerations of the "national interest"—not by moral, philosophical, or ethical considerations. I do not share that view. Certainly in the past we have made grievous mistakes when we have allowed righteousness and the crusading spirit to influence our foreign actions. Nonetheless I believe that, unless underlying our foreign policy and all other national policy there beats a strong pulse of faith in the essential ideas of brotherhood, love, social justice, and individual dignity, then our whole existence becomes meaningless, individually and nationally, and the very roots of our strength and character die.

Given the importance and practical possibility of helping to shape the policies of the United States—this great and determining influence in the world—what should the Christian community do?

There are three appropriate tasks which seem to me of great importance and urgency:

The first is to help maintain a balance and perspective between the several major elements of our foreign policy and programs, especially the diplomatic, economic, and military. With the fearsome increase in Russian power that has now occurred, the military aspects of the East-West contest have become crucial. Our response in countering the Russian military threat must be strong and clear. But as military considerations move to the forefront, and as already vast military expenditures expand, there is a subtle danger that our thinking may become to a degree militarized. We may depreciate the diplomatic function and forget the role of negotiations and compromise. Faced with the heavy burden of military outlays, we may overlook the equally important need, in the long run, of maintaining and improving our foreign assistance programs.

Christian concern can be of particular importance in giving these programs the status and recognition they deserve. It is commonly lamented in Washington that "economic aid programs have no constituency" and that they are therefore disadvantaged in the political process. But their constituency should be the conscience and the understanding of every true Christian and citizen.

Second, Christian elements in our population can play an important part by giving sturdy endurance and calm confidence to our national policies in the face of international adversity. For the struggle in which we are engaged will be of long duration and may outlast the lives of most of us. It is a struggle which may involve defeats, serious defeats, before the tide finally turns in our favor. It will test not only our resources and productivity, but our convictions and our character. Unless we have a firm base of beliefs and values, as well as an understanding of what ultimately is involved in the struggle, we cannot prevail.

It should be a cause for reflection and concern on the part of Christians that every time the Communist threat becomes acute, every time the clouds of the world situation darken, there are more than a few of their fellow believers who seem immediately prepared to scuttle and run. The glorious name of Christianity is currently lettered on the banners of some so-called crusades which seem to have no faith at all in the deep strength and durability of Christian principles and Christian society. They give themselves readily to panicky feelings of fear and hopelessness; they consequently seem ready—eager, almost—at the first sign of trouble to abandon the distinguishing elements of our freedom, to deny the necessity for social and racial progress here at home, and to manifest their lack of conviction in democracy by sowing to all winds their suspicion and distrust of some of our most important institutions and most honorable leaders.

It is urgent that in the troubled years ahead we begin to see as much vigor, as much organized concern about national and world problems, on the part of responsible, undaunted elements in the Christian community as the frantic fringes seem periodically to display.

Third and finally, I believe that the Christian community can and must turn itself to a re-examination and re-evaluation of the meaning and the faults of our modern mass society—modern technological, scientific, materialistic, industrial, urban society.

One of the fundamental reasons we find ourselves in a grave predicament today is that we have become lost in our thinking and our understanding. We have fallen victim to outmoded and invalid conceptions of our problems. We have been dazzled by scientism and materialism, partly perhaps because of our dazzling success and progress in these directions. We have become indifferent to injustice because of the familiarity of its forms. We have become ineffective in our collaboration with our fellow man of different color, different culture, and different convictions because of the effects of wealth and comfort upon our view of life. We find ourselves discontented in the midst of plenty, and our society turning about in circles, dissatisfied with itself, but bewildered about where it wants to go and how to get there.

I have read and reread the recently issued twenty-year program of the Soviet Communist Party. With sadness and some apprehension, I have studied this masterpiece of cynicism, this incredibly skillful exploitation of human idealism.

And then I have asked myself: what have we, the free men of the free world, done to formulate our convictions, to define our view of society in modern terms, to hang in the sky a statement of our goals and ideals? What have we done to inspire our fellow men with a statement of the things in which we truly believe and for which we are striving?

Thus we return to the point from which all things begin—man himself. Ultimately, the heroic and eternal task is within ourselves, in the purification of our faith, the clarification of our understanding, and the dedication of our lives. To the extent we can do these things, to that extent we will render our greatest service to a revolutionary world, to all mankind, and to the will of God.

Part II

THE RAPPROCHEMENT
BETWEEN SCIENCE AND RELIGION

5

The New Rapprochement
between Science and Religion

AS WE LOOK AT THE PATTERN OF EVENTS IN THE WORLD AROUND US
today, it is easy to find considerable evidence that the two most important factors currently shaping the course of human life on this
planet are science and religion. Science has placed in our hands the
key to ultimate power, the power of the atom. Religion, or the lack
of it, will ultimately decide whether this power is used to build a
brave new world or misused to leave a world totally destroyed.

In view of this critical juncture, it seems worth while to take a look
at the relationship between science and religion and at what it may
mean for our future. Are they destined always to be implacable
enemies, as many were convinced a century ago? Or can they become
allies, fighting side by side in our struggle to attain peace on earth,
abundant living, and a new order of understanding of human
destiny?

In seeking the answers to these questions, we discover signs of reorientation today in both fields. Science is developing new perspective
as it approaches the inner and outer boundaries of the universe. It
looks within at the atom and without at the distant nebulae and discerns new elements of design in the cosmic structure. Religion is likewise concerned with the inner and outer boundaries of life. It looks
within at the human heart and without at human destiny and also sees
new vistas of the divine plan. Moreover, there is persuasive evidence
that these changing perspectives in science and religion are at last
approaching a common focus. If this is true, it is a bright ray of hope
in this rather gloomy world in which we live today.

SCIENCE AND RELIGION IN THE NINETEENTH CENTURY

To see the nature of the recent changes in the relation of science and religion, it is helpful to recall some nineteenth-century attitudes. A hundred years ago scientific and religious thought certainly did not have a common focus, and the issues on which they split were sharply defined. The thinking of science, at least in its more mature aspects, was dominated by a mechanistic slant. A succession of powerful intellects—Galileo, Descartes, Newton, Leibnitz, Lagrange—had attacked the basic problem of matter and motion, and in its solution they had produced the science of mechanics, a structure of analytical logic that was beautiful in its simplicity and rigor, and powerful as a basic explanation of phenomena far beyond its own bailiwick. For example, it formed the basis of a kinetic theory of gases, a wave theory of optics, a vectorial electrodynamics, and a chemical thermodynamics. Extended to technology, this stimulated the invention of the steam engine, the electric generator, and the internal combustion motor; and from all these new sources of power came the industrial revolution. We cannot, naturally, give all the credit to mechanics for this profound change in the shape of civilization, but certainly mechanics was at the core of it. Without the co-ordinates of Descartes and the laws of Newton it is hard to see how any of these other developments could have happened.

Moreover, when these new theories were used to study the internal economy of the atom, it was found that the atom itself appeared to obey the laws of mechanics. The evidence from spectra and from experiments with radioactivity indicated that the atom was a miniature solar system. At its center there was a nucleus acting like a little sun. Around this nucleus electrons circulated like planets in orbits, under the same laws of mechanics that governed the movement of the earth and its sister planets around our sun. Since the atom obeyed the laws of mechanics, it seemed necessary to conclude that it was in essence a little machine. And since in particle mechanics the whole is no more than the sum of its parts, the next conclusion was that man, being made of atoms, was just a big machine. Finally, pushing the argument to its cosmic end: the universe was composed of atoms and was therefore just a supermachine.

Another binding principle in mechanics was the law of cause and effect. Every cause had an effect and these were linked together in an inexorable web of determinism governing every action in the universe.

Thus, according to this logic, one was forced to conclude that man is a puppet dancing on the strings of determinism in a mechanistic universe—a Petroushka dumbly twitching in response to the fluctuations of the cosmos—and that there is nowhere any trace of evidence of a master of this mechanical carnival.

In assessing the weight of this argument in retrospect, not only must we look at the areas where the mechanistic scientists worked with such success, but we must be equally aware of the areas they neglected. For they passed rather glibly over a whole class of questions that today we would call boundary problems. For example, they accepted infinity as the outer boundary for both space and time. They treated space as a linear three-dimensional manifold extending in every direction without limit. Likewise, they treated time as a linear dimension extending both backward and forward without limit. Space, they thought, went out indefinitely in every direction. Time, they said, had been flowing on forever and would continue to flow on forever. They claimed that no one could possibly think of any other answer. But as we can see today, no one in this period actually thought at all about the precise meaning of ascribing infinity as an outer boundary.

There was a similar vagueness about inner boundaries, such as the extent to which either space or matter could be subdivided. The ancient Greeks were aware of this problem and accepted a limit on the subdivision of matter; this limit was called the atom—the uncuttable particle. The concept of the atom proved to be a well-anchored axis holding subsequent thoughts about matter in an orderly pattern for centuries. It certainly was the basis for the mass-particle idea that was the cornerstone of Newtonian mechanics. Today we see that this focus on the particle, this *particulate* cast of thought, stimulated a large part of the progress in scientific theory of the eighteenth and nineteenth centuries; but it also blinded the scientists of that time to the danger of extending particulate thinking beyond its proper sphere. And it was precisely in this treatment of the inner and outer boundaries of time, space, and matter that the thinking of men of science and men of religion in the nineteenth century diverged so sharply.

Religion properly could claim a right to speak about these boundaries. They included the problems of creation, the Creator, eternity, and human destiny as the encompassing concepts of life. They included the human spirit, the essence of life, and man's relation to his

Creator as the inner core of existence. For many thousands of years men of religion had struggled to express more clearly these relations of man to that which surrounds him. They could only see dimly; words and images were inadequate; but what they saw and understood was enough to provide them with a dynamic for life that in faith and in works testified to a profound truth.

Now place this core of religion's analysis of cosmic boundaries over against the comparable analyses of nineteenth-century science. Ask about the initial boundary in time. How did things begin? Religion answered positively that they were initiated by a Creator. Science answered negatively that there was no beginning, only a dull, flat, monotonous flow of time from no definable source into no definable sink.

These statements oversimplify the arguments, of course, and ignore many complications. For example, if one takes the first chapters of Genesis as the official pronouncement of our own Christian religion on the problem of creation, the scientific antagonist can have a field day by throwing stones at literal interpretations of the text. The calculation by Bishop Ussher of the exact moment of the beginning of creation as 4004 B.C. has been the source of many a smile. But is it any worse than asserting that there cannot have been any creation because it is impossible to think of an initial point in time. One may grant the nineteenth-century physicists that, if time is indefinitely linear in measure, then to talk about a simple initial point in time is impossible. But it is precisely in the assumption of linearity and continuity that classical physics fails in dealing with boundary problems; and the progress of nonlinear scientific thought in our own century makes this increasingly plain. We have no justification for assuming that when apparent linearity and continuity prevail over the central area under consideration, we will then find linearity and continuity no matter how far we explore the fineness of texture toward an inner boundary, and no matter how far we explore the extension of the area toward an outer boundary. By way of contrast, I think religious thought at least implicitly recognized the deeper significance of boundary conditions. And I believe that the change of attitude in science toward boundary conditions is one of the most important aspects of the rapprochement between science and religion. This is illustrated by the shift from particles to harmonic forms as the basis of our thinking about the mass and energy of our universe, by new concepts of space, and by new vistas in cosmology. I should like to discuss each of these areas briefly and then examine the conclusions to be drawn that are changing our views on the philosophical orientation of science.

THE NEW REALITIES OF NATURE

The concept of the atom as a small planetary system reached its peak of popularity early in the 1920's. But the same experiments that provided the best evidence in favor of this planetary atomic picture also proved conclusively that there were serious flaws in its basic pattern. First of all, these planetary electrons should have radiated energy as they moved in orbits, but they clearly did not. Next it was found that they moved in only a few of the total possible number of orbits. In the language of physics, the motions of the electrons were *quantized* or restricted; and classical mechanics and electrodynamics could offer no explanation for this strange restriction.

The first suggestion to provide a way out of this difficulty came from the French physicist Louis de Broglie. He pointed out that this quantized behavior might be explained far more completely if the electrons were treated as waves rather than as particles. This was a revolutionary idea, as no one had previously regarded electricity as composed of anything but particle-like electrons. These waves, proposed by De Broglie, were something completely new in nature—not like water waves, sound waves, or even light waves. But De Broglie contended that if light exhibited both a wave and a particle aspect as made clear two decades earlier by Planck and Einstein, it was reasonable to suppose that electrons and other particles, such as the protons composing matter, should likewise have both a particle and a wave aspect. Almost immediately after De Broglie put forward this startling hypothesis, experimental evidence was found showing that electrons and protons did behave like waves under many circumstances; and mathematical theories were developed which explained is a most convincing way how these waves gave rise to the quantum restrictions on the energy of the electrons in atoms. So almost every scientist accepted the fact that particle mechanics was dethroned as the fundamental law of motion in the universe and that wave mechanics ruled in its place.

How does this scientific revolution affect the orientation of science with repect to philosophy and religion? One may reply that the primary force of the old mechanistic argument has been knocked out at several points. First of all, in the new wave mechanics there is no longer a deterministic law of cause and effect applicable on the atomic scale. This law remains only as an approximation which the movements of large bodies of matter come very close to obeying. On the atomic scale, at the inner boundary of the very small, we no longer believe that a given cause is always followed by a precisely determinable effect; instead we believe that the nature of the effect is, to a degree, *uncertain*. On this microscale the effect of a cause cannot be precisely predicted. This is the famous Heisenberg principle of indeterminacy or uncertainty.

Some physicists still say that there is more uncertainty about the uncertainty principle than there is in it. They maintain that this Heisenberg imprecision is really only a kind of cosmically imposed ignorance. What must happen, does happen, they say; it is only that we are prevented from knowing the deterministic mechanism. But this invocation of ignorance to shore up the collapsing structure of determinism smacks of a rearguard action. If we are realistic, we must conclude that a door has opened, leading to some new operational structure different from determinism. Just what this new structure is, we cannot say with certainty on the basis of our present knowledge, but the signs point to a structure containing an element of behavior that strongly suggests freedom.

Another important aspect of wave mechanics is its emphasis on the whole rather than on the parts. To see this, let us take a look at a sound wave. Its basic character is rhythm. Let us suppose that this wave of sound comes to us from a vibrating piano string so that it constitutes a musical tone. Now the tone is produced only because of the sustained rhythmic movement of the piano strings, a series of vibrations, of regularly repeated movements up and down. One can argue that this whole tone is made up of parts, each part being a single flip of the string. But produce only *one* such flip itself alone and one finds that there is no tone, no frequency, no pitch. As contrasted with sustained rhythm, a single flip is a boundary situation, approached when one reduces the whole to a single part, a kind of inner boundary, where entirely different laws obtain for a part than for the whole. We conclude that the whole is more than sum of the parts, when we deal with waves.

Now the electron wave in the atom appears to have a nature closely resembling that of the piano string in sustained vibration. Just as the pegs that hold the string at each end are the physical boundaries of vibration, the positive and negative electrical charges in the atom are responsible for the boundaries for the electron wave.

Again, you cannot localize the string wave in a single place or part; it must be sustained all over the string or it does not exist at all. Similarly, you cannot localize the sustained electron wave; it must extend through space, perhaps throughout the entire universe, or it does not exist.

We see that this kind of fabric of law leaves science oriented quite differently from the position established on the basis of the laws of particle mechanics. The new emphasis is on wholes, and wholes that cannot be localized either in space or in time. The fabric of reality is a fabric of the relations of wholes, a fabric utterly different from that woven from the relations of point-particles moving in familiar space and time. We conclude that the old familiar particles—electrons, protons, and even atoms—are illusory shadows, perceived in something like particle form only when matter is torn apart under the artificial conditions of the laboratory.

All this is reminiscent of the words of Mephistopheles' advice to the student in Dr. Faustus' study, just before the devil and the professor leave for their long journey. The student is getting comments on the different branches of study. As regards science, Mephistopheles is scornful:

> Tear nature to parts, says Chemistry,
> Mocking itself, not knowing why.

NEW MANIFOLDS OF EXISTENCE

During the last thirty years wave mechanics has developed into a reasonably mature branch of science. Its mathematical structure is largely unambiguous and its physical meaning generally clear. Moreover, the many successful applications of wave mechanics have established beyond a doubt that its concepts have a significant content of truth. But although everyone is in pretty good agreement on how to use it, there is no comparable agreement on the philosophical meaning of wave mechanics.

A skeptic may ask, "Do these electron waves exist in the same fullness of reality as light waves and sound waves?" Some answer yes, some no; but almost everyone agrees that electrons in atoms behave in the way that we would expect waves to behave; and to me this is the equivalent of electron waves *existing*.

Well then, continues the skeptic, must we now regard both man and the universe as made of these waves, just as we once regarded man and the universe as made of atoms? I answer again: *yes*. Then, concludes the skeptic, we are back in an even deeper pit of mechanism. Where is there room for a soul in a complex of waves?

To answer this question we have to examine the way in which the concept of a universe made of waves changes our concepts of space and time. We normally think of the universe in which we live as existing in the three dimensions of length, breadth, and height. We do not hesitate, however, to consider special situations where fewer dimensions are significant. The piano string ideally has vibrations significant in only the one dimension of length. When sounding, it contains one-dimensional waves. We analyze these waves with mathematics employing only one dimension. The ideal planar drumhead has vibrations significantly in only two dimensions, length and breadth. In giving out sound it contains two-dimensional waves. We use two-dimensional mathematics to analyze these vibrations. So the presence of less than three dimensions does not disturb us.

I have not happened to hear of three-dimensional drums; but I can imagine using a child's toy balloon as a kind of vibrating hyper-drum. It would, of course, have vibrations in three dimensions—length, breadth, and height—i.e., in three-dimensional waves.

In our immediate sense experience these three dimensions of length, breadth, and height are the only ones of which most of us are aware. Yet there is no reason for mathematical analyses to stop at three dimensions. Just as a normal square is two-dimensional and a cube three-dimensional, so there is an extension of this rectilinear form that can be defined in an imaginary space of four dimensions. It is called the *tesseract*. Just as a cube has squares for its sides, the tesseract has cubes for its "sides." There are similar extensions of rectilinear form in spaces of five, six, or as many dimensions as you choose. Moreover, we can predict the precise form of the four-dimensional waves that a tesseract drum would contain if it vibrated elastically in four dimensions. The mathematics of this problem is relatively simple.

These examples and a host of others from modern mathematics demonstrate that the analysis of relationships in multidimensional space is practical and meaningful. Given a number of different patterns of relationships, one may analyze them and say that in a certain group of patterns there is a content that may be regarded meaningfully in terms of two-dimensional space; in another group, patterns suggest three-dimensional space; in still another, four-dimensional space; and so on, running up to a space of perhaps even an infinite number of dimensions.

If some of these patterns so analyzed represent physical observations, we ask next whether a meaningful content, suggesting a space, say, of six dimensions, implies that the part of nature observed actually *exists* in a space of six dimensions. This again calls for a clear understanding of what we mean by existence, and what we mean by space.

Now it is to a considerable extent through such studies of waves that our concepts of space have been broadened. In order to illustrate this further, let us briefly examine a few of the wave patterns in a piano string. Suppose that we have a string that normally sounds the note of middle C. If we could look at it with magic glasses that permitted us to see clearly the exact form of its rapid vibrations (instruments like this called stroboscopes are in common use), we would see the string first making an arc down, then an arc up, and then back down again, the center of the string moving up and down with the greatest amplitude of motion. If the string were tuned to "scientific" pitch, we would observe 256 of these trips up and down taking place each second. This frequency of 256 vibrations per second is called the fundamental frequency of the middle C string. In executing this vibration there is only a single arc either up or down between the ends of the string.

If we pluck the string not at the midpoint, but halfway between that point and the end, we can set up another type of vibration known as an overtone. In this vibration the string shows two arcs: the left half may move up while the right half moves down. Each arc is just half the length of the arc formed in the fundamental vibration. If we count the number of vibrations we find 512 per second; the string is moving just twice as fast, and the note sounding is C', one octave above the original note of middle C.

If we continue a series of experiments along these lines, we can make the string show three arcs (768 vibrations per second at G'); four arcs (1024 vibrations per second at C''); or five arcs (1280 vibrations per second at E''). At this point we have produced the musical chord of C major: C, G, E. This is the type of chord that characterizes the one-dimensional harmony of the string and is the basis of so much of occidental music. We could continue this series of experiments indefinitely and produce six, seven, or eight or more arcs.

Consider now the form of vibration when the string is sounding E''. There are five arcs distributed evenly along the string. We shall refer to this total group of arcs as the *wave*. Thus by wave we do not mean a single *crest* in the sense that one may say, "I was knocked down by a wave at the beach." By wave we mean the whole group of crests or arcs on the string.

Now think of the problem of distinguishing the dymanic form of the wave with five arcs sounding E'' from the wave with four crests sounding C'', if both are vibrating on the string at the same time. You cannot distinguish one from the other by saying one is *here* and the other *there*, for both are spread out over the entire string. You cannot distinguish them by a space location (technically speaking, by a space co-ordinate). You can distinguish them, however, by their *form* co-ordinates; one is characterized by the number 4, the number of arcs in its dynamic form; the other is characterized by the number 5, the number of arcs in the other dynamic form. Thus in dealing with waves we are forced in this sense to abandon the ordinary dimension of space and think in terms of a dimension of form.

It takes quite a leap of imagination to toss overboard the familiar three dimensions of space of our universe and substitute form co-ordinates in an almost inconceivably large number of dimensions. Yet there are reasons for believing that this is exactly what we must do if we search for the most significant way in which to express the structure of our dynamic universe. So there is a strong implication in this new wave perspective of the universe that everything is everywhere all at once. Separation of two objects in space is an illusion. Granted, there are certain aspects of behavior that make it convenient to think in ordinary affairs that one thing is here and another there! But this is only superficially true; it holds only when we focus on the macromaterial properties of things. There is a deeper unity in the universe in which there is neither *here* nor *there* but only omnipresence. This is one of the new perspectives of wave mechanics.

But the skeptic is not yet convinced, though I hope he may be a bit shaken. You still have not shown me, he says, any sign of a dwelling place for the freedom that lifts man above the level of puppet. Yes, I reply, we have to go still further. Freedom implies freedom of choice; choice implies action; and action implies time. Let us examine the nature of time in this new perspective.

The relation of a sustained wave to time is much like the relation of a sustained wave to space. You cannot say the wave is here and not there; because it is *everywhere* in the vibrating medium. Similarly you cannot say it is *now* and not *then*, because it must be sustained—it must have continued motion to exist. As a thing may have a superficial focus in space, though basically existing everywhere, so a wave may have a superficial focus in time, though basically existing at all times. We may recognize more easily a fleeting aspect of its changing form at some one moment, but basically, as T. S. Eliot puts it, "All is always now."

To make this more specific, I want to describe some experiments that a friend of mine and I actually carried out. We got a high speed motion picture camera that took pictures at the rate of five thousand frames a second. With this camera we photographed a vibrating violin string. In one series, the first photograph showed four arcs in the string at their maximum height. The next picture, taken a five-thousandth of a second later, showed the arcs considerably smaller. In succeeding pictures the arcs were shrinking still more, until in the tenth frame the violin string was perfectly straight. Then in the eleventh picture the arcs reappeared, continually growing until in the twentieth they were back to original maximum size. Because the wave was a dynamic form, its aspect changed from moment to moment. It could not be fixed in time. I could not say of the wave with maximum amplitude at ten o'clock, "Now is the wave." The wave existed with equal reality a five-hundredth of a second later when the camera showed only a straight string. Momentarily the wave form had disappeared, but the wave's existence included all stages from *maximum* form to *no* form.

This sketchy description may give a little understanding of the difficulty of characterizing waves in terms of precise location in space and time. You can say of your fountain pen and your pencil: "My pen is lying on the table and my pencil is in my pocket, at this moment, 8:56 A.M. today." This is a statement of significant information in a practical situation. But with two waves instead of two objects like pen and pencil, the significant information is not where they are and when they are, but what their form co-ordinates are that express their harmonic relations. If reality is associated with significant relationship, then we must seek the reality of waves, not in the dimensions of space and time but in the dimensions of harmonic form. If we focus not on the class of material relations between things in everyday life, but on the class of the significant relations of living human beings, then there is a strong implication in this new wave perspective that we will find the reality of man not in space and time but in some other dimensions.

To explore this idea further, let us now consider the nature of the living human body, regarding it as composed of waves that cannot be localized in space and time, waves in which the whole is more than the sum of the parts. If the nature of the electron waves follows the pattern of delocalization that we have just discussed, then a human being is somehow in contact with the entire universe at all times. We must admit that it is difficult to assess the significance of this contact, but we must acknowledge that it exists. Of course, for most practical purposes, there is more sense in regarding myself as localized. If I am thirsty, I either move my focus to the vicinity of a glass of water or I get someone to move the glass of water to me. That is the practical way of satisfying my thirst. Yet I cannot help recalling that every atom in my body is tied by an invisible thread of gravity to every atom of H_2O in all the reservoirs, all the lakes, and all the oceans of the entire world. My electron waves overlap the waves of all water, even though there are restrictions on my association with water, expressed in conventional language by saying that at this moment, as I write these lines, I am high and dry in my study and the water is far away. In wave language: I do not know how to "tune in" this water and make it satisfy my thirst without relocating either myself or the water to bring about physical juxtaposition.

If my desire is for mental rather than physical refreshment, however, the situation is different. With a few motions of my hand, I can turn on my FM radio and tune in music coming from a broadcasting studio two hundred miles away. True, in this act I am employing a process that usually is expressed most satisfactorily in terms of classical electrodynamics: I am rearranging radio waves in a manner that no longer seems mysterious because it is so familiar. But in terms of realities, I am operating at a different level; I am not seeking a certain kind of matter—physical water—but a certain kind of energy organized in a rhythmic and harmonic pattern: a Mozart symphony. This symphony is not brought to me in a container like a glass of water, but in wave form by tuning in.

In the process of life as displayed in the human body we can see both matter and energy playing significant roles. We have to convey both water and food frequently to our bodies so that the atoms of these necessities of life may be juxtaposed with our own atoms. We also need the energy in calories that our food contains. But if we probe more deeply into the nature of life we see that by far the more significant aspect lies in the perspective of *tuning* relationships, rather than in simple juxtaposition of mass and energy. There is increasing evidence that the mysterious force that directs and sustains the life of a human being has its reality centered in harmonic rather than material relationships. We are not matter but music.

Consider the flow of atoms that is part of your life. With every breath you inhale quintillions of oxygen atoms and join a large number of these to your body in various ways. As you exhale, you expel other quintillions of oxygen atoms from your body in the form of carbon dioxide. This exchange is only one small part of the metabolic process by which you are constantly swapping old atoms for new. It is estimated that, in effect, every human being gets a whole new body every five years. This is only a rough estimate, and some parts change faster than others, but it gives you the feel of what is going on within you all during your life.

Now in spite of this vast atomic ebb and flow, you do not change your *inner* self in any comparable manner. In the midst of this incredible flux there is an inner invariance, something that directs the course of these countless atom exchanges and maintains order and coherence throughout the body as a whole. Thus life, thought of in terms of the moving point-particles of classical mechanics, is an almost incredible miracle of unfathomable complexity; but life thought of in terms of the intermingled dynamic forms that manifest its rhythms is far more understandable. If we think of life as the movements of the octillion atoms of the human body, we are faced with a maze of complexity as illegible as the images of the pages of an octillion books, superimposed in a mad jumble; but if we think of life with its reality centered in dimensions of form, we see the signs of a dominant and supremely real vector core steadily and purposefully directed in the midst of micro-chaos.

As the form of nature around us has been more carefully scrutinized and analyzed, particularly with the help of multidimensional mathematics, the principle has been recognized that invariance under transformation is one of the supreme tests of significance. As Henry Margenau has pointed out in a number of discussions, invariance under transformation is the essence of law, and law expresses significant structure. In the phenomenon of life we see an impressive example of invariance under transformation through time; we see the inner core of life somehow invariant, dominant, and directive amid the almost infinite complex of atomic changes through which it is manifested. If invariance under transformation is a test of significant reality, here in the phenomenon of man is evidence for a supreme reality.

In view of this evidence one can say that the perspective for viewing life must be reoriented still further from that of classical mechanics or even simple wave mechanics. If we accept the attitude of wave mechanics that the significant dimensions are not the superficial dimensions of space-time but those of form, then we must be prepared to accept the further orientation that in these new manifolds of form there are realities of a kind beyond the mass particle, beyond the throbbing electron, beyond the complexes of waves that make up inanimate nature. We must accept the fact that the most potent dynamic fiber of the universe is the fiber of the human soul. Here is a reality that transcends time and space and nature, a reality that lives and moves and has its being in the dimensions of the spirit. It is in this reality and in this dimension that we find freedom. Thus freedom is not found as a property of, or created from, material nature. Freedom is the fundamental fiber out of which the spiritual life of man is woven. Freedom is a reality in its own right.

Freedom is dynamic, and dynamism is the essence of time. So in order to see more clearly the nature of freedom, let us examine more closely the nature of time.

THE NEW FRONTIERS OF TIME

We have had a brief look at the inside of the atom; let us complement this picture with a glance at the outer part of our universe, the stars and the nebulae. What can observations of the very large and the very distant tell us about both space and time?

Two thousand years ago men were inclined to believe that the space of the heavens was limited. It would carry us beyond the bounds of this essay to analyze in detail the space concepts of classical thought, but I think it is correct to say that nearly everyone in that age was satisfied with the idea of a finite empyrean and felt no particular urge to ask what lay beyond. And almost everyone felt much the same way about time. To men of that era it seemed obvious that there must have been a beginning and that there probably would be an end to time. It was more comfortable to accept this finite concept than to say that time had no beginning and no end.

During the Renaissance the pendulum of thought swung the other way. Adopting Descartes' idea of a rectilinear three-dimensional space measured with numbers, both scientists and philosophers were in general agreement that the only proper limit to space was infinity. Number increased without limit, they argued, and so must a linear space dimension. Set up any finite limit and there must always be a beyond.

Naturally they adopted the same attitude toward time. Time could be measured by number; set up any beginning and there must be a time before that; set up any end and there must be a time after that.

Given a linear measure, then the only possible bound of time was infinity—in other words, no bound.

During the early years of our own century this attitude again began to change. Just as mathematical analysis showed that there was sense in talking about more than the three dimensions of length, breadth, and height, the extended concepts of geometry showed that there was sense in talking about nonlinear space. If it made sense to talk about theoretical curved space, why not have a look, Einstein said, to see if this physical space in which we live might be curved?

Once scientists started looking, they quickly found startling evidence that space does have curvature. The displacement of light images at the time of eclipses and the displacement of light frequencies in atomic radiation both verified the hypothesis of the theory of relativity and supported the idea of curved space. This, in turn, led to the possibility that space may curve back on itself in such a way that total space may be unbounded but finite in extent. Thus there may be a boundary condition on space that involves a structure of relationships that in the limit is different from the structure observed in the space of everyday living.

A similar situation has recently developed with respect to time. A shift in the frequency of radiation toward the red has been detected in the light from distant nebulae. A regularity has been observed in the radioactive decay of atoms. This evidence from both the very large and the very small points to the possibility that, in going back toward the initial boundary of time, the structure of relationships may be quite different from that observed in familiar duration measured in days, years, or even millennia.

Our present fabric of scientific and philosophical thought is admittedly inadequate to deal properly with this problem, though some bold attempts have been made. For example, it has been suggested that we might imagine some initial cosmic event, roughly describable as the appearance of all cosmic energy and matter in the form of a ball of light. This event is thought of as taking place at a time that, linearly speaking, is now placed roughly about ten billion years ago. As this ball of light expanded, space and time were themselves created in their present familiar form; light congealed to matter, and soon the image of the universe emerged much as we know it today. In this picture there is a startling resemblance to the first chapter of the book of Genesis: "In the beginning . . . God said, 'Let there be light'; and there was light."

Once when I mentioned this resemblance to Paul Lehmann, he

suggested that the writer of Genesis not only anticipated modern cosmology, but also foresaw wave mechanics; for the prophet also wrote: "Darkness was upon the face of the deep; and the Spirit of God was moving over the face of the waters."

At any rate, whether we insist on a literal interpretation or are willing to read these passages with some poetic license, it is clear that the problem of creation is of a kind that concerns both science and religion. Men of science and men of religion can each derive benefit from the other's way of thinking when trying to understand better the nature of these ultimate encompassing boundaries of man and the universe. As Amos Wilder puts it, the boundary situation in life is the necessary focus of revelation and redemption. For if there is a significant initial boundary of time, it is surely logical to ask whether there may not be a significant final boundary. Creation and Judgment Day may well share a common morphology.

This brings us back to our skeptic's still unanswered question. In a universe more properly thought of not as particles but as waves—not as matter but as music—are there signs that man is more than a puppet? Is there a reality in the human soul that surpasses the finite in both space and time?

We have seen that it makes sense to say there is an invariant core of reality in human life that is deeper than the transient transformations of appearance which we ordinarily call *matter in movement*. Let us identify this deepor core of human reality with *soul*. When these transient transformations of life terminate in death, are there signs that the soul still persists? Does this vector of the spirit still point unswervingly along the trace to a destiny beyond time and space.

We have seen that the significant delineation of this invariant of life is to be found in the dimensions, not of space, but of form. Is its significant delineation of duration also to be found, not in time, but in another dimension of change? Surely this already has been sensed by men of vision down through the centuries. St. Augustine puts it: "In thee my soul, I measure time."

We can see that the proper perception of form often involves the proper choice not only of perspective and dimensions but also of scale. This is especially true with phenomena involving changes in time. Play back a record of human speech at the same speed at which it was recorded and the diction is clear and intelligible; play it back four times faster and it is as unintelligible as the chatter from a cage of monkeys. The perception of form has been destroyed by a change in the time scale. Recall that the cosmological calculation tells us that we must go back some ten billion years to find the time when time transforms to an origin. Next, think of an atom of hydrogen in the skin of the tip of your finger. The electron wave in this atom is throbbing with nearly a quintillion beats during each second of your existence. Thus in *one second* of time your hydrogen wave pulses more times than your heart would have beat if it had been throbbing continuously down through all the billions of years since the dawn of creation.

Three score and ten years, the age span of human life, may seem but an instant compared with the ten billion years that is the age of the universe. Yet if human life holds within its structure events of less than a quintillionth of a second's duration, is it unreasonable to think that human life also has a core of reality that may embrace more than quintillions of seconds?

Calculations based on the theory of relativity yield a rough figure of 10^{68} cubic miles (one followed by sixty-eight zeroes) for the size of the universe under the hypothesis that the cosmos is finite but unbounded. Calculations based on observations of the atomic nucleus show that the smallest significant volume appearing in microrelationships may be something like 10^{-60} cubic centimeters. Proportionally, man with a half dozen cubic feet of flesh stands about halfway between the extremes of the very large and the very small. In the same manner of speaking, the span of human life may stand midway between the extremes of the very short and the very long in time.

We now recall that in the new dimensions of form we cannot pinpoint a location of reality either in space or in time. There is no precise *where* or *when*. Reality transcends both space and time. Moreover, it is in this intersection of space and time that determinism disappears; and in the new perspective of this intersection, in the deepest dimensions of form, we see emerging the image of the reality of freedom. In this image that has neither where nor when, that spreads its wings over all space and over all time, we have a vision of the immortality of the soul.

Kierkegaard wrote: "But what is this myself? It is the most abstract and at the same time the most concrete of all realities. It is freedom." In this new structure of cosmology we see intimations that through the creative power of life, through the vital power of love, the spirit escapes from the prison of determinacy and leaps beyond the walls of time into the mansions of eternity.

The structure of eternity is admittedly beyond expression in human language. But we can project the structure of human life and of the universe in which it is lived, and in that projection see the suggestion of an eternity far richer than the undifferentiated infinity of mechanistic philosophy. Reinhold Niebuhr has emphasized the significance of this aspect of our cosmic boundary.

Finally, if we recognize the evidence for a significant invariant core at the heart of individual human existence, would it be any greater miracle to find a core of cosmic spirit at the heart of the universe? If the human soul transcends where and when, surely to this spirit of the universe must be ascribed ultimate transcendence. If the invariant core of human life dominates its vast sea of atomic changes, surely there must be ascribed to the cosmic *changeless-amid-change* all might, all power, and all dominion. Yet somehow, in the dimensions of the spirit, the infinite divine and the finite human join. In the words of Vincent Van Gogh, we have a Father, we are brothers.

In his treatise entitled *Philosophy of Mathematics and Natural Science,* Hermann Weyl, the associate of Albert Einstein in Princeton, wrote: "Whether the view is tenable that the organizing power of life establishes correlation between individual atomic processes, there is no doubt that wherever thought and the causative power of will emerge, especially in man, power is increasingly controlled by a spiritual world of images." In the course of this discussion, we have seen some of the images that take shape in the merging perspectives of science and religion. One message from these images is plain. We must ensure that science and religion go forward hand in hand in their continuing search for truth. Only then can we be confident that the future for humanity is bright, not only here on earth, but out among the stars, as a new generation of astronauts crosses the threshold of space into the universe.

6

Can Science Aid Religion?

ÉMILE CAILLIET

SCIENCE HAS INCREASINGLY RESTRICTED ITSELF TO THE TASK OF achieving a rational interpretation of the aggregate of phenomena, with a view to turning the resulting data to a unitary representation. Hence the expression "the universe of science." Actually, natural scientists would seem to understand the processes and influences of their discipline better than they do its meaning. Their over-all activities may be said to combine brilliancy of achievement with a large degree of obscurity of understanding. While outstanding scientists together with the technicians who work out their findings have been legion, genuine philosophers of science have been scarce. Men of the caliber of Mach, Pierson, and Duhem may be counted on the fingers of one hand; and their writings are not as widely or as deeply read as they should be, even by scientists. Moreover, natural science has progressed by such tremendous leaps and bounds that there has been little time to evaluate the bearing of the progress made on the understanding of the world of nature and of man—still less on the understanding of religion

It has become commonplace to say that, while scientists attempt an exhaustive account of what the cosmos seems to be, they cannot concern themselves with the problem of why things are as they are, or even why they are at all. This last question, it is pointed out, is an existential one. As such, it calls for a religious solution, that is, for answers that lie beyond the jurisdiction of the scientist, whose sole business is to find out how things actually work. Alfred North Whitehead had this distinction in mind when, in *Science and the Modern World,* he remarked that Galileo "keeps harping on how things happen, whereas his adversaries had a complete theory as to why things

73

happen."* Even so, I have always felt that to postulate a dichotomy between the questions *how* and *why* amounted to a misleading over-simplification. All depends on whether the question is asked in a meaningful way or not, and there is no doubt that any genuine inquiry can involve the question *Why?* meaningfully asked and calling for a meaningful answer. Any married man whose wife has ever lost anything knows this to be the case.

Where, then, does religion come in? The trouble at the outset is that it would be difficult to think of a more misleading term. There is no synonym for it in the languages of those societies one would associate with the spiritual qualities it currently suggests. The ancient Hebrews knew of no such designation. Neither did the Hindus, the Greeks, the Germans, or the Celts. Current translations of the Greek *threskeia* in Acts 26:5 and in James 1:26-27 notwithstanding, it is fair to say that the word *religion* is foreign to the New Testament. Neither does it seem to have been used by Christians before the third century, and this after it had taken on proper connotations. Where did it come from, anyway? Scandalous as this may seem, it was borrowed from the Romans, who were of all men the least religious. This questionable kind of ancestry no doubt plays a large part in the confusion of tongues encountered in the use of the word *religion*.

Those of us who have raised the question of a common referent for it in the banter of college discussion groups will remember how eagerly practitioners of semantic analysis would press forward and around, as if longing for a slanging match. They would not allow their abrasive feelings to dwindle until their own characterization of religion had been singled out for consideration amid a multiplicity of others, if for a brief period only. It is noteworthy that Paul Tillich, who perhaps more than any other professor in our generation has had to cope with this state of affairs, has tried to extricate himself from the thicket by cutting down his definition of religion to two words, namely, "ultimate concern." To do justice to his own wisdom, which is great, he might as well have cut down the definition to the two-letter sound that expresses the Sanskrit character for God, uttered in rapture: OM! Yet, even to have done this would have amounted to taking sides.

In the last analysis, all definitions of religion are governed by two magnetic poles, the naturalistic and the theistic. Even in regions where the magnetic field intensities are weak, it is possible to dis-

* Alfred North Whitehead, *Science and the Modern World* (New York, 1925), p. 12.

tinguish between effects which should be ascribed to a north pole and to a south pole. For example, a man like William Ernest Hocking is governed by the theistic pole even as he takes a firm stand on nature, for he makes it clear that his is a wider "nature" that includes supernature. Such was also the case for the late Mahatma Gandhi when he answered invitations to become a Christian by saying that God had placed him in India. On the other hand, there are theologians who would deny the use of the word *religion* to those who use it with reference to naturalistic views and to whom religion merely stands for distinctive cultural activities or functions freed from "superstitious" beliefs in the existence of a divine being. The bitterness engendered by the issue may be sensed in Emil Brunner's sharp pronouncement that pseudo-religion, so called, has done more harm than all the alcohol drunk by Americans during prohibition—and, mind you, a large part of the stuff was wood alcohol, too!

It stands to reason that in a series of lectures such as this, issues cannot be disposed of in terms of what may amount to name-calling. All that can be said for the present is that answers to the question as to whether science can aid rather than hinder religion are bound to take a different course according to the context in which religion is considered—whether the naturalistic or the theistic.

NATURALISTIC FORMS OF RELIGION

As we begin with the consideration of naturalistic forms of religion, we find ourselves confronted at the outset by a situation likely to becloud the issue. Most elementary forms of religion imply belief in supernatural beings. It is only with the passing of time that such forms are pronounced naturalistic in their basic inspiration, and this in the measure as monotheism comes into its own. To the Greeks, for example, the world was full of gods, but these were parts of nature in the first place.

The whole Greek countryside, its groves and streams, its hills and the blue Mediterranean sky over them, teemed with spirits suggested by local myths and wonderful stories. The rustic life thrived on nature spirits, as did the metropolitan life on its gods and goddesses. Even great gods of mythology such as Apollo changed in nature and priesthood according to whether they were worshiped in Delos or in Delphi. The Homeric epics were born in such a world. So were the dramas of Sophocles and even the dialogues of Plato. In due time, Orphism came to be expressed in terms of Pythagorean philosophy.

But then, the Greek universe was not a created universe, while the assertion of creation is the original feature of the biblical outlook.

Even so, Hellenistic philosophy remained for a long time a way of salvation. Disraeli in his early novel *Venetia* has happily emphasized this essential aspect. "You said of a man that he was a Stoic or an Epicurean, as you say of a man now that he is a Calvinist or a Wesleyan." How was this notion lost? The record speaks for itself. It even points to the official date of the event, namely, the year 529 A.D., when Justinian excommunicated philosophy as heretofore conceived. Indeed, what the emperor felt constrained to discard was not philosophy in itself, but philosophy as it assumed a religious character and accordingly appeared incompatible with the Christian religion. There could be room in the Roman empire for only one of the two religious organisms demanding allegiance.

A magnificent evocation of this revolution may be found in the eighth canto of Dante's *Purgatory*. At sunset the souls in the valley of the kings devoutly join in their evening hymn. Looking to heaven at this quiet hour of prayer and meditation, Dante notes that the four stars representing the moral virtues have vanished behind the mountain, and the three stars that symbolize the theological virtues have taken their place. The immediate implication is that the proper function of Purgatory is to reclaim a sound moral will. The deeper symbolism, however, can hardly be missed. The four cardinal virtues of ancient Greek philosophy, whose glory was typified by the four stars that had been deemed worthy of illuminating the venerable face of Cato in the first canto, had been superseded by the three theological virtues of Christianity now shining in the deep blue of the heavens. The proclamation of Christian theism had at long last triumphed over the religious naturalism of ancient Greece.

The fact remained, nevertheless, that the realities this religious naturalism stood for had to be properly assessed. This task was actually achieved as an aftermath to the ascendancy of science.

Indeed, there was reality in the faith of the ancient Greeks, in its sincerity, its grandeur, and the poetic charm of its naturism. Readers of Greek literature still exult with contagious enthusiasm in a life infused with spirit and divinity, such as glows in the fragrant grove and in the ripening grace of the garden. Once freed by natural science from mythology and obsolete cosmological connotations, however, Greek speculation was found to have spoken all along of transformism. To the Greeks, everything indeed came about by transformation—the transformation of something into something else.

In this manner the Aristotelian soul became the realization of potentialities in which the universe manifested its existence. The clue to
this mood of panpsychism has in our day been found by Bergson in
an *élan vital,* and by Whitehead in the notion of process. And lo and
behold, as we find the old creed of the Greeks transposed by Whitehead, not only has its naturalism come into its own, but it has done so
in scientific terms. In *Religion in the Making:* "We know nothing
beyond this temporal world and the formative elements which jointly
constitute its character. The temporal world and its formative elements constitute for us the all-inclusive universe" (p. 90). The identification of this naturalistic religion with science becomes a *fait accompli*
in further excerpts: as Whitehead sees it, religion attempts to evolve
"notions which strike more deeply into the root of reality." Progress
in truth is at the same time progress in "truth of science and truth
of religion" (p. 131). Again, this progress reaches its final principle
in the conviction that "there is a wisdom in the nature of things,
from which flow our direction of practice, and our possibility of the
theoretical analysis of fact" (p. 143). There are those who may feel
that a naturalistic creed of this sort sounds rather weird in our atomic
age. The least that can be said about it is that its optimism goes
beyond what would be allowed by such a guarded scientist as Sir
Charles Sherrington in his Gifford Lectures (1937-38), *Man on His
Nature.*

Enough has been said, however, on the impact of science on naturalistic forms of religion, to allow these preliminary conclusions: The
ascendancy of science has increasingly demythologized elementary
forms of religious naturalism. In so doing, it has exposed the fallacies
of paganism and by the same token indirectly helped the rise of
monotheism. On the other hand, because of the limitations inherent
in the epistemological status of the scientific enterprise, the only
way for science as such to turn its interest to religion is the naturalistic way. This last conclusion is bound to affect the impact of science
on theistic aspects of religion, a subject to which we now turn, with
special attention to New Testament Christianity.

THE IMPACT OF SCIENCE ON CHRISTIANITY

At first blush, an earnest Christian is likely to laugh off the suggestion that the ascendancy of science may in the least affect his
religion. How could the faith of a man who knows himself to have
been overpowered from on high be shaken by the assertion that

science, or anything else, could interfere with a certainty whose originator is the living God? Our man's answer will most probably turn out to be a variation on the retort well known to New Testament readers: "One thing I know, that though I was blind, now I see."

We have imagined the hearty laughter with which our earnest Christian—call him a Calvinist for the sake of argument—would be likely to greet the suggestion that science could ever interfere with the Almighty. Now, when a Calvinist begins to laugh, there surely is reason to pause. Our man might say in the manner of Sarah that God had made him to laugh, then further direct attention to the psalmist, who thinks of the Lord himself laughing as He sees what must come to pass. The laughter that now concerns us is laughter at the preposterous. And admittedly, the insinuation that men like Paul and Calvin could have gone astray in what they characterized as the bondage of the will would strike a man of faith as preposterous.

Think only of the five points of Calvinism as vindicated by the Synod of Dort: (1) God elects individuals to be saved; (2) He deigns complete redemption for these elect only; (3) fallen man is of himself incapable of true faith and repentance; (4) God's grace is efficacious for the salvation of the elect; (5) a soul once regenerated and converted is never ultimately lost. How could the ascendancy of science begin to weaken an edifice of faith resting on these five unshakable pillars? The reverse position would rather be in order. Thus Calvin, who showed real interest in science, was willing to acknowledge its relevance as a manifestation of God's wisdom. Only the strong can afford this kind of recognition.

And yet it would seem that Calvin himself was not quite without misgivings as he took notice of the ascendancy of the science of his own day. It is noteworthy that he continued to assume the correctness of the cosmology of Ptolemy, even as the cosmological views of Copernicus were on the rise. Centuries before our own Franklin D. Roosevelt practiced the tactics and strategy of not mentioning the names of his adversaries, Calvin had already made it a point never to breathe the name Copernicus. Could it be that he vaguely discerned in Copernicus a possible adversary? All that can safely be said on this thorny subject is that the great reformer was uneasy at the thought that an uncontrolled concern for science might detract attention from the Creator. Uncontrolled, that is, inasmuch as science may in the long run cease to view its findings in the setting of their theological context and accordingly fail to acknowledge God even in the consideration of His handiwork.

In order to appraise these misgivings more correctly, let us remember that the haunting vision had not as yet developed its sting. The reformer could not possibly anticipate the tensions that men like Galileo and Newton would bring about for those who did not differentiate between the cosmological settings of the Bible and the Bible's witness to Christology. Calvin, moreover, formulated his biblical theology long before Richard Simon and John Astruc inaugurated the methods of modern criticism—that is, before the impact of the new science of the universe, of man, and of social realities had been felt. In the admirable *Dictionary* of Moréri, completed in the middle of the eighteenth century by Abbé Gouget, there was no mention of subjects such as Brahmanism, Buddhism, Confucianism, Sanskrit, Egyptian religion, Germanic mythology, and so forth. Two hundred years after the death of Calvin there still was no discussion of linguistics, mythology, philology, prehistoric archaeology; no inkling of comparative religion, sociology of religion, psychology of religion, history of religion, philosophy of religion. Only in the second half of the eighteenth century would Diderot, d'Alembert, and the Encyclopedists complete their integration of the data that had emerged from three hundred years of modern erudition. Calvin died one hundred and thirty years before Voltaire was born. The latter's *Essai sur les moeurs et l'esprit des nations,* the first masterpiece of the new philosophy of history, was not published until 1756. Hume's *Essay on Miracles* had come out in 1748. The German professor was as yet undreamed of. Calvin, therefore, did not know the pangs and inhibitions of a biblicist confronted with the flat contradictions of a daring liberalism.

To grant the reality of such tensions—and it is hard to see how any of us could avoid granting it—is to admit that the ascendancy of science throughout this modern age has raised difficulties for Christianity. The whole issue has come to a head in the Kantian critique, with reference to commitment to any organized theistic creed; ultimately with regard to the factualness of Christianity.

Our age lives, moves, and has its being under the lengthening shadow of Immanuel Kant. His critique has provided science with a rationalized formulation of its modern status. Within experience, science makes it its task to probe, along useful and convenient causal lines, those appearances in nature which are apprehended in the a priori forms of sensibility in space and time. Since God is not such an object of cognition, not a phenomenon, His existence cannot be so perceived. It may indeed be postulated, either as a unifying principle of knowledge or as a necessity of practical reason. Yet there will always be those who see no reason for taking advantage of these postulations.

From here on, God may be said to have been replaced by experience, if not by a utilitarian activism. Thus Schleiermacher was led to emphasize a divine immanence stirring up within man a pious feeling of dependence upon the Infinite. Hence the mystical experience of apprehending delicate vibrations which harmonized in his case with the inwardness of the Moravians. So did it, incidentally, with a prevalent mood of romanticism. Soon Tieck and Novalis would suggest the same experience in terms of an inner music. In the same vein, William James would suggest an intimate sense of companionship with the invisible through the analogy of a quiet music playing in the back of his mind. A Mendelssohn might well have characterized that music as being "without words."

The point, however, is that since this and similar experiences occur within the natural order, science will claim them as fair objects of investigation. This kind of approach has been attempted many times in our modern age. There comes immediately to mind a masterly work that leaves all other similar endeavors far behind, for it sums up and integrates to a rare degree of perfection the best information they have yielded. This book of course is William James' *The Varieties of Religious Experience,* which provides a comprehensive treatment in the place of monographs and partial views in previous works. It would be hard to imagine a more able and thorough study coupled with more disappointing results. Take the book again from that slightly neglected corner in your library and judge for yourself as you peruse the conclusions. No doubt the author realized this and was the first to be disappointed, if we may judge from the postscript he added to his reluctant summing up. Precious pages they all are, rich in new insights into a vital subject, yet the net result is here for all to see. One can almost feel the disappointment of the good, honest master workman as he put the finishing touch to his bulky manuscript. There he was, empty-handed, offering at best the suggestions of a pragmatic agnosticism to the trusting souls who had lived in expectation of perceiving, at long last, some tangible divine reality.

And yet that inquiry of William James has not been in vain—far from it. It provides a vivid demonstration of the startling reversal that is bound to occur once a science bent on the naturalistic way assumes the appraiser's role and proceeds to take the measure even of theistic views. Whatever factualness may for a time seem to remain in them is bound to dissipate in thin air. An emphasis on religious experience, together with its projection in symbol and myth, implies a corresponding minimization of dogma. For in the new context, dogma is merely the language spoken by faith, a language conditioned by an ever changing social and cultural determinism, and at this point the academic approach to the phenomenon of religion takes over. Neither will it help a Christian to look for further "safe" lines of retreat—for instance, to seek refuge in so-called "unformulated experiences." Anthropologists, sociologists, psychologists, psychoanalysts, pathologists, and even the biochemists of the glands will invade the scene, now their own, and explain away in scientific terms whatever may seem to be left of these unformulated experiences. One may, with apology, offer a blunt illustration: when Huysmans became worried about the soul of Anatole France, the master of contemporary skepticism sneered, "Tell Huysmans to have a urinalysis!" Thus we may understand why William James had to be disappointed and disappointing. Hardly was the ink dry on his pages when they fell into the hands of oversolicitous specialists who ascribed the varieties of religious experience he had been concerned with to the workings of social consciousness, if not to some deficiency in iodine or iron salts. Vitamins were not as yet on the agenda. Neither, of course, were myth-generating father symbols, mother symbols, or combined father-mother symbols.

The great merit of Karl Barth is to have been so perceptive in his diagnosis of the rout. Implied in a liberal approach which so stressed religious experience as to brush aside the factualness of the objective revelation of God in Scripture and Creed was the presupposition that man may derive a valid religious knowledge from his own concepts, ultimately from his own certainty. In Schleiermacher, Barth identified a spiritual heir to Descartes; and in the latter's "I think, therefore I am," the perennial principle according to which the theology of the Word of God, reasserted by the Reformation, had been reduced to anthropology. According to Barth, however, there is no way from anthropology to Christology; there is only a way from Christology to anthropology. God is only known through God. This authentic knowledge can only be the knowledge of faith, a knowledge energized and conditioned at every step by a sovereign and utterly prior Word. Thus man—the truth of man—has been once for all determined by God in Christ. The crucial weakness accordingly detected by Barth in the liberal approach is that it concerns only the phenomenal man, not the real man. The same critique extends a fortiori to all scientific and secular disciplines, in so far as they deal with phenomena as viewed by Everyman. However impressive and useful they may prove to be, they must be characterized as radically incapable of telling the ultimate truth about the landscape of reality. Indeed, these extreme views of Barth vindicate Calvin's misgivings, already pointed out, with regard to the ascendancy of science. Yet they do more than this. They suggest that all scientific and secular disciplines may well conceal God and the things that are God's—that is, everything that truly matters.

Each must assess for himself the value and relevance of the Barthian critique. Let me just draw attention to the possibility that its origin in the setting of two world wars—the official, perhaps one should say the existential, version—may be purely coincidental. The conclusion immediately suggested by what has already been said is, rather, that the ascendancy of science had ultimately forced modernism into an impasse, and that, as a result, a theology worthy of the name had to reconsider its whole position. It may even be that God had something to do with the chastisement and at least part of its aftermath.

The preceding remarks further invite the thought that Rudolf Bultmann's concessions to the spirit of modern science are destined to the same fiasco that sounded the death knell of nineteenth-century subjectivism. For Bultmann did not invent demythologizing. Natural science, as we have seen, practiced it long before he was born. And just as nineteenth-century liberalism sought in vain a line of retreat in "unformulated experiences," the disciples of Bultmann are greatly mistaken if they think that the existentially inspired substitution of myth for factualness can ever be restricted to those gaps which seemingly appear in the event-structure of Christian beliefs.

We are now ready to conclude our consideration of the impact of science on theistic aspects of religion with special attention to New Testament Christianity. The record of four centuries of scientific progress shows that it is wishful thinking on the part of Christians to suppose that natural science can ever help to establish the truth of their creedal affirmations. What the ascendancy of science has done and promises to keep on doing is to expose the deception of all attempts on the part of New Testament Christianity to save its life by sacrificing its objectivity, or even satisfy its imagination at the expense of a committed intellect. In so doing, science has indirectly saved Christianity from the snare of substitutes, by the same token as we have seen it indirectly help monotheism to displace paganism.

Let me ponder with you this naked fact: New Testament Christianity lives on, lives on with all the rough edges of the apostolic proclamation, lives on with all the foolishness of its otherworldliness. When the theologians and natural scientists have done their best, or worst, the fact is still there, staring them in the face.

It was suggested earlier that an earnest Christian, confronted by the suggestion that science or anything else could possibly interfere with his faith, would be likely to echo the well-known New Testament retort: "One thing I know, that though I was blind, now I see." Now let me ask: can it be fortuitous merely that Galileo, rising from his knees after repeating the formula of abjuration, should have fallen into a similar form of speech as, according to legend, he stamped on the ground and exclaimed, "*Eppur si muove!*"

Granting the extreme possibility that the activities of nature may be illusory and what we call reality but a subjective geometry we have discovered in ourselves, natural scientists nevertheless continue to work on the assumption that there is something out there. An irreducible and stubborn sense of objectivity carries them along. Their steadfast quest is bent upon the use of their intellect. This is why they become so wary of models likely to be confused with pictures of "reality" that they restrict the use of the word "model" to a set of mathematical symbols. In other words, they become increasingly aware of our human propensity to substitute "imaginable" for "conceivable," and vice versa. As they further see it, the correspondence or correlation of our concepts and our sensations becomes all the more indirect as purer mathematical models are devised. Yet this very remoteness allows a closer, more adequate approximation of this world. It therefore would never occur to a genuine scientist to pronounce reality inconceivable because it does not prove "picturable," to use a term coined in this connection by Dirac in his *Principles of Quantum Mechanics*. Neither would it occur to him to deny objectivity to that reality on the ground that it is not imaginable.

Contrast now the frame of mind of an existentialist theologian who reduces such mysteries as that of the Resurrection to the mythical, on the ground that our apprehension of them does not square with the ways of anthropomorphic picture-making. Even as he deigns to continue to use the traditional language, provided the same be transposed in terms of meaningful symbols accessible to his subjectivity, does not such a condescending defeatism on his part provide an important clue to the plight of Protestant theology today?

Once a quantum physicist who was doing research work at the

Princeton Institute of Advanced Study expressed to me great surprise
at the sight of theologians bent upon reducing mysteries to familiar
anthropomorphic views. Said he, "Why, we often find ourselves confronted by mysteries as baffling as those that trouble many theologians,
if not more so. Some of the events we have to cope with actually
sound absurd and perverse to the point where common sense would
seem to play us false."

"What do you do then?" I asked.

"We first do our best to ascertain available data as accurately and
as faithfully as is given to us."

"And then?"

"And then," he added, as if sounding the very depths of the
unexpected occurrence, "we try to make out what the world of
reality must be like, to account for such happenings."

Let there be no mistake about it. This attitude of mind and spirit
stands behind the ascendancy of science—this expectant faith, this
spirit of submission to fact coupled with a readiness to proceed upon
the resulting situation, however perplexing it may be. And only in
the measure as Christians make such qualities their own, may they
expect science to smile upon their endeavor.

Part III

THE RELATION

OF PSYCHIATRY AND RELIGION

7

Psychiatric Understandings of Man:

A THEOLOGICAL APPRAISAL

SEWARD HILTNER

THE MATERIAL THAT ANNOUNCED THIS SERIES REPORTED IT AS dealing with "controversial issues facing Christianity." But the specific announcement of this session on psychiatry and religion stated that "new emphasis upon their co-ordination holds promise for improving man's personal ills." Can both these things be true, or are they contradictory? It is my thesis that this is not a contradiction—that better understanding between psychiatry and religion does hold forth promise, but that such understanding cannot be achieved by evading the actual or potential realms of controversy.

Let us first consider the nature of modern psychiatry, the stages in its developing understanding of man, and the assertions about man that now seem to have consensual status. From this procedure three kinds of outcome may legitimately be expected. First, the clarification of what psychiatry is and is not may produce sympathetic understanding and appreciation where misunderstanding and hostility have appeared before. Very much about psychiatry seems to me to fall under this heading and I shall stress it without apology. Second, we may find some issues in the understanding of man in which we shall have to demur or disagree. And third, we may find places where we are not sure we are talking about the same or about different things, that is, where confusion becomes greater even though better informed. Following this kind of a look at psychiatry, we may consider those points at which the psychiatric and the theological understandings of man actually hold some hope of co-ordination without a violation of either.

THE NATURE OF PSYCHIATRY

Psychiatry is a branch of medicine. This means that, above and beyond whatever knowledge or understandings or viewpoints it may possess, it is also a professionally oriented practice. The psychiatrist or other physician deals with patients, with sufferers, and not solely with facts or ideas or views about illness and health. It is this need to mobilize all available resources in the interest of a real situation that most plainly distinguishes a profession from an "ology."

In other respects a profession moves backward if it fails to have continuing kinship with the sciences or "ologies" that provide its basic principles of knowledge. Both science and profession are concerned to find out basic principles, whether in the detachment of the laboratory or the heat of clinical observation. The profession with no concern for research is on the way to becoming a mere trade or craft. For it is the unique business of a profession to link basic principle with concrete situation.

In all good professional practice, which does move from basic principles and not simply from rules of thumb, a peculiar thing tends to happen. The complexities of concrete situations drive the practitioner, if he is alert, into considering orders of resource that may be relevant to his needs, but which have not hitherto been structured as relevant to his kind of practice. Think of some illustrations of professional practice in other fields. City planners, for instance, at first drew mainly upon architecture, engineering, and esthetics. But the complexities of their "patient"—the city—have now driven them also to various social sciences as well.

Much in the present state of psychiatry is incomprehensible if we fail to see this same tendency at work. Again and again, in the interest of helping its patients, psychiatry has had to mobilize resources not otherwise related to the structure of scientifically oriented medicine. To those defining medicine as structured by fixed means, rather than as mobilizing all resources in the interests of alleviating illness and enhancing health, many of these moves seemed at least trans-medical and perhaps even heretical. But psychiatry has taken the position, quite rightly, that medicine is not properly defined by the nature of its means but rather by bringing together all available means in the interest of health. The Hippocratic oath certainly seems to be on this side of the fence. In contrast, those who want to dissociate psychiatry from medicine ordinarily have a puristic conception of medicine that is not only belied by the facts but also rests on a kind of eschatology:

"Give us time and we'll find out about that." The trouble is that suffering is always *now*.

As it has sought, in unlikely as well as likely places, for resources that may help its patients, psychiatry has developed a content which, while including traditional medicine, also embraces material from "ologies" not traditionally regarded as medically relevant. It is not merely that there are differences of content. Every medical specialty has such differences. But the differences between urology and gynecology or otolaryngology are all of the same order. They are the same kinds of differences. Between psychiatry and other medical specialties, however, the kinds of differences are themselves different. In my judgment, psychiatry simply *must* proceed in this way unless it wants to restrict itself to purely neurological work. And in that case some other group would have to step in and play the role of physician, whether so called or not.

An even more important development in psychiatry, as a result of trying to mobilize all possible resources in the interest of the patient's health, is the emergence of the psychiatric team. At first glance this appears to be much like the team operation in other branches of medicine. The surgeon associates with himself anesthetists, nurses, bacteriologists, laboratory technicians, and others. Around the psychiatrist work clinical psychologists, social workers, occupational or adjunctive therapists, chaplains, and others. But there tends to be a difference, of great importance although it is not categorical. The surgeon, for instance, gets laboratory findings about his patient; then he makes a decision and performs the decisive acts designed to be therapeutic. That is, both appraisal, or diagnosis, and treatment are in his hands. His associates provide data, but he decides.

As captain of his team, the psychiatrist too must finally decide. But the process preceding decision is much more consultation than mere reporting of facts. Thus the appraisal is much more a group process, even though structured and under the guidance of the team captain. Similarly, when it comes to treatment—the execution of the critical procedures on which improvement most depends—any member of the team may, on occasion, be assigned the crucial role. And he may be so assigned for various reasons: because of his special knowledge, or because of the relationship he has established to the patient, or because of what the patient believes him to represent.

Thus the emerging conception of the psychiatric team is profoundly important if we are to understand psychiatry. Let me say at once that I see no tendency on the part of psychiatrists to abrogate the focal medical responsibility. But true consultation is not confined to colleagues of the same profession; it is extended to all whose background, knowledge, and resources can possibly shed some light on the concrete patient. They, too, have contact with him as professional persons. Even those who are not now considered genuine professionals are moving in that direction. The psychiatrist is head of the team. Indeed, if he chooses he may even today make lone-wolf decisions and refuse genuine consultation. But to do so is to risk failure to mobilize all resources for the welfare of the patient. Hence if he acts in just the way some other physician may legitimately act in another situation, he may be guilty of subverting the service ethics of the medical profession.

All this is of vital interest to the team members associated with psychiatrists, as well as to the psychiatrists themselves. The surgeon who failed to call upon laboratory people and the psychiatrist who had no clinical psychologist working with him would be equally reprehensible. But the latter is very much more a colleague than the former, in professional terms. Here a whole new qualitative meaning is given to the notion of team practice. Whether this may have effects back upon other branches of medicine, one cannot say. But it is the most vital growing edge of psychiatry, and at the same time the fact most difficult for many other physicians to comprehend as necessary to good medicine itself.

This is stressed because, indeed, within a generation lone-wolf practice by psychiatrists, in whatever setting, will be regarded as malpractice. Will all this movement toward genuine democratic consultation in the interests of the patient mean that some day a psychiatric team will make its psychiatrist just one of the boys, and vote some one else as its leader if they like him better? I do not believe so; and if they did, they would misunderstand both the problem and the reasons for consultative team practice.

The target we are approaching in this discussion is the psychiatric understanding of man. It now becomes clear that this is not necessarily the same thing as the understanding held by men with M.D. degrees who specialize in the diagnosis and treatment of mental diseases and emotional disorders. It does mean the views of people who work, in one way or another, on a psychiatric team.

STAGES IN RECENT PSYCHIATRIC THOUGHT

It was in part social accident, but a most fortunate one, that put physicians in charge of institutions for the mentally ill. Had the job been foisted instead upon either of the other possible candidates—clergymen or matrons—we should surely be much worse off than we are today. Quite possibly psychiatry as we have been describing it would still be unknown.

Until very recently, indeed, there was no possibility that psychiatry could have anything to say to the understanding of man at a level that would be of general interest to theologians, either pro or con. Long before our century dawned, the demon theory was dead (although twitching occasionally). It had been replaced in medicine by a kind of organicistic eschatology: "Some day we shall find all specific causes for specific diseases." This was eked out for the demands of current practice by heavy reliance upon descriptive classifications, usually accompanied by the (to the doctor) comforting words that the patient *had* dementia praecox, or depression, or paresis, or hysteria. In the instance of paresis this way of speaking has since been proved partially correct. But with the others even suggestive evidence seems nearly all the other way round.

Then, near the turn of the century, came the two men who have done more to shape American psychiatry than any others, Adolf Meyer and Sigmund Freud. An increasing amount of the content of psychiatry is Freudian in origin—not necessarily just Freud's ideas and no others, but ideas stemming from Freud's contributions. But an increasing amount of the form and practice of psychiatry is, in my judgment, derivative from Meyer. He held that, to get its data, psychiatry had to become a "psychobiology," and the notion of a social history, of getting expert colleagues who were not necessarily physicians, received its greatest impetus from him. It is the ideas of Freud that are talked about today. But it is Meyer's lead that gives us the teamwork conception and practice of psychiatry.

Meyer's influence was exercised through the professors and practitioners of psychiatry who studied under his direction. He wrote relatively little. Even when he did, his erudition, his broad philosophical orientation, and his irenic inclusiveness prevented people such as theologians from hearing him at all. One of his ideas—"spontaneity"—might well have sparked some new orders of theological thought about both creativity and freedom. But since Meyer's material contained no attacks, the theologians left him strictly alone. This, I suppose, is letting a theological cat out of the bag: that theologians are unlikely to pay attention to you if you agree with them, unless you do so vigorously and in a way that makes them ashamed of their own lukewarmness. On the whole, you can get their attention much more easily by attack.

Quite in contrast to Meyer, Freud and his early students quickly captured theological interest. This was mostly for the wrong reasons. Those who did pay attention to him, barring theological collaborators like Oskar Pfister, feared that he was advocating sexual promiscuity, seeing little children as monsters, and generally breaking down the morals of civilization. Since even Freud's worst enemies can no longer get away with such distortions, I shall not dignify these early charges with a reply. But it has taken us a long time to grasp what Freud was really driving at and to separate it from more subtle forms of misunderstanding than those suggested above.

The most crucial contribution by Freud, among the many that have rightly been named by various students, can be put more accurately in terms of a method than of a content. We might paraphrase it this way: In trying to understand psychic life, do not assume that the obvious is the significant. Instead, find ways to explore the significant, wherever it lies. And the significant, he added, is dynamic, which should be translated from its original Greek meaning of energetic—having strength and push and drive. Using this general method, and mostly the specific technique of psychoanalysis, Freud found many a significant psychic stone that previous builders had rejected, which collectively have come very close to becoming the head of the modern psychiatric corner.

In his later years Freud's writings included many on what he called "metapsychology," about the nature and prospects for men and civilization, about the origins of society, about religion and art and education, and even about the god "logos" spelled with a lower-case "l." But he never failed to indicate that these were his own views and speculations, not inevitable conclusions drawn logically from psychoanalysis or psychiatry as he had developed them. Some of his early students were less cautious. In the grip of a fascinating new idea and method, it was natural that they should reach out to explore its range of relevance. Some of them thought the word they pronounced upon art, religion, mythology, anthropology, ethics, or literature was a substitute for all the experts knew. This period was understandable, probably inevitable, but it was unfortunate and some negative consequences are still with us. This was not, to put it bluntly, either psychiatry or psychoanalysis at work, in theory or in practice. It was, instead, a group of converts swinging out to convert the pagans before they had developed a meaningful and coherent theology of their faith.

Although there may remain a few relics from that period of rash missionary outreach among Freud's pupils, both the small company of psychoanalysts and the much larger company of psychiatrists influenced by psychoanalytic thought tend today to have a quite different cast of mind. They may have put Freud's stones safely at the head of the corner, but they are thoroughly aware that a building needs more than cornerstones or keystones. They have learned, for example, that psychological tests may now disclose important aspects of the psyche as clearly as psychoanalytic technique and in much less time. They are considering the integrating as well as the dividing forces of psychic life. They find related disciplines emerging with theoretical formulations that are useful, such as the field theory, open systems theory, homeostatic theory, and even biochemical theory. In practice we have already noted the shape of the new psychiatric team.

Two footnotes are necessary to balance this truncated account of the stages in recent psychiatric development. For one thing, what has been described here is Western, and above all American, psychiatry. It is not Soviet psychiatry. And so far as the development of the psychiatric team is concerned, it is still mostly American and British psychiatry. The other note is that this account has inevitably dealt only with the dominant trend, and not with the many variations and divergencies. These latter, if serious, seem now to be both more numerous and more promising—since some one of them is bound to pay off—but less embarrassing or plaguing than before. Psychiatry seems to have reached enough maturity to welcome some rebels, left-wingers, and stand-patters, lest it become too orthodox and uncreative.

PSYCHIATRIC UNDERSTANDINGS OF MAN

If we ask what a group really believes most deeply about something, it is never safe simply to look at what its members say is most important. For what is said is often provoked by controversy within the group, or in reply to outside criticism, and therefore magnifies out of proportion certain issues and leaves unstated others that are deeply believed in. Theological history is by no means innocent of the same sort of bias. Without derogating the truth and clarification that have often emerged from the fires of controversy, one is forced to realize that a picture of the Christian faith derived only from statements concerned with such issues would be very biased indeed.

In what immediately follows, therefore, an attempt is made to get at the convictions about man that most psychiatrists, and most members of psychiatric teams, hold to most tenaciously, not infrequently at such a level that they are never clearly articulated. This procedure is risky but necessary.

∘1. *At least as regards illness and health, man can be studied.* At first glance, this may appear a tautology. But it is very important. When something goes wrong, if you believe this, you cannot immediately do any of the following things: treat him the way you treated the last fellow who seemed roughly similar; regard him either as hopeless or as simply having growing pains and let it go at that; get his detailed account of the matter and assume that everything else is irrelevant; fix up whatever you are an expert in and disclaim responsibility for everything else; ignore the trouble and talk to him about getting right with God, the universe, and his own existence as the only proper course.

To say that man is studiable need not mean either that study will produce everything about him that is worth knowing, or that his studiability cancels out our respect for his uniqueness and individuality. Both reductionism and exploitation are distortions of this affirmation. It is true that man could be neither objectivized nor brain-washed if he were not studiable. But neither could he be helped or healed. That Western psychiatry assumes the one and disclaims the other is an indication that its value system is still based, however remotely, on the Jewish, Christian, and later democratic valuations placed on man and on the human person as individual.

To affirm that man is studiable does not imply that all ways of studying him are known. Thus there is always an openness in regard to method and a self-criticism about methods currently employed. There is also a sensitivity to, and alertness about, either potentially new methods of study or even old methods that may have virtues beyond the vices that led to their earlier discarding. For example, Freud may indeed have been right in discarding hypnosis and using the couch and free association instead. For what the couch can accomplish, hypnosis is a poor and temporary substitute indeed. But perhaps hypnosis has an area of usefulness of its own. By similar logic some psychiatrists have been brought to reconsider such outrageously old-fashioned things as the biblical understanding of man.

The phrase "at least as regards illness and health" has been prefixed to the affirmation that man is studiable, mainly because this is the proper focus of the psychiatrist's endeavors. But it does not mean that man can be studied solely from the point of view of illness and health. No doubt most psychiatrists would say that man in any aspect can be studied—i.e., that there is something to be learned about him that we do not now know and that is worth knowing. But health is not necessarily the highest value in all hierarchies of value, and this statement, with its qualification, simply protects the psychiatrist from even an unconscious imperialism.

2. *In relation to illness and health, man is adaptively and dynamically bipolar.* We can almost convey the meaning of this by saying that, no matter how rough things may be, man tries to cope with them, although at a price. Thus psychic illness in itself is bipolar; it is an indication on the one side, that man is trying to cope with life and has not given up, and on the other side, that the symptoms are the price of remaining alive.

This is not, it should be noted, a sentimental assertion of man's infinite worth. Whether or not a particular adaptation or compromise has become so fixed as to be, with present skill, irreversible, we cannot know in advance. Many that seem at first to be irreversible prove **not**, if this principle is seriously put into practice. Others remain recalcitrant. But even when they do, we are not shocked into either cynicism or hopelessness by the fact, provided we believe in and understand this principle.

Let us put the principle into extreme illustrative forms. Even the person who is most sick or removed or distorted is not so from sheer perversity, or completely so. His illness, however severe, began as a bad form of intended adaptation. He may now be stuck with it. But something of him transcends the illness or he would not be alive. Whether this something can be located, fortified, and strengthened or not, we can assume its presence. His essence, to use an outworn terminology, is more than the demon that possesses him.

At the other extreme the most loving, useful, creative, and stable person still, upon close inspection, bears the marks or scars of having had to cope with stresses. The very success of his coping may make his scar tissue all but unrecognizable. But if he himself forgets it altogether, he will get a new scar of large proportions, for he will thereby rule himself out of emphatic membership in the fallible but imaginative human race.

When psychiatry started, under Freud's stimulus, to become alert to these dynamics of conflict, it tended to use mechanical models to account for the phenomena. The modes of coping and compromise adaptation were "defense mechanisms." Such a term is not entirely false, in so far as it connotes that the processes go on apart from conscious control and are directed against strong instinctual forces. They do "run themselves," just as does the autonomic nervous system

—a term that simply denotes the fact that it runs itself. But the over-all process that takes place in man is not adequately described by a mechanical model. Freud's own models became less mechanistic as his understanding deepened and as both physics and biology made their models more subtle and abstract. This is also now, with some exceptions, a general trend.

3. *Man develops—he does not just unfold, and he does not just freely create.* The notion of development came into our vocabulary through biology, where at first it meant the opposite of envelopment— that is, it connoted regular, gradual, and uniform unfolding. But inspection showed that creatures far less complex than man move through their life pilgrimage in complexities to which the unfolding idea does scant justice. As a result "development" has come to suggest the total course of movement from the birth of an organism to death—with the question left open as to which aspects of this are slow and uniform and which are sharp and decisive.

The chief early contribution of Freud to the understanding of development was his understanding of sexuality. In finding that sexual responsiveness goes through stages, that it is learned and does not automatically unfold, but that there are pushes and nudges from inside as well as outside—Freud laid the theoretical groundwork for solving an immense number of important practical problems. Homosexuality, for example, is not the result of unfortunate glands save in the rarest instances. It is, instead, a result of learning through relationships. And if this is so, it is not inconceivable that it can yield to re-education.

When we say *man* in the generic sense, we mean adult men, women, children, babies, teen-agers, older people, and all the varieties. But although folk wisdom has never failed to notice these distinctions, the precise study of developmental sequences and the function of various factors in development (including personal initiative) involves a great deal more than common sense. What man is depends in part, psychiatry might say, upon where he is; not least upon where he is in the developmental sequence. If this is forgotten in allegedly general statements about man, then they are bound to be imperialistic projections from particular points and not truly general and comprehensive.

4. *Man has depth, in the sense both of complexity and of the continuation of early influences.* Freud compared man to an iceberg, with something like eight-ninths not visible. But if the iceberg hits you, every ninth has as much momentum as every other. Whatever

man may be, his uncriticized rational processes are not enough to guide him. This does not mean that more rationality is all he needs, or that all reason is a corrupt guide. It does mean that more true rationality is better than less rationality, but that any specific instance of rationality is suspect of special pleading unless proved otherwise.

To say that man always shows, upon close examination, the continuation of early influences on his life is another way of calling him an inevitably historical creature, who can regress as well as progress. And since a historical and remembering creature is, in the present tense, one of self-transcendence, and in the future tense, of imagination, this is testimony to the fact that all three of man's time dimensions are both animal and self-transcendent at the same time. Indeed, his membership in the animal series, no less than his self-transcendence, is an evidence of his depth.

To call man complex may mean only that we have not yet classified him. But as this is discussed in psychiatry it means much more. It implies a respect for individuality and an awareness of its mystery. Any man is a mystery. Even the apparently simplest case presents, if we look hard enough, baffling elements. But this is realism, not a renunciation of inquiry or retreat into detachment.

5. *Man is a creature of society and culture, but he molds them as well as being molded by them.* Psychiatry is fully convinced of the social origin and nexus of man's selfhood. And yet, whether through factors of temperament, powers of imagination and intelligence, ego strength, or whatever, it is equally recognized that the description of a set of environmental circumstances will not lead automatically to a description of individual behavior in relation to them. Further, in however slight a way, a culture does not remain unaffected by any individual, though some affect it more than others.

APPRAISAL OF THE PSYCHIATRIC UNDERSTANDINGS

The first things to be noted, from the theological point of view, is that these statements are at a lower level of abstraction than is customary with theological statements about man. If we took statements of this order and stacked them up against the usual Christian statements about man, they would meet only in part. Paul Tillich, who believes as I do that theologians can learn about man from psychiatry, has a very neat gimmick at this point. He says that theology deals with the ultimate dimensions, while all other disciplines, including psychiatry, deal with preliminary dimensions. This is very attractive; it is surely not false—yet I find it unsatisfying.

The trouble with the ultimate-preliminary distinction is its subtle suggestion that anyone with red blood will be dissatisfied with the preliminary, so why waste much time on it at all? To continue using Tillich's terms, I believe, on the contrary, that such vision as we have of the ultimate comes only through our winning through to it by way of the preliminary. When it comes to substituting the ultimate for the preliminary, one can easily demonstrate the fallacy of that. You want the surgeon to make a competent stab at you before he invokes God's blessing upon your demise. And if you are a theological student, you had better not conclude too quickly that what you feel is pure ontological anxiety, which you nurse to your bosom as a mark of your superiority in relating existence to essence—at least until you have consulted someone to trace the dregs of your particular neurosis.

So-called "neurotic anxiety" and "ontological anxiety" come from two different levels of experience and represent different orders of abstraction from that experience. This does not mean that they are wholly separate, have nothing in common. But it does mean that any attempt to bring them together that fails to deal with the difference of levels is doomed to distortion. In the same way, the psychiatric understandings of man as delineated here are not, in my judgment, wholly different from theological understandings; yet neither are they of the same order. A theologian who would dismiss them as irrelevant seems to me as wrong as another theologian who would try to merge them without noting the difference in level of abstraction.

It seems to me that understandings of man of the order and kind cited must be taken seriously by all thoughtful men. Even if they are, in some respects, preliminary rather than ultimate statements, belief in them may make ultimate differences to a lot of people. To believe that a sick man is studiable only up to a point can mean physical or psychic death to some persons, while a deep and persistent conviction about man's studiability may mean life. Besides, how could an ultimate be known without preliminaries? To understand man's psychic ills as the unintended price of intended coping with life is to drive us forward in hopeful and realistic search for resources. All five of the enunciated principles seem of equal significance. Not to believe deeply in them is to become apathetic, or detached, or hopeless, or superficial, or one-sided. The big news to theologians should be that these are the basic principles on which members of the psychiatric team proceed, because they believe deeply in them. Understanding of them ought, therefore, to mean their inclusion in any truly comprehensive statements about man.

But, one may ask, though all that is very well, what about these areas of controversy? Does not psychiatry hold that man has some interior part that never learns anything and never gives up, and that man is therefore bad? Or perhaps it believes that psychiatric therapy, if we had enough of it, could help every man to become the good self he potentially is? Is it not one or the other? Again, is not psychiatry pessimistic about man's future, with aggression flying all over the place whether the lid is on it or not? Or is it optimistic, rather—because man would have a great future if culture did not bind and distort him? Surely it's one or the other—?

Let me concede at once that various psychiatric interpreters have taken both kinds of positions and a great many variations in between. One may go even further and say that it is much harder for a psychiatrist to avoid ideas and convictions at this level than it is for a chemist or even for most other physicians, for he deals every day with people to whom one kind of optimism or one level of pessimism may spell the difference between progress and regress, and with persons reluctant to acknowledge the good in themselves, as with others clinging defensively to the notion that they contain no bad.

But general and abstract conclusions about whether man is good or bad, his future rosy or dark, do not follow by simple implication from psychiatry as such. For instance, two psychiatric and psychological colleagues, Karl Menninger and Carl Rogers, appear to differ radically on just these issues. Yet both men at work, whether in teaching, research, or the direct helping of people, have an immense similarity in their realism, their patience, their hope, and their indefatigability. Manifestly, both believe in the five principles of psychiatry enunciated above. But beyond that, both believe very deeply in the valuation of man that is our heritage from the Jewish-Christian religious tradition and the democratic political tradition. There are important differences between them. But they share the principles that have been stated, plus a particular kind of valuation of man that transcends psychiatry or psychology as such.

If we assume these three variables—the five psychiatric understandings of man, some position about man as good or evil, and the Western position on man's value—and present them to a Soviet psychiatrist, we will be likely to have the following result:

Most clearly, his position about man as good or bad, and optimism or pessimism about his future, would not come from the Soviet psychiatrist's psychiatry but from his philosophy. Similarly, he would

accept or reject this or that of the Jewish-Christian-democratic valuation of man on grounds other than his psychiatry. He would apparently agree with the five principles, at least so far as they are
merely formal in nature. He would say that he studies man, that the
bipolar description of psychic life contains truth, that man does
develop, that he is complex and is a social as well as individual being.
But his exposition would negate nearly everything important that
has been included in our description. Our principles, therefore, while
apparently formal in nature, actually carry a great deal of content
the minute we try to say what we really mean by them. These overtones are part of our perspective and cannot be categorically separated
from our valuation of man or from our underlying view of man's
potentialities and problems.

In its long-term history, psychiatry is as much a part of the Western
valuation of man as is literature or theology. Over the shorter term,
as observers like Albert C. Outler have rightly noted, a large number
of its interpreters have held naturalistic and even reductionistic assumptions derivative from the eighteenth century, and scientistic
assumptions from the nineteenth century. In so far as such assumptions are present, they do run counter to the theologian's understanding
of man and must be rejected. But even the statements by some
psychiatrists most arrantly implying reductionistic and naturalistic
views of man cannot be understood if considered alone, apart from
the larger and longer-term context of evaluation in which they are
set. And even here, the differences among psychiatrists are great;
it is false to assign one view to psychiatrists in general as if they stood,
collectively and universally, against the theological understanding of
man.

On a question such as being optimistic or pessimistic about man's
future, the wisest psychiatrists are inclined to be agnostic about what
psychiatry says, but they are also inclined to work and discuss and
collaborate with all intelligent men of good will to increase the
grounds for a realistic optimism. But they know that society and
nations and culture and institutions, and even men who sit in front
of push-buttons, can now crucially guide man's future—over and
above the factors in man that psychiatric study reveals. Is this not
humility, and courage, and ethical concern—in the Christian sense?

Individual psychiatrists, or even groups of them, may say all kinds
of things about man. They may even say things with which one
agrees, but for what seem the wrong reasons. But the real dangers
or temptations of psychiatry seem to me rather different from those

mentioned. The crucial danger seems a subtle one, difficult to describe, especially because it is the reverse side of a good intention. Perhaps it is best to begin with that intention.

Clinical work makes psychiatrists aware of the dangers in views of man that, whatever their content, have become fixed, rigid, or dogmatic and exclusivistic in tone. They want, therefore, to give no aid and comfort to views that are rigid in this sense. Often it seems to them, therefore, that various views of man set forth by people such as theologians are misleading, not so much because of their specific content as because they appear to be fixed, closed, rigid, and final. From this point the inference may be drawn that the best way to avoid such premature closure or finality is to have no views at this level of consideration and abstraction. It may then be concluded that the mark of an open mind is the absence of views at this level.

What many psychiatrists actually do is to become so deeply immersed in helping people, and so understandably attached to whatever they have found useful in the process, that they are suspicious of orders of conceptualization that are not obviously useful in the helping. Combined with this are the great strain of psychiatric clinical practice and the hope that they may quit thinking about man after office or clinic hours.

It is a mistaken diagnosis that every view of man at the theological level inevitably becomes rigid, closed, fixed, and final. Our views can be open to new understanding as well. When system becomes a Procrustean bed, it is not because it is attempting to be systematic, that is, to bring coherence out of data and relationships, but because there is some inner emotional need to round things off even at the price of sacrificing truth. Here psychiatric insight ought to help us to distinguish between a distorted system and a systematic or disciplined attempt to articulate relationships, including the unknowns among them. But this very important distinction is unlikely to be made if every attempt to think systematically is interpreted as a symptom of something reprehensible.

Important as are the five basic principles of psychiatric understanding formulated above, it is also true that, left entirely on their own, they could be interpreted as purely formal—and the underlying valuation of man which they presuppose might conceivably be changed even by one who found them useful. That is, the valuational presupposition comes at a different level of discourse, and the tendency is for psychiatrists not to articulate it. Yet their actual use of these five principles would mean something quite different if the

Western valuation of man were not present in the background. An articulation of it will, of course, approximate the theological level of discourse concerning man, whatever the specific content.

Most of the significant understandings of man that have been formulated in the past have emerged as generalizations from particular perspectives. Very few of the great philosophers have studied only what a department of philosophy now teaches. Very few of the great minds in science have been concerned about nothing but their scientific object. The generalizations may have come from an immersion in mathematics, in a particular science, in theology, or in literature; but these have been particulars explored for the generality they might reveal.

Psychiatry seems uniquely rich in such potentialities. But most psychiatrists hesitate to think at all at such a level, for the reasons suggested, which are partly praiseworthy but must ultimately be rejected. The relatively few psychiatrists who do work and think at this level are under the temptation to move too far and too fast away from their psychiatric insights in making generalizations. Psychiatry has potentially important contributions to make at the general level of theological thought, but we are only at the threshold of doing this adequately.

IS CO-ORDINATION POSSIBLE?

In Christian theological circles there is a wide area of agreement concerning man's nature. Statements like the following are made by nearly all concerned, even though every person and group would reserve the right to make others as well:

Man was created by God, and is still being created by God, in God's own image; therefore man is inherently free and not a doll or puppet. He is also capable of love, which means that his nature is not an isolated entity. Man, however, has sinned and does sin; he has both rebelled and fallen short. As a result, his actual situation involves isolation and estrangement from God, isolation from his fellows, and even estrangement from the essential nature of himself as intended by God. The exemplary picture of man's essential nature comes from Jesus Christ, fully man but God incarnate. And the actual power of grace that can rescue man from sin also comes from the same Jesus Christ, released to man through the Holy Spirit. The power that sets man on the new path, that makes him a new being in Christ and not the old Adam, is not his own. In his old nature he cannot command it. But the man who is renewed or sanctified by the grace of his Lord Jesus Christ can, even though he is not free of sin, nevertheless act in a freedom and with a responsibility of which he was previously unaware. While he had best not rest on his oars—as if he commanded grace instead of grace empowering him—he is nonetheless truly a new creature in Christ, a new being. His traits—tidiness or untidiness, affability or reserve, bullheadedness or receptivity—continue, though probably not unmodified. But what is changed is the very center of his character, his ultimate commitment and loyalty. He may still marry the wrong wife or vote for the wrong senator, but if his faith is what it ought to be, he will not worship the wrong god or focus around the wrong center of his selfhood.

If this Protestant statement summarizing views of man's nature is inspected by an Eastern Orthodox Christian, he is very likely to find it unduly preoccupied with the problems of sin and guilt and the processes of redemption from them. But it is precisely this Western bias or slant that makes us Protestants take psychiatry so seriously, for there also is to be found a preoccupation with rescue from inner psychic distortion and with the processes whereby this may be assisted. In this respect Roman Catholic thought is also Western and shares the Protestant and the psychiatric bias.

As has already been stated in more general terms, the content of Western Christian statements tends to be at a higher level of abstraction than the five principles we have enunciated on behalf of Western psychiatry. Yet the parallelism within that difference of levels should not be overlooked. Time will permit only one or two illustrations of this, beyond the manifest preoccupation that both have with man at the point where rescue is needed.

Psychiatry, rightly, does not talk about sin; for the basic meaning of sin is incomprehensible apart from a theological context. "Against thee, thee only, have I sinned." Even though my act or my failure or my withdrawal may have alienated me from my fellows, or from important aspects of myself, what is crucially wrong about it is its alienation of me from the source of all fellowship and integration, which is God. The forms and dimensions of sin are very real, but they are consequences of the isolation from God and not just ways of talking about it.

To a psychiatrist this way of assessing man's capacity for getting himself into messes may or may not make sense. But whether the theological way of putting it is meaningful to him or not, we must call his attention to his belief in a phenomenon of human life that in a sense is very much like the Christian sin, even though discussed at a lower level of abstraction. Our five psychiatric principles in understanding man have considered this under statements 2 and 5. Principle 2 concerns the bipolar nature of symptoms. They represent the best idea one had at the time; but their consequences can be fantastically worse than one expected. Generalized, this is sin. For safety's sake one value (or coping device) was hit upon rather than another more difficult or elusive. Immediate result: relief, like catching flies on flypaper. Eventual result: an incubus, even when the flies are gone, for the flypaper continues to stick. Nobody begins to sin in order to become a bad man. Instead, he makes peaceful co-existence treaties with the devil. That is sin. And although psychiatric experience does not exhaust the meaning of this process in human life, it certainly illuminates very important aspects of it.

On the more positive side, we may look at the theological assertions about the priority and sufficiency of grace. If a man is rescued, it is not because his skill as a carpenter has enabled him to build ladders from the bottom of the pit to the surface. It is because ladders have been thrown down to him. Modest as members of the psychiatric team may be, they know the immense difference between the patient who receives a proper ladder and the one who does not. They have a great variety of ladders—rope, silk, pine, oak, hemp, or even electronic— but they know that their initiative in finding the right ladder may make the difference between life and death to the patient. Beyond this they may not wish to generalize, and we cannot blame them. But they can hardly say that they fail wholly to understand what the Christian means by grace, if they are willing to generalize on this little matter of throwing out the lifelines.

The question of co-ordination of the efforts of psychiatrists and theologians is, therefore, a very subtle one that may be rendered impossible on either side by introducing the wrong set of ground rules. If theologians insist that all statements about man, to be meaningful, must be of the same order as their own, and otherwise may be quietly absorbed or ignored, then the psychiatrists may rightly regard us theologians as methodologically narcissistic, with a strong tinge of paranoia or obsessionalism. But if psychiatrists should insist that their agreed-on understandings of man, at least as delineated in this discussion, are not only all that is known but all that any one needs to be perceptive about, then they too may be accused of a great psychological error, namely, dishonesty—that is, failing to acknowledge the valuational assumptions about man without which they could not assert their principles.

If co-ordination is desirable, merger is most undesirable. It is of the most immense significance that we have dedicated persons, believing deeply in the dignity of human and personal and individual life, who are working hour by hour to save and rescue people in grievous suffering; who study and work and inquire to improve their means, and who are understandably reluctant to accept any formulae that would appear to make rescue either impossible or automatic. Merger is entirely the wrong notion, because we do not want psychiatry to "aid" religion, or religion to "aid" psychiatry.

But co-ordination holds promise. This means a proper ordering of the contributions, the activities, and the understandings of man that have been and will be discovered and set forth by both psychiatry and theology. From a mutually respectful inquiry of this kind, both we and the welfare of mankind are altogether likely to profit.

8

The Power of the Personal: A STUDY OF
THE RELATION BETWEEN RELIGION AND PSYCHIATRY

REUEL HOWE

THERE ARE MANY WAYS OF COMPARING RELIGION AND PSYCHIATRY, but the meaning of each and the relation of each to the other will become clear as we apply them to some common point of focus. That focus, is seems to me, is man and his need.

MAN'S NEED FOR THE PERSONAL

What do we need? We need the full relationship for which we were created. We need to be reunited to ourselves, to our fellows, and to our God, and restored in the unity of our being. Because we have lost it we are afraid. We know a deep separation and are profoundly anxious. As we go through life we try to find ourselves and become what we believe we were meant to be. But we are beset with enemies from within and from without. We experience much in life that threatens us and opposes any full realization of ourselves. As we seek life, death crowds us. We would love, but our resentment and hostility inhibit us. In the very moment when we seem close to God the devil seems most active. The presence of the negative raises questions about the positive. The contradictoriness of life produces in us a deep anxiety. What truth about man, about ourselves, lies beneath these conditions?

First, we are centered in ourselves, and when anything seems to attack or threaten this center we react as if life itself were being attacked. Each of us needs to preserve his centeredness, which is the need to affirm ourselves and is best seen in the courage with which we will fight or otherwise seek to protect ourselves. We need this

106

centeredness in order to participate in the life and meaning of others. Our need to participate is important because the realization of one's self is possible only in relation to another. We long to know and be known, to accept and be accepted, to love and be loved, and this can be done only in relation. We sense a risk in such relationship because we are afraid that we will lose our own centeredness, our own sense of being. We may try to protect ourselves by hiding from encounter, which we do by either withdrawing or overextending ourselves. Our struggles for self-actualization through the various birth-growth crises are the means by which we become conscious of ourselves as distinct and participating persons. Only in relation to others can we grow in the knowledge of who we are. The experience of relationship may either call us forth as persons or send us into hiding—either cause us to be reborn or cause our death as persons. The power of the personal can both give life and destroy it.

The power of the personal for destruction is well known. When something has gone wrong between us and another, when we have been hurt and have hurt another, we may experience fear and guilt, both of which send us into hiding. We hide because we are afraid and because we are ashamed. And we hide by withdrawing from relationship. The pain of it has become so great that we are no longer available for its healing power. The only true medicine for personal hurt is personal healing. Thus withdrawal from relationship removes us from the source of healing. The purpose of the retreat, of course, is to protect us from further hurt and to reduce our responsibility for personal relations. The burdens of personal life have become so great that we throw them off and withdraw. Withdrawals take many forms, from mental illness to pouting and sulking. People's inhibited and reserved attitudes, for example, are ways of keeping themselves aloof and from getting hurt again.

For most of us these periods of withdrawal are momentary and sooner or later, unless the condition has become chronic, there occurs an act of courage on our part which may be described as a "counterattack." Like an army commander who has temporarily to pull his troops into a more limited territory in order to survive, and then counterattacks, we too, after retreat, may seek to break into the world of the personal again. This act of courage should be regarded as an attempt on the part of a person to affirm himself again against all the odds that seem to be lined up against him. And he needs someone to affirm him in this act of courage and to meet his counterattack with encouragement. To a greater or lesser degree we all live this way.

At one time we are more out on the frontier of life and at another we have to some extent withdrawn and retreated. Then we counterattack, facing with courage the enemies that maintain their position both within and outside of us. How we fare depends in large measure upon how we are met.

This insight had profound meaning for the pastor and the psychiatrist. When a person who is in trouble and may therefore have withdrawn from life comes for help, his act of seeking help should be regarded as an act of courage and a counterattack in which his resources for relationship have been marshaled. Pastors, psychiatrists, and others to whom men may turn have the opportunity to affirm people in their acts of courage by helping them to understand what it is they are really doing and to congratulate them on having done it.

The practice of religion by many of us, unfortunately, is not conspicuous for its affirmation of people, but rather for its rejection of them. Although we may use religious and liturgical language to refer to ourselves as sinners and in need of God's forgiveness, we find it next to impossible, outside of formal religious observance, to acknowledge and accept our weakness, sickness, or sinfulness. We are readily and frequently embarrassed by evidence of our humanness. We think it shameful to be disturbed by life's experiences and to have problems for which we need help, so that we often pretend a well-being we do not have. We may even undergo years of suffering and agony rather than ask for help, because to do so would be to admit we are in trouble. If we cannot accept ourselves we cannot accept others. If we will not allow ourselves to be affirmed, we will be unable to affirm others who might come to us as a part of their attempt to counterattack and find their place in human relationships again.

We also find it difficult to accept or affirm what people are and have, because of what they are not and do not have. We reject people because of their failures, and we fail to see their yearning, their courage, and the effort that they do make. No matter how little anyone brought Him, Christ was able to recognize it, affirm it, and use it to lead the person on to greater acts of courage and commitment. Would that we might practice the same power to call persons into being!

The deterioration of religion into moralism also crowds out the power of the personal. Many practitioners of religion live under—and put others under—the demoralizing demand of the "ought," and lose sight of the need and power of forgiveness. Those who have been hurt in human relationship and have gone into hiding, and have finally mustered the courage to seek the aid of a healing person, need the re-assurance of men and women who, because they have been forgiven, are forgiving; who, having been accepted, accept; who, having been loved, love. These are the affirming people, the saints in human relationship.

Then there is the religious emphasis that substitutes a system of ideas about God for God, and talks about religion as a substitute for a life of responsible personal relation. Religion thus becomes academic and monological and loses touch with life and its questions.

These are some of the perennial temptations of religion that lead to its becoming moralistic and formal so that the dynamic of faith does not touch the dynamic of life. Sometimes when men come to us for bread they receive stones, and when they turn to us for an enabling relationship they are given moral imperatives and a system of ideas. The personal becomes institutionalized. Through the centuries the struggle has gone on between the formal and the vital, between the institutional and the personal, and each age must rediscover for it-self the power of the personal.

PERSONS AS MEANS OF GRACE

In our own time the understandings of psychodynamics have helped religion to rediscover the meanings of the truths it represents. The process of rediscovering the power of the personal has brought psychiatry and religion into exciting new dialogue.

Perhaps one of the most powerful insights in which psychody-namics and religion meet is that of acceptance. Many of us mis-takenly think that acceptance means unqualified approval. Acceptance does not mean to condone. Acceptance is a relationship in which we are accepted in spite of being unacceptable. Acceptance includes judgment. Although judged and found wanting, we are affirmed in ourselves. The experience of feeling unacceptable and yet being ac-cepted frees us from self-rejection, so that we are able to accept ac-ceptance. Furthermore, the experience of being thus accepted enables us to accept others. Understanding of the dynamics of acceptance has given religion a fresh understanding of the dynamics of forgiveness which is central to the gospel. Here, too, is a way of understanding anew the meaning of grace, which has the power, thus demonstrated, to change and transform lives. And we begin to understand that the dynamics of relationship are the same between man and man and man and God. Some interpreters would say, and I agree, that the relationship between man and man is more than an analogy of the divine-human encounter; it is a means by which God reveals the way in which He works and the way in which He would have us work in His Name.

Thus a second, most powerful contemporary insight recognizes persons as agents of grace or acceptance. This insight was born out of the study of the relation between therapist and patient. One person, the healer, communicates with another person in such a way that the hurt one may be affirmed and gain courage for a new attempt at life. Having been loved, he begins to love and to participate in the power of persons to heal. Thus the power of the personal in the crucial issues of life and death has been revealed to us during the last fifty years and has restored vitality to the forms and practices of ancient beliefs.

How amazing, however, that these insights are news to religion! They are news, for a number of reasons. Christian theology and ministry had become suspicious of the human and the personal, and had sought to bring God's healing to men through sacraments, rites, ceremonies, preaching, programs, and institutions, as if these could be conducted independently of the role of persons. We had lost sight of, or shied away from, the truth that preaching is not only exposition of the gospel but is also a part of the gospel event. And our pastoral relationships are also a part of the gospel action.

It is curious how little we think of our relationship with one another as a resource. When someone in trouble comes to us, we often say, "I wish I could think of something to do or say that would help him," not realizing that the greatest thing we can do is to be with him. I have frequently observed that ministers confronted by some problem, such as an estrangement between themselves and their people, look for remedies that include almost everything except the employment of themselves and their relation to the people involved. Unfortunately, their training for the ministry did not acquaint them with the personal as a basic resource for ministry nor train them in the employment of it. And because ordained ministers and teachers of the church are unaware of persons as agents of grace, they are unable to awaken and train lay members of the church for employment of the personal in their part of the church's witness. Naturally, therefore, many people think of religion only in terms of ideas, programs, and practices. No wonder the forms of religion capture and crowd out its vitality. The vitality of faith can find expression only through the interpersonal.

Although contemporary insights into the role of the personal in ministry have come mainly from the field of psychotherapy, it is nevertheless true that many psychiatrists and other psychotherapists fail to recognize and employ the person-to-person dynamic in the conduct of their own work. Some avoid dialogue by pleading the need for an objective attitude in relation to a patient and do not seem to realize that the relationship which they call objective is experienced by the patient as rejection. Without the bridge of relation between person and person there is no way for God or the renewing power of life to reach us. Our belief is that God created us to live in a structure of relationship and to be maintained by it. Since we can be both hurt and restored by persons, the role of the personal is crucial.

That persons can be instruments of acceptance or means of grace should not seem amazing to religion, for the Scriptures are about the encounter between God and man. And as we look closer we see that God is always speaking to men, and through them to other men. In the words of Scripture, God makes "His appeal through us"; that is, He seeks persons through persons. "God's purpose is such and He so made humanity in accordance with that purpose that He never enters into personal relationship with a man apart from other human persons."* "God's personal approach to men and women is always through other persons, or more generally through history, which is the sphere of persons in relationship, the sphere where decisions have to be taken and choices made in relation with other wills."† The personal approach of God is found in both the Old Testament and the New Testament. The people who had a covenant relationship with God were not only witnesses to Him but instruments as well of His will among the nations of the world. And Christians believe that the love and healing of God was incarnate in Jesus, whom we call the Christ. God chose that which He created, namely, human relations, to be the instrument of His reconciliation. And the Church is meant to be a fellowship of such reconciling relationships.

The Church came into being, according to Christian belief, by the Holy Spirit, who incarnates and embodies Himself in the relation between men to continue the reconciliation of men to themselves, to one another, and to God, the source of life and light and truth. The primary vocation of church members, therefore, is to respond to the call to be persons living in responsible relation. The ministry of the Church is a ministry of persons to one another and through persons to the corporate structures and institutions of our culture. The content

* Herbert H. Farmer, *The Servant of the Word* (New York, 1942), p. 37.
† *Ibid.*, p. 56.

of the relationship is life. The gift of the relationship is love and acceptance, truth and judgment, and repentance—which is acceptance of acceptance. Thus we are freed for responsible service to others—whether religious, psychiatric, educational, or whatever—which is the true vocation of persons and the personal.

THE TECHNIQUE OF MINISTRY—PARTICIPATION

Thus far we have observed and discussed briefly two insights: first, that persons need to be affirmed, welcomed, and empowered; and second, that persons themselves are the instruments of acceptance and the means of grace. The question now remains: is there a way of life, a kind of relationship, a technique of ministry, that is peculiarly appropriate to a ministry of persons calling each other into being?

There is, and it is the relationship of participation in which two people confront and are met by each other to their mutual benefit. That one of these may be a psychotherapist or minister or some other professional should in no way diminish the quality of mutuality of the relationship, but means only that one of them has more responsibility for what happens. The attitude of the counselor cannot be one of condescension, but rather one of partnership in which, to some degree at least, the benefits are mutual. The healer is also healed, and the healed also serves as healer. Real meeting between person and person must inevitably bless both. If real meeting does not take place between person and person, therapy or pastoral care cannot possibly occur at the level at which they are needed.

Remember that a person in trouble is looking for a healing person, whether he can admit it or not. He needs to be met by someone who is able to be really present to him and participate with him in all the meanings of his life. The pastoral relation, therefore, must be a two-way street, an honest dialogue in which each person encounters the other. The *experience of relationship* stands in sharp contrast to that in which there is only *talk about* relationship. One is appalled at how much both pastors and therapists engage their parishioners and patients in conversation *about* relationship with other people but ignore the relationship that exists between them. A man, for example, who had gone to a therapist for help in his marriage because of his dependence on his wife and others, exhibited the same need in his relation to the therapist and wanted constantly to be reassured. He was told to confine the discussion to his relation with others and not to evade that by references to the therapeutic situation. Yet the relation with the therapist was a more natural curriculum, exploration of which would open the man to new understandings and patterns for other relationships. The therapist in this case refused to be present to his patient as a person and was unwilling to participate with him as an agent of healing.

How can one be really present to another person?

1. By listening. There is nothing startling about this observation, but it is indispensable and fundamental. The capacity for listening is rare among us. Ministers and psychiatrists talk about its importance, but listening does not occur as frequently as one might expect. Too many of us listen out of our respective agenda anxieties and our pre-occupations. We listen through our images of people, so that the meaning of what they say has to be sifted through our image of them and is distorted. We also listen with what we want to say, and look for openings that give us an opportunity to make our speeches. And sometimes we listen with the fear of hearing, because if we really heard another human being we would be confronted, judged, and called forth by him into unknown possible changes.

Listening is an act of love, a commitment of ourselves to another. To do it truly, we listen with every sense alert, with ear and eye and every sensitivity of being, so that we may responsibly and reverently participate in the mystery of another. Listening is not a one-sided activity. The other person calls to us in all kinds of ways. He wants to be heard, because to be heard is to be known and to be known is to live. Listening is a two-sided responsibility. The speaker respects the listener by trying to speak his meanings clearly and honestly, and the listener respects the speaker by giving his whole attention to what the speaker is trying to say.

What does listening accomplish? Not only does it gives us information, but it is also an act which itself enables us to participate in the reunion of man with man. Listening bridges the loneliness of man and heals the alienation that makes him a gaping wound. The reunion accomplished through listening is also a reunion of man with himself and with the source of his being, whom we call God; for reunion in any part of the personal must include reunion of the part with the whole realm of personal being. Poets, philosophers, and other interpreters have witnessed to this truth, for those who have participated in a true meeting between person and person have a sense of being united in that meeting with all other men and with God. Thus psychotherapy has explored the use of listening in the work of healing; psychodynamics has interpreted its meaning, the process and effect of listening; and theology identifies its ultimate or religious purpose and significance.

2. Another way we can be really present to a person is by participating with him in a true meeting, which, as we have seen, begins with the act of speaking and listening. Participation means being another's partner in the enterprise of healing, or to state it more generally, in the enterprise of becoming. It is required of a partner that he have something invested in the enterprise, which means that he as a person, with all his resources, is committed to it. So is the minister and psychiatrist committed to the enterprise of care.

First, he commits what he is as a person: his life, his being, his values, his beliefs, his knowledge and skill. Second, he commits himself in transit as it were. In the act of giving himself he takes the risk of creativity, he gives love, understanding, and guidance, and risks not having it accepted and rewarded. Too many would-be helpers estimate the rewards before they make the gift. Rightly did our Lord ask, "If you love those who love you, what reward have you?"

The purpose of giving oneself is to affirm the other, in order that he may affirm himself. The self thus becomes the agent of healing and of reconciliation. Affirmation, however, does not mean unqualified approval of what a person thinks or does, and participation does not mean that we become emotionally involved in another's predicament. The experience of being affirmed and accepted must include the experience of being judged. Participation includes the giving and receiving of judgments, not in the spirit of condemnation, but in the spirit of being accepted in spite of everything about which one may feel guilty.

We all have our areas of guilt and with them our sense of guilt. And when we seek to break out again into a fuller experience and participation in life, this part of our life needs to be met, too. It is not adequately met when acceptance is misunderstood to be approval. It *is* adequately met when the reality of our guilt and our feelings about it are taken seriously, and in spite of our guilt, accepted. Thus, true repentance is response to the acceptance of acceptance and makes possible restoration to relationship.

Third, listening and participation are dependent upon dialogue between persons which accomplishes a meeting of meaning between person and person. Dialogue is to relationship what blood is to the body. When the flow of blood stops, the body dies. When the flow of dialogue stops, the relationship dies. The only way to restore a relationship is to restore the dialogue, so that the fundamental meanings of each person may become available to the other and reactivated. Thus dialogue between doctor and patient, pastor and parishioner, is indispensable not only for their special relationship, but also for the resumption of communication between them in their respective natural relationships.

We are now brought to the threshold of the religious dimension, because the power of the personal is the power to accomplish, through dialogue, a meeting of meaning between the word of man and the Word of God. This dialogue in turn renews the power of the personal. Honest dialogue between man and man creates in them conditions that make them more responsive to the work of the Spirit of God in them.

THE FRONTIER FOR RELIGION AND PSYCHIATRY

I have tried to describe the simple but profound truth of the power of the personal as seen in the self as the agent of acceptance and in persons as a means of grace, and have identified this insight as coming from both religion and psychodynamics. I have concluded that, since God created the structure of relationship for the purpose of calling persons into being, and according to Christian interpretation accomplished His great work of reconciliation in and through the person of Jesus of Nazareth, whom we call Christ, He intends personal relations to be the basic means of grace upon which all other means of grace depend.

This is a tremendous insight, more than we have realized and more than many want to admit. Certainly it is an insight we are called upon to explore and to which the studious attention of generation after generation may be profitably applied.

Unfortunately, there is a prevalent state of mind in the fields of psychology and religion that would block any such study. It is the attitude of mind that tends to dogmatize and institutionalize the fragments of truth that we have. Religion has perhaps more difficulty at this point than do other disciplines because it prizes divine revelation and emphasizes its once-and-for-all character. It fails, however, to distinguish between revelation and religion—that the latter is the human response to revelation and not the revelation; the understanding of the truth, not the truth itself. The revelation may be complete from the point of view of the Revealer, but while the receiver may acknowledge its completeness he may fall far short of understanding it. The true religious response to revelation, therefore, is to hold its reception of revelation openly, with the expectation that, as human experience and study continue, more will be understood. Thus reverence for revelation and devotion to study of the data of human experience are compatible.

Let religion and psychiatry, therefore, continue to study persons in relation, persons as agents of acceptance and as a means of grace, and hold what is now known about these with both reverence and openness, realizing that in ten generations from now our understandings will be deepened and broadened, while truth now understood will be affirmed.

CONCLUSION

The doctrine of the Incarnation which underlies all Christian life is really the doctrine of the personalization of love. By it is meant the embodiment in man of the life of God, who is love. The Incarnation makes life personal, and persons are of primary importance to its existence and meaning. In each generation men are called upon to reaffirm their faith in the power of persons living in relation to God and man. Our own generation and the generations to come have and will have special need for a reaffirmation of the personal because of preoccupation with science and technology and with vast space and enormous power. One wonders and hears others wondering how a single person can be valid in the face of all these masses, spaces, and complexities. But it was revealed in Christ, and every now and then is revealed to us afresh, that the whole vast structure of life is dependent upon the power of persons and upon our exercise of the power of the personal. The character of man, expressed in his relations with his fellow man, will finally determine whether we use our vast powers destructively or creatively.

If there is to be a creative world revolution, it will come as a result of men accepting their role as agents of divine love and living their lives as sacraments of the personal, through which they may find reconciliation and love and thereby escape from the bondage of materialism and institutionalism.

Part IV

COMMUNICATION

9

Communication

EDGAR DALE

It was the best of times, it was the worst of times, it was the age of wisdom, it was the age of foolishness, it was the epoch of belief, it was the epoch of incredulity, it was the season of Light, it was the season of Darkness, it was the spring of hope, it was the winter of despair.

—A Tale of Two Cities.

It was the year of the 50-megaton bomb, of the conquests of space. It was a year when two great nations, India and the United States, both used force and aggression—one successfully—to impose their will on another nation. It was a time when knowledge in health, medicine, agriculture, education, and human relations was increasing faster than we had learned how to distribute it. It was a time when love and hate were, as usual, drawing compound interest. It was a period when in many, many meetings some one stood up and said sagely, "Our problem is basically a problem of communication." And many people nodded in agreement.

The statement is true, but truistic. It does emphasize and underline the importance of communication, yet there still remains the vexing and complex problem of how to communicate, when to communicate, how to test the effects of communication.

Communication is the sharing of ideas in a mood of mutuality. Thus it is democratic, not authoritarian. It emphasizes the flow of ideas. It promotes empathy, getting into the other fellow's shoes. It puts one-way, imitative reaction at the low end of the scale and creative interaction at the other.

In the past twenty years we have begun to work in earnest on these questions of communication. We have approached the problem from the psychological, sociological, and philosophical points of view. There has been extensive research on the mass media, beginning with the pioneering Payne Fund studies in the early thirties. Let me summarize, though without adequate qualification in this brief space, some of the major findings of these studies.

STUDIES IN THE MASS MEDIA

1. In all communication we must distinguish between (a) the precipitating experience, the final triggering action in a chain of related events; and (b) those influences which have a "persistent, shaping effect upon the thought and behavior of human beings, singly or collectively."* Thus a television program might trigger a boy to commit a delinquent act which in turn was the result of the "persistent shaping effect" of a disturbed family relationship.

We can also classify effects as reminders or reconstructors. Thus the recent television series on Shakespeare, "The Age of Kings," which originally appeared over the BBC, may remind us to read or reread the plays in the series. Would a carefully developed series of television programs on key characters in the Bible have similar reminding effects?

The mass media may satisfy or amplify a present taste but only on rare occasions be able to create a major shift in taste, as for example from light entertainment fiction to a taste for classic literature. Samuel Johnson put it this way over two hundred years ago: "What is new is opposed, because most are unwilling to be taught; and what is known is rejected, because it is not sufficiently considered that men more frequently require to be reminded than informed."

We are likely to fall into error in religious instruction if we conclude that, because the advertiser can get the planned results through radio or television, then religious communicators can, too. We must distinguish between what people want and what they need. They may not need what they want, or want what they need. The advertiser presents a message to a person who already has a taste in a particular field and merely shifts from one product to another. The channel is already dug. Further, you don't change your life pattern when you buy perfume, aspirin, automobiles, soap, or cigarettes.

2. The situational factors are highly important in effective com-

*Louis Gottschalk, *Understanding History* (New York, 1950), p. 223.

munication. Remember that a few years ago parents and educators were up in arms against certain kinds of comic books. Today a sermon on comics would draw polite yawns. A sermon that left an audience cold five years ago may warm them up today.

Are the "persistent shaping effects" of the culture noted by Gottschalk working with you or against you in the communication of the Christian idea and ideal? Do you say the same things in church or on the air that are said by big businessmen, by college presidents, by heads of television networks or heads of unions? If not, where do you differ? Do they reinforce your ideas, neutralize them, or directly oppose them?

Let us not forget that we are living in a world of prize-fixing in television, of price-fixing in business, of point-fixing in college basketball. Are these merely abnormalities in a healthy society, or do they represent the norm? Is naked force now the norm in international life? If we are in fact living in a decadent society and a decadent world, then the role of the minister and the Christian in a community is a difficult one. You must ask yourself whether you wish to be prophetic or popular. There is no easy way of stepping on the conscience of a congregation without stepping on its toes. You can, of course, say that there are two sides to all questions, and then try to occupy both of them.

The communication issue here is clear. Do the leaders of our churches have a responsibility for diagnosing in Christian terms the great issues of the day? Certainly they need not keep the nerves of the congregation raw with exhortations; nor need they pose as experts and give neat solutions. They must, however, clarify the issues as they see them. The minister must comfort the troubled and trouble the comfortable. In an age when comfort is often deified there is a conflict between comfort and conscience. Jack Paar recently spoke very highly of Albert Schweitzer, saying that he was probably the greatest person in the world, and then added, "I'd like to go and work with him—and I would, too, if I could commute."

3. People read, see, and hear selectively depending upon their past experiences. These experiences have been conditioned by their age, sex, location, organizational grouping, income, education, and native ability. As a result of these differences in background few television programs, motion pictures, or newspaper articles are seen or read by as many as 50 per cent of our population. We have, in effect, a series of minority audiences—not one public but many. "A program selects its own audience."

If this is true, then we must have varied programs for people to select from; must develop religious programs that reflect the varied needs of viewers. We must also look at our own church programs and outlooks and ask whether we have developed exclusive or inclusive programs in our churches. Is the message of the suburban church "Come if you are like us, stay away if you are not"?

When a message strikes close to home, it may be either accepted and acted upon or rejected. When a situation is really threatening and anxiety-producing, the communicator must set up some channel through which the anxiety can be realistically allayed. If there is no channel for action, rejection or evasive behavior may occur. One study showed that when smokers read about the relationship between cigarettes and cancer, they did not quit smoking. They quit reading. When burdens become unbearable and no way out is suggested, we may either anesthetize ourselves to the situation or evade it in some way or other. A pathological search for pleasure may mask hidden anxieties which we seem unable to resolve.

4. The communication likely to be most effective in the long run is that which causes feedback, critical and creative interaction. The mood is one of problem-solving, not furnishing pat answers. This leads us to the difference between a mass and a public. C. Wright Mills, sociologist at Columbia University, has pointed out in *The Power Elite* that we have a mass and not a public when (1) a few speak to the many, (2) the many cannot answer back—do not interact, (3) public opinion cannot shape powerful decisions, and (4) the state effectively controls the individual.

Obviously our concern here is to create or cater to a variety of religious publics whom we help in problem-framing and problem-solving. A quest begins with a question. The aim of religious communication is to develop people with mature minds of their own; critical-minded, not sponge-minded. The more forums we have, the fewer arenas we shall need. It is better to talk it out than to fight it out.

5. A personal message is likely to be the most effective of all means of communication. Person-to-person contact is followed in order of effectiveness by television, films, then radio. Print is especially valuable for a message which requires careful critical study. You can't turn back the page with television, films, or radio. Person-to-person contact permits greater clarity of the message, permits interaction to clarify ambiguity, and provides the trust and authority so necessary

for effective communication. "If you want to send a message, wrap it up in a person."

6. The more specific the message, the more likely it will be to elicit a response, move to action. This relates, obviously, first to understandableness, and second, to its value in meeting a specific need. But complicated messages, however clarified, require time for communication. This means careful, long-range planning of ends and means.

Too many sermons are vague and discursive; they do not leave the individual with suggested specific responses that can be made. There are no handles for using the ideas presented in the sermon. Define the expected responses and thus help the members of the church—or your readers, listeners, or viewers—to translate them into reality.

But isn't the sermon or TV presentation supposed to be inspirational? Yes, it should be. But to present desirable ends without suggesting specific means for reaching them is mere sentimentality. Keep facing the question: how can this idea be made relevant to the varying needs of the members of the congregation? A specific message can meet a specific need. This does not leave out of account the necessity for developing generalizations that individuals can translate into conduct for themselves. But we must approach the universal through the particular.

7. Repetition with variation is an effective method of communication. This provides what the psychologist calls reinforcement. Repetition in itself may become very boring, but in a variety of interesting forms it induces effective learning. It provides more chances for catching on to the meanings communicated. It may also enable us to reach more and differing publics.

A multiple-media approach provides repetition under varying conditions. Coupled with face-to-face contact, it furnishes us the most effective method of communication. Peter Odegard of the University of California told me that studies of the U.S. Treasury during the war disclosed that the person who could give most reasons for buying bonds did in fact buy most bonds. There is scientific evidence, too, of the value of using a multisensory approach. Sight and sound may reinforce each other.

8. Securing a believable message is a key factor in communication. Children say, in effect, in rejecting an unfavorable comment by a playmate, "I consider the source." So do adults. "Who said it?" or "Who wrote?" is a key question in effective persuasion.

There are, of course, a number of factors about the credibility of the message which do not relate to its original quality. The data on fluoridation of water, even though accepted by the highest medical authorities, may be rejected by an individual. The factors within the control of the church, however, are those relating to the scholarship of the material communicated, the skill with which sound ideas are marshaled and presented, and the reputation of the minister for thoughtful, considered statements.

EFFECTIVENESS OF COMMUNICATION

We have noted eight factors that influence the effectiveness of communication. They are:

1. The level of changed behavior sought—a reminder or reconstruction.

2. The situation, the cultural context.

3. Selective perception—we see and hear what we want to see.

4. Opportunities for participation and critical and creative involvement.

5. The personal quality of the message.

6. Specificity of the message, ease of translation into action.

7. The use of repetition and variation through many media and multisensory experience.

8. Credibility.

How do these eight key factors apply in communicating religious ideas and ideals? Let us look at the steps from the preparing and delivery of the message to a check or evaluation of the effectiveness of the procedure. When I speak of a message I am not thinking only about sermons, but of all the kinds of Christian messages that are transmitted through speaking and listening, through writing and reading, and especially through visualizing and observing—the rituals, the liturgy, the church atmosphere. Much communication will and should occur in small face-to-face groups.

Let us now look carefully at the messages we plan to communicate. Remember: the more specific the message, the more likely you can communicate it. What, then, is the specific message that your church wishes to convey? It is not enough to refer in general to *the* Christian message. The Christian message varies in interpretation all the way from the sacerdotal caterwauling on many radio stations on Sunday to the vigorous, clear-cut messages presented by able leaders in the National Council of Churches or the United Church Women.

Let us suppose that your message emphasizes the Christian responsibility to see that boys and girls, men and women, everywhere in the world live a fulfilled life, that no roadblocks are deliberately thrown in their way. What, specifically, can a single individual or a group in your church do to see that a Korean, or Congolese, or Bolivian boy or girl lives a fulfilled life? Is your church going to do something specific about world literacy, about world health, about the world food supply, about world peace?

Suppose your message is that there can be no peace in the world unless there is shared power and shared respect, unless we recognize the dignity and importance of all individuals. How do you convey it? Certainly by believing confidently in it yourself. Self-respect precedes respect for others. A few years ago in a workshop for ministers I asked those who felt they were indispensable to raise their hands. About one in ten did. Then I said, "I thought that the essence of the Christian doctrine was the indispensability, the dignity, the importance of all persons. Why do you exclude yourself? If you don't believe that you are important, can you convince other people that they are important?"

A good many years ago a teacher in the Pittsburgh schools was having her fifth-grade class tell what they would like to be when they grew up. They had just started when the superintendent of schools came in to visit the class. Row by row they told about wanting to be nurses, doctors, firemen, engineers, and so forth, Suddenly the teacher realized that the last boy in the last seat would probably say something out of key with what the others had said. He wasn't prepossessing, he wasn't able. Perhaps the superintendent would go before he reported—but the interested superintendent stayed on. When it came the boy's turn to speak he said, "When I grow up I would like to lead a blind man." His was the only reply that directly considered the helping of others.

What publics are you trying to serve? Let us suppose you are clear as to your message and that you are now ready to prepare it for an audience. You are certainly kidding yourself if you consider your basic public those reached by the Sunday sermon. You must think also of the nursery school and its parents, of the camp programs for young people, of the choir, the church school; of small face-to-face discussion groups, the mission board, the guilds, and individuals whom you are counseling. One church refers to its serving of a wide range of publics as a "full-guidance" program.

What will be the form of the message? As noted above, the sermon comes readily to mind. But the sermon, fruitful as any lecture can be, usually lacks creative interaction, feedback, critical evaluation. A progressive church must provide regular means for discussion, conversation about what has been said in the pulpit or presented elsewhere in the church.

The sermon should be seen as the starting of a dialogue, a continued conversation. The sermon is not the last word. It should be a regular installment of a continued story which integrates all the work of the church.

The Christian message will also be presented in church school lessons, on film, by recording, drama, dance, a well-organized series of church meetings, and the like. For the nonchurchgoing public we are not adequately exploiting the full range of radio and television. Nor should the minister overlook the possibility of making the sermon available through mimeographing, and later, if the publishers are willing, through a book. Remember the importance of the multiple-media approach.

Will your message be understood? Boswell recorded in his *Life of Samuel Johnson* the following exchange between himself and his subject: "I have talked of preaching, and of the great success which those called methodists have." Johnson replied, "Sir, it is owing to their expressing themselves in a plain and familiar manner, which is the only way to do good to the common people, and which clergymen of genius and learning ought to do from a principle of duty, when it is suited to their congregations; a practice, for which they will be praised by men of sense."

All professional people are likely to believe that everybody understands their own jargon. The words community, dialogue, the I-Thou relationship, ecumenical, witness, and hundreds of others are really in-group words. Most people do not know what they mean. Many college students do not even smile when you talk about the great love affair of Dan and Beersheba, Sodom and Gomorrah. Many do not even know the meaning of "prodigal" in the parable of the prodigal son. Sermons should be aimed to express an idea, not to impress the congregation with your scholarship or speaking ability.

If you are speaking to or writing for the average congregation in the United States, they will have had less than a high school education —one-third of the younger members of your congregation will not even have graduated from high school. Seven or 8 per cent will be college graduates. Do you know how to talk to the man on the street, get into his shoes?

Don't make sermons any harder than they need to be or any easier than they need to be. Herein lies the great value of the parable. It is a "comparable"—it is both simile and metaphor. It can be understood at a concrete level and is capable of wide generalization. It has both primary and secondary meanings. It is "suffused with suggestibility," a phrase used by Alfred North Whitehead.

A story has a beginning and end. It is easy to remember because it usually is well organized and has a time or cause-and-effect sequence. It serves as a reminder to call up the rest of the message.

You will be understood if you tell not only what is on your mind but what is on your heart. If you are a young man, tell us what you have concluded up to now. Don't fill us full of what other people have concluded. Speak to the congregation and not to your professors back in the seminary.

Will your message be believed, or critically evaluated? It may be rejected, of course, because it is contrary to one's present beliefs. It may be evaded if your listener or viewer on TV sees no way to begin on a series of steps leading in the right direction.

Here we also face the credibility of the minister himself or the materials prepared for church use. Are you careful in your statements in the pulpit? Can your facts be depended upon? Do you draw conclusions with care? Do your either-or's need more qualification? Have you read anything important lately?

Is your message about the right length? Do you agree that if you don't strike oil in the first twenty minutes you should stop boring? Are you filling their cups so full of your ideas that they are beginning to slop over? Are you sensitive to signals from your audience or congregation that they have had about enough?

Finally, *how do you get action?* Your church message may have been presented in a favorable situation; you may have prepared it to meet the specific needs of a congregation; it may have been clear and easily understood; the congregation may have nodded in approval as the message was presented. But will they act? Will their attitudes and outlooks be changed?

Let me first answer this question indirectly. What is your own action index, the per cent you get when you divide what you do by what you know you should do—what is your D/K score? Did you write that letter to Columbia Broadcasting System complimenting them on their wonderful year-end program from Chicago? Did you write a letter congratulating a member of the community on his recent promotion? Why didn't you visit your sick friend in the hospital as you resolved to do? All of us will have to admit to a good deal of slippage—our D/K scores are not as good as they ought to be.

Communication would be made more effective if we helped people organize their lives for action, helped them become translators of ideals they already have instead of frustrating them with more things to do. Some of us are driving with the brakes on and can't act the way we know is right. Some of us do not know how to use wisely the time of our lives. Time is our greatest capital, but few teachers or ministers show us *specifically* how to invest it wisely.

We could save huge amounts of time if we sharpened our focus on the kinds of goals we think are worth spending our time on. Many travel a social jungle without an adequate map. If you don't know where you're going, the chances of getting there are poor.

When we feel guilty about how little we seem to accomplish, we often resolve to work harder. But we might first plan not to work harder but to work smarter. In a letter to George Washington dated April 23, 1794, Jefferson notes that he is now back on his farm and cannot write his usual ten or twelve letters a day, but must postpone answering letters until there is a rainy day. Where did he find the time? He wrote to his daughter Patsy: "Determine never to be idle. . . . No person will have occasion to complain of the want of time who never loses any. It is wonderful how much may be done if we are always doing."

But Jefferson also took time for the reflection needed to precede doing. Dumas Malone reports that when Jefferson was in France he retired from time to time to a hermitage kept by lay brothers beyond the Bois de Boulogne. Here he cut himself off from outside contacts until he caught up with his work. Ministers and church workers must do the same.

Justice Holmes once said, "The great thing is to have an eye for the essential." What is the essential aim for communication in the effective church? It is not only the informed church member; it is chiefly the transformed church member.

The church member should be an actor, not one who is acted upon; a participant, not a comfortable spectator on the side lines; a member who is a part of the church, not apart from it.

Emile Gauvreau, a well-known newspaperman of the thirties, wrote: "I was now definitely a part of that strange race of people aptly described . . . as spending their lives doing work they detest to make money they don't want to buy things they don't need in order to impress people they dislike."

In a time of conflict, those who have something to say regarding the great issues of that conflict have a chance to come into their own. That conflict relates to the revolution of rising expectations, to the values and hazards of nationalism, and to communism. Listen to this comment:

There is only one cure for the evils which newly acquired freedom produces, and that cure is freedom.
. . . .
Many politicians of our time are in the habit of laying it down, as a self-evident proposition, that no people ought to be free till they are fit to use their freedom. The maxim is worthy of the fool in the old story, who resolved not to go into the water till he had learned to swim. If men are to wait for liberty till they become wise and good in slavery, they may indeed wait forever.

This makes good sense today, as it did when Macaulay wrote it more than a century ago in his essay on Milton.

We are deeply concerned about the creative use of the communication process. The program we recommend is one which respects the mind and the personality of all individuals. This is the essence of the democratic processes and the essence of the Judaeo-Christian philosophy.

The outcome of effective communication will then be a growing person, a person moving toward spiritual and intellectual maturity. Our task is to be an active participator in this process. This means setting up the conditions that provide access to excellence. It means building a society in which people can work and think without coercion, a society where there is a free flow of ideas and abundant opportunities for creative interaction.

In a revolutionary period do you say with Hamlet: "The time is out of joint; O cursed spite,/That ever I was born to set it right!" Or do you speak with the same hope Wordsworth had, speaking of revolutionary times: "Bliss was it in that dawn to be alive,/And to be young was very heaven. . . ."?

Today we must take both the short view and the long view in our communications. The possibilities of nuclear warfare make the short view critical. But neither must we forget the long view that helps to give us a compass and guide to the future. Let us remember the words of Marchal Lyautey, who, when he was in Africa, asked his gardener to get him a certain tree. The gardener objected that this tree did not reach maturity for two hundred years. The marshal replied, "In that case there's no time to lose. Plant it this afternoon."

10

The Mass Media
and the Churches

DALLAS SMYTHE

THE CHRISTIAN, WHEREVER HE LIVES, HAS THE RESPONSIBILITY TO stand in critical detachment from the works of man. This necessarily means that his life should not be complacent and soft, but rather sensitively critical and even uncomfortable. My own position, then, is that of a primitive Christian. In this way I approach the mass media and the Church.

Under the auspices of the American Friends Service Committee, Milton Mayer went to study the churches in Eastern Europe. On his return he said, "All over Eastern Europe one hears the same agonized words from churchmen: 'The atheists had to come to teach us the Social Gospel.' "[1]* What did he mean? As I understand him, his meaning is close to the core of the relation between the mass media of communications and the Church in the United States.

The reader will need no reminding of the power of mass media, and in particular of broadcasting and film. We know that broadcasting tends to monopolize over time the sensory attention of the population and to condition it to materials produced by highly integrated organizations. There are now TV sets in over 90 per cent of our households, and the average viewing in a TV home is at least six hours a day. In any average minute between 7:00 and 11:00 P.M. in January 1961, 29 million American families were watching TV. This means that an audience of more than half our population is always watching TV in the evening. Next to time spent in work, TV literally monopolizes more of our time than any other waking activity. We know that the

* The notes for this chapter will be found on pp. 144 f.

130

mass media tend to narcotize the population, to reinforce the status quo, to filter out and water down efforts to change our basic policies and institutions.[2]

The policy of the business organizations that operate the TV-radio industry, the press, comic books, and so on is the same as that of cultural industry in general, of which it is a part. The term *cultural industry* refers here to the mass production of consumer goods as distinct from goods used in further production. Elaborate technology and heavy capital investment require mass production when applied to entertainment or to automobile manufacturing. Mass production requires the largest possible market. And it is because they are mass producers that we call them the mass media of communication. Mass production for a mass market means that the product is shaped to offend as few as possible. Because the largest number of potential consumers is in the portion of the population with median or lower incomes, the design of the mass-produced commodity or service is especially geared to what are supposed to be median taste levels.

Standardization of product is a necessary condition to mass production. And standardization of the product of cultural industry as we practice it robs the product of diversity, spontaneity, and individuality. Even more, it constricts the scope of permissible topics, characters, and styles of treatment. Thus, General Mills tells the writers of its TV and radio dramas:

In general, the moral code of the characters in our dramas will be more or less synonymous with the moral code of the bulk of the American middle-class, as it is commonly understood. . . . There will be no material that may give offense either directly or by inference to any organized minority group, lodge, or other organizations, institutions, residents of any state or section of the country, or a commercial organization of any sort. This will be taken to include political organizations; fraternal organizations; college and school groups; labor groups; industrial, business and professional organizations; religious orders; civic clubs, memorial and patriotic societies; philanthropic and reform societies (Anti-Tobacco League, for example); athletic organizations; women's groups, etc., which are in good standing.

We will treat mention of the Civil War carefully, mindful of the sensitiveness of the south on this subject. No written material may be used that might give offense to our Canadian neighbors . . .

General Mills' audiences are to see only the best of all possible worlds:

There will be no material for or against sharply drawn national or regional controversial issues. . . . Where it seems fitting, the characters should reflect recognition and acceptance of the world situation in their thoughts and actions, although in dealing with war, our writers should minimize the "horror" aspects. . . . Men in uniform shall not be cast as heavy villains or portrayed as engaging in any criminal activity. There will be no material on any of our programs which could in any way further the concept of business as cold, ruthless and lacking all sentiment or spiritual motivation.[3]

This is not caricature; it delineates the serious policy of cultural industry—a policy of providing content that is smoothed out—or homogenized—so as to offend nobody and to cater to the presumed taste of the largest possible number.

Not only must today's mass media product be standardized; it must be differentiated from yesterday's. For our media men live in a one-day world. Audience loyalties must be evoked by using "images" which promise that tomorrow's product will be both the same as, and better than, today's. To this end superlatives are used to make the insignificant differences that distinguish the two seem real and important. Sensationalism, as it used to be called when it was introduced by "yellow journalism," tends to reduce all experiences to a flat level when linked with the presentation of news in snippets, flanked by commercial announcements. Yesterday's local murder story receives the same scare headlines as today's international crisis which may actually extinguish us all in a nuclear holocaust.

The mass media of communication and the mass producers of other goods and services are not only similar; they are functionally indispensable to each other.

The mass production systems for refrigerators, automobiles, clothing, and so on depend for their markets on the advertising carried to the audience by the mass media of communication; without it they could not function. The mass production system for communications depends for its support on revenues from advertising which provides the context for and agenda of your entertainment, your information, and your guidance; without this support it could not function. As a mass production enterprise, the first duty of the mass media of communications is conceived to be the pursuit of profits. What ties the two parts of the whole system together—the mass production of cultural goods and the mass production of communications—is a common policy: the education of the American people to loyal and dutiful consumership of advertised goods.

Now materialism is a dirty word, whether used in reference to the Communists or to ourselves. Raymond Williams, the Oxford profes-

sor, says in effect that the materialism in our capitalist mass production society is both excessive and insufficient.⁴ He distinguishes between use and consumption. If we buy soap for its cleaning properties, this is use. If we buy it as a means to becoming an attractive
sexual object, this is consumership. If we buy clothes for comfort,
grace, and durability, this is use. If we buy them because they are the
mode set this year by Jackie Kennedy, this is consumership. Consumption is an artifact of advertising. So our materialist emphasis is
really a perversion of materialism. We try to inject our intangible
values into materialism. In the process they are degraded and homogenized. If our materialism were functional we would not be so preju-
diced against production for public use, here and in the underdeveloped areas of the world.

Our consumption-based culture is also obsessed with technology.
The teaching of consumership in our marketing and mass media
systems rests on the techniques of manipulating people to consume
as lavishly as possible. Our concern with technique is evident from
our worship of know-how—from our devotion to the development
of technology and its productive potential for personal pleasure as
well as destructive potential in war. This concern for technique makes
sense of the problem of violence and sex in the mass media. The
Mickey Spillane kind of violence for the sake of violence is technique
stripped of meaning. By contrast, in Shakespeare there may be much
violence, but it is used for its human meaning, not for its own sake.
Similarly, the exploitation of sex symbols for the sake of the thrill
is a play on the technique of love, minus the self-respecting meaning
of love. Linked with technique in our values is the importance of conflict. In domestic affairs conflict is typically disapproved—for example, in the form of strikes or Freedom Riders—unless cast in the
form of games. Our recreation and entertainment revolve around the
conflict in games to a high degree. Our political elections, under the
influence of TV, are becoming like a World Series. And here one sees
how our concern with technique and with games is integrated. Our
passionate interest in the statistics of the World Series or of political
convention and election voting is a concern with the technique of
the game. It is no accident that "games theory" is one of the few
uniquely American developments in economic theory and that our
military strategists try to apply it to cold war situations. Also note
that, half-humorously, businessmen refer to business as a game.

Even the cold war is perceived in terms of some kind of box score,
with our team pitted against its rival in what is geographically a World

Series. A study by Dr. George Gerbner of articles in the *New York Times* and the Hungarian Communist Party daily newspaper for the period in the fall of 1961 when heads of state were attending the UN reveals that the *New York Times* was more concerned with keeping score in the cold war, while the Hungarian paper was more concerned with substantive issues. When possibly our best newspaper devotes relatively more attention to procedural and tactical gains and losses in the cold war than to such substantive issues as the real conditions of peoples throughout the world, one may be sure that the bulk of our mass media oversimplify the box score even further. This dangerously oversimplified view of life makes for an ominous irrelevance to the real problems of living in a world which will either develop mutual accommodation for diverse political and economic systems or suffer the calamity of nuclear war.

Harold Innis once remarked that the function of popular culture and our institutions is to serve the need of the individual to "appraise problems in terms of space and time," and to enable him to "take the proper steps at the right time."[5] Our mass media should contribute to this function. In large measure we depend on our cultural industry to educate, inform, and entertain us, and to provide the basis for our government policy as well as for electing men to public office. When human values are subordinated to the process of obtaining profits from the mass production of these communications services, it is not surprising that a moral basis for national policy is uncertain and often absent. Witness the U-2 incident. Witness the "Bay of Pigs" invasion. Witness the cruel deceptions in our fall-out shelter program. And note that the mass media of communications serve to merchandise to the American people our undemocratically arrived-at bipartisan foreign policy.

How is the Church related to these aspects of our popular culture in the United States today? Does it stand and act in critical detachment? Does it recognize its kinship with Christians even in the socialist countries?

We note the high level and rapid growth in the past fifteen years of professed attachment to religious faiths. Will Herberg mentions a recent opinion survey which found that 95 per cent of the population in this country identified itself as Protestants, Catholics, or Jews.[6] Church membership is increasing and new church buildings keep being built. "Godless" is a powerful epithet. The old tradition of antipathy to having a Roman Catholic as head of the state was finally broken in the last presidential election. And it is doubtful that a man with the views on religion held by Thomas Jefferson could be elected to any substantial public office today. Even the academic community, traditionally secular, grows more concerned with religion.

In searching for the significance of churches and religion today, however, one notes that in the survey, while more than 95 per cent of Americans believe in God, more than 80 per cent are most serious about living as comfortably in this life as possible rather than about the hereafter. More than half assert that they follow the rule of loving one's neighbor as oneself "all the way." At the same time, more than half of the same Americans who said that religion was something "very important" said that their religious beliefs had no real effect on their ideas or conduct in politics and business.[7]

Will Herberg finds that the effective religion in America is the American way of life. He contends that it is an organic structure of ideas, values, and beliefs that is genuinely operative in American lives, which both influences and is influenced by the "official" religions.[8] This American way of life, summed up in the word *democracy,* means on the political side the Constitution, on the economic side free enterprise, on the social side mobility and competition in consumership, and on the spiritual side a humanitarian, optimistic idealism. The predominant object of faith in American religion is faith itself: we worship not God but our own worshiping. We should not be surprised, then, that the identity of democracy and religion has been explicitly recognized by a number of writers in recent years; we find, for example, J. Paul Williams insisting that

Americans must come to look on the democratic ideal (not necessarily the American practice of it) as the Will of God, or if they please, of nature. . . . Americans must be brought to the conviction that democracy is the very Law of Life. . . . The state must be brought into the picture; governmental agencies must teach the democratic ideal as religion . . . primary responsibility for teaching democracy *as religion* must be given to the public school, for instance . . .[9]

Another professor sums it up: "For the communicants of the democratic faith it is the religion of and for religions . . . It is the religion of religions, all may freely come together in it."[10]

What has this in common with Christianity, with Judaism? Is this not, as Herberg says, a particularly insidious idolatry?

It seems obvious that this identification of religion with the American way of life is in part at least a reaction to the perceived threat of Communism to the American institutional pattern. Thus we find

Herberg saying that in America "religion commends itself as our greatest resource and most powerful secret weapon" in the cold war. Religion is repeatedly referred to as the "shield of the nation," "more powerful than the H-bomb," and "America's strongest weapon against atheistic Communism."[11]

Obviously, also, not all faiths and denominations take such positions explicitly or even implicity as official Church policy. Such an identification of culture and religion is more the outcome of the total role of the churches and their members than a matter of conscious policy. The hard fact seems to be that American churches tend to be prisoners of their cultural context.

Within the churches themselves there are tendencies that lead to the identification of religion with culture, to say nothing of failure to implement the Social Gospel. These are the characteristics of the institutionalized Church. There is the tendency on the part of both laymen and ministers to regard the Church as a place for the "pro's" —to wall it off from the profane world. There is a tendency to regard the local church as a physical center for fellowship in a sense which makes it a competitor of the country club and the athletic club. There is a tendency to take refuge from the problems of the real world in a private world of ritual and dogma. There is no articulated policy for the implementation of the Social Gospel, employing all the vast educational and influential power of the Church and assigning to this policy a priority of urgency consonant with the needs of the times. There is a tendency for the Church to become preoccupied with its internal bureaucratic concerns. Within the local church this is evident in the trend to model the organization on the business corporation. Like the businessman, the minister becomes an executive, concerned primarily with public relations, with budget, with personnel, with physical plant, and with committees. In this setting, psychological counseling is the counterpart of employee counseling; juvenile delinquency work the counterpart of the work of the schools and courts with this by-product of urban industrialism. In the higher Church echelons bureaucracy becomes evident in a form more elastically resistant than in business, and much more so than in government. Concern for status and security breeds the habit of listening, conferring, and occupying oneself with paper work within the ambit comfortably permitted by the mores of the supporting popular culture.

Whatever position the Church feels called upon to take on the issue of the relation of the Church to popular culture, this position would seem to constitute a policy for the churches. The word *policy* is used here to mean the total policy of the Church in using its energies and resources. In this sense priorities need to be assigned to resources, just as you might well assign priorities for your perceived problems. The role of religious use of the mass media must be that of tools for the implementation of Church policy. The mass media of communication have no magic messages for Church problems; the nearest thing to magic in the mass media is the incredible efficiency they have in influencing people, because of their massproduction character. By themselves they are neutral, just as a knife is neutral: it can kill, or in the hands of the surgeon it may save.

It would be presumptuous to say what the policy of priorities should be or just how the various possible uses of mass media might serve, as a kit of variegated tools, to bring these policies to reality. All one can do is to suggest certain dimensions that may exist in the re-evaluation of the task and the resources of the churches.

In the book *The Television-Radio Audience and Religion,*[12] the same demand on the churches was made. As a result a Study Commission was created by the National Council of Churches with an agenda which would have accommodated a drastic self-examination and prescription of appropriate changes. The reality fell far short of the potential. The Commission often found itself dealing with platitudes and with such minor questions as the extent of desirable intervention by the Church in the making of Hollywood movies. It is dangerous frivolity to be concerned with the permissible depth of a plunging neckline when the shadow of plunging intercontinental missiles hangs over us all. If the report of the Commission deals with some crucial aspects of policy of the Church, it does so tangentially and without tackling the centers of institutional inertia in any way that challenges their traditional procedures.[13] Such an outcome of the effort to set churches in motion toward currently valid objectives, incidentally, illustrates again the point made earlier. For while the words of the Study Commission report are brave as far as they go, what effect have they had? The output of a temporary committee at the highest organizational level has, apparently, precious little impact on the minister in his community church.

What were the important points made in that report? It viewed the problem of the Church as one of sharing responsibility for the moral disease of policies which assume man's end to be material advantage, power, and pleasure achieved through competing with, manipulating, and exploiting his fellow man. In mid-twentieth cen-

tury, TV, film, radio, and so forth have created a system for mass-
producing the material that now provides people with the basis of
their values and attitudes—the practical substitute for the former
function of the schools and the churches. The Church was urged
to come to grips with the reality of this mass-produced culture; to
eliminate the lag that makes Church policy and structure tend to
irrelevance in this regard. What is required to eliminate that lag?
It would involve a number of reforms within the churches:

1. The Church should actively influence national and international
policy on the vital issues of our nuclear age toward the elimination of
war and nuclear terror.

2. The Church should actively influence national policy on problems of communications. For instance, what instructions have congregations or seminary students been given on the merits of Newton
Minow's efforts to improve what he called the "vast wasteland of
TV"? Has the Church used its influence to improve the quality of
TV-radio performance in the community through using the FCC
licensing procedures? Do you even know what you could do in this
way? Has the Church instructed congregations or students in the
implications of communications satellites for a peaceful Christian
world? Has the Church told the White House or Senators what it
thinks of the issue of private privilege versus public benefit, which
is at the heart of the controversy over who should own and operate
the first American communications satellite system? On problems such
as these the Church's voice should be heard.

3. The Church should influence the many men and women in
positions of leadership within the communications industry and in
related governmental, educational, and other organizations toward
achieving the creative possibilities inherent in the mass media in
speaking to man's condition. This is obvious and important.

4. The Church should employ the mass media to illuminate the
major thrusts of the gospel into the modern world. Basically, this
means that the churches must approach the mass media with respect
for the integrity of the terrible power these techniques possess. Specifically, this means a number of related changes in Church policy:

a. In their production of material for the mass media the churches
"must deal with genuine contemporary issues . . . interpreting the
judgments and healing of the Gospel in relation to these issues, and
not speak merely in inoffensive and innocuous terms."[14]

b. In sermons, in pastoral counseling, in committee meetings,
the minister should be conversant with, and where appropriate talk

about, the content of the secular mass media fare which fills the time of his congregation and provides them with attitudes and values.

c. In planning and operating the local church the regional and local councils of churches, and the national Church organization, there must be a reorientation of Church resources to cope with the problems that the mass media present. This should include planning for the local utilization of nationally and regionally produced religious TV-radio programs. What do the members of the churches do about discussing, criticizing, evaluating, and acting on their conclusions concerning the content of specific Broadcasting and Film Commission programs? Under this heading also comes the matter of the separate agencies that all major denominations have set up to deal with media programing. These broadcasting and film commissions have tended to become isolated from the general program departments of the denominations and the National Council. Instead of being in effect detached, these commissions should be interacting closely with the general program departments, giving them the reorientation toward the reality of our mass-produced culture which would restore to the churches as a whole some of their lost relevance to the real world.

d. The churches should undertake and adequately support continuous research, analysis, and experimentation to discover what is effective programing and to evaluate their own offerings through the media. Included should be basic research into the relationship between the mass media and contemporary value systems, including the effects of the performance of the business operators of the mass media on the substance of the educative and political processes and on the image of the good man and the good life.

e. And last, the churches and especially the seminaries should give more attention to the esthetics of the mass media and of our mass-produced culture. The Roman Catholic Church does this. Protestant churches generally do not, and this default implies a degree of irrelevance to the real world which is dangerous. If the suggestion were taken seriously, nothing less than a general reorientation of the curriculum of the seminaries would result. From this nothing but good could come.

All human institutions suffer from what we used to call cultural lag. We go on following group habits of thinking, feeling, and acting when the real situation has changed and old ways of thinking and acting are no longer relevant. Local government units were slow to relinquish their obsolete policies and attitudes when the national state became the dominant governmental form. Today the national state continues to act in ways which were serviceable before 1945 but are so no longer. The use of violence in international affairs ought to be now substantially impossible. Yet we are blinded by a thought barrier from seeing and acting in ways that would replace violence in international relations by nonviolent sanctions. If we get out of this crisis intact we will look back on it incredulously. How, it will be asked, could people who assumed the impossibility of equipping New York and New Jersey with atom bombs to use against each other be slow to see the inevitability of adopting similar policies for the United States and the U.S.S.R., or for Israel and Egypt? What is needed here is no reliance on fuzzy idealism or utopian dreamers. It is simple hardheaded practicality.

What is the position of the Christian churches in relation to this situation? If we look back on our policy toward war, we find we have been moving in two directions at once. In principle, war is contrary to Christ's teachings. Yet exceptions have been made for wars in self-defense. And, sadly enough, national armies with conventional arms have almost always marched to war with the blessings of the Church—even when they were fighting each other. A Roman Catholic scholar at Loyola in Chicago has demonstrated, for instance, that his Church—the same Church—found World War II morally justified in both France and Germany.[15] The best that could be said of the churches' role in relation to war was that they at least occasionally spoke against it. But let us remember that in all history before 1945 the churches' antiwar pronouncements were running against the real technological situation: they were bucking an otherwise viable institution—national defense.

Today, however, it is a constant source of amazement to note that the Church does not talk and act as though nuclear deterrents were its greatest asset in seeking the outlawing of force in international relations. For the first time in history, technology is on the same side as the Church. We have the once-in-a-million-years chance to put Christ's teaching about love to work. It is our first good chance. It is also our last chance of any kind to do it. For if we fail now, at best we go back to the level of primitive savages with permanently damaged genes, and at worst we eliminate all animal life from the planet.

To sum up this part of the argument, a few propositions seem self-evident:

1. Nuclear war is totally unacceptable. It would be fatal to civilization.

2. Nuclear deterrents will inevitably lead to nuclear war if they are continued long enough. The probability of accidental or unintentional nuclear war is not great in any given month. But if things go on as they are going now the probability rises almost to certainty, given ten to fifteen years of increasing competition in deterrents.

3. The aspirations of former colonial peoples, seeking the benefits of industrialization and of political freedom, guarantee that for the immediate future there will be a continuation of the process of popular revolutions—of which Cuba and the Congo are examples—and these revolutions would continue to take place if all Communists were suddenly transported to Mars.

4. While the revolutionary process may be accelerated or slowed, may be assisted in peaceful ways or repressed with violence, it is irreversible. It is quite unrealistic to think of restoring colonial control to the Congo, or of restoring capitalism in Russia.

If these propositions are accepted, then a fifth must follow:

5. The qualified and miserable "peaceful" co-existence that has prevailed for the past ten years under the threat of deterrents must quickly be organized on a more stable, enduring basis: we must build the structure and attitudes for international relations based on sanctions other than armed force.

Why, if this is so logical, do we not take the fifth step? The reasons seem to fall into two categories: psychological and politico-economic.

Dr. Jerome Frank has argued that we are blocked by a thought barrier of psychological mechanisms from taking the obvious steps.[16] He explains our massive indifference to the threat of nuclear destruction by saying that we react to armaments as an alcoholic does to drink—neurotically. We know that eventually, if we continue along the same line, they will kill us. But fatalistically, or through habituation to the thing, we continue to approach our doom. Sometimes we try to exorcise the danger by denying it. Sometimes we try to argue that the weapons are too awful for anyone to use. When we do, we are reaching for straws. Underlying these neurotic devices is an insensitivity to the remote; we are reluctant to forego an immediately available palliative (e.g., giving nuclear arms to West Germany) although we know that the long-run effects may be bad. (But what happens when Israel and Egypt have the bomb, or Cuba and the Dominican Republic?) Implicit in all these mechanisms that set cultures at each other's throats is the one Robert Merton calls the "self-fulfilling prophecy." Each major hostile act or speech in the cold war tends to make the hot war more probable. The old adage still holds good here: if you give a man a dog's name he tends to act like one.

Apart from the psychological blocks of a thought barrier there are some politico-economic blocks. Without in any way implying that there is malice or evil intent involved, it is still true that there are clashes of interest between the ways in which business organizations like to operate and the courses of action that our technology implies in the field of international relations. Take one example: we followed a policy toward Cuba more solicitous of sugar and oil investments by our citizens in that country than of the needs of the Cubans to develop a multiproduct economy and to achieve general literacy and adequate health protection. As a result we have forced the Cubans to look elsewhere—to China and the Soviet Union—for economic and technical assistance. And this kind of example could be multiplied. The ideology of our popular culture stands in the way of Christian action to implement the gospel in our nuclear crisis.

In addressing groups of churchmen, I have learned from their reactions that there are several additional mechanisms in the thought barrier that sometimes inhibits religious people. The first of these is the question: maybe God intended that mankind should go out with a nuclear bang. Maybe a nuclear holocaust is God's will. I put this question, in turn, to Dr. Joseph Sittler, professor of theology at the University of Chicago. His answer was, in essence, that while he claimed no monopoly as spokesman for God, he knew of nothing from God that supported this view and much that would contradict it. In Sittler's opinion, nuclear war is the ultimate blasphemy.[17]

The second mechanism implicit in the thought barrier is the argument that it is better to die on your feet for freedom than to live on your knees as a slave. The answer to this kind of reasoning is given in the pamphlet *A Christian Approach to Nuclear War* prepared by Buttrick, Wyckoff, and other theologians, published by the Church Peace Mission, from which I quote briefly.

... enslavement and individual physical and mental suffering which might be imposed by a conqueror ... could not be as acute and meaningless a form of suffering as that bound to occur in an eruption of atomic warfare. This is not simply because some life is better than no life. It is not bare survival that ultimately matters for the Christian who does not fear death. What matters is that the survival of life under tyranny could be creative, being deliberately chosen in consonance with Christian faith and hope. The risk of enslavement at the hands of another nation is not so fearful a thing as the risk of effacing the image of God in man through wholesale adoption of satanic means to defend national existence or even truth. What would be the substance of "freedom," "truth," "love," after we had used atomic weapons in a general war?[18]

The third and last peculiarly religious block in the thought barrier concerns the relation of the Christian in North America to Christians in the socialist countries. And now I return to my opening quotation from Milton Mayer's article in *Harper's* reporting on a study of the churches in those countries.[19] He asks what is a proper attitude for the Church in the Western world to take toward religion in the Communist countries, and gives his answer in various ways. For us to call upon religious peoples in those countries to choose between treason and damnation is, he says, a call by those who need not choose to those who must—a call which will not be answered there or anywhere. While Americans tend to boycott it, the Christian Peace Conference meeting annually in Prague speaks in these terms:

. . . The atom bomb of Hiroshima . . . lit up in a flash the road of Christendom. . . . All of us share the guilt. . . . We have not loved Him Whom God loved so much. Being of little faith we have thought that weapons and human power were our help. . . . The bomb . . . has become a summons.

When, therefore, we come together with our congregation and churches on the day of Hiroshima this year to hold a service of penitence and prayer, we ask all of you, both in East and in West, and all over the world, not to withhold your communion from us. Let us stand together before God as His children and make a new beginning through His forgiveness. . . .[20]

Mayer goes on:

Before I left Eastern Europe, I asked an elder, and a very old elder, what the Church in the West can contribute to our time.

"I do not know the West," he said, "but I know that there, as here, all Christians sing the hymn, 'In Christ There Is No East or West.' So I shall simply say what I think the Church, West and East, can contribute. If the trouble of the world is too deep and too desperate for self-interested negotiation, then there is something left which neither capitalism nor communism offers, but only the Church: brotherhood. But the Church must learn before it can teach."[21]

The relation of the churches to culture in the socialist countries offers a reversed image of our situation which may illuminate our predicament. There the Church stands in critical detachment from the popular way of life. Mutually interlaced, our popular culture and our churches seem to have more in common with each other than does Christianity in the East and in the West. For us the crucial issue may be: shall the Church be estranged from the Social Gospel and the rest of Christianity because of its permeation and vitiation by popular culture? Should the Church act effectively to reshape our popular culture in accordance with Christianity and the Social Gospel? Is it possible that the paramount religious problem in the Western world today is, as Mayer implies, that of the Social Gospel (and Christianity) in its relation to capitalism?

Quoting the tenth chapter of Isaiah, Mayer raises the question:

Could this—this professing Anti-Christ—be the Profane Reformation, bent so terribly upon accomplishing the alteration of society as the Sacred Reformation accomplished the alteration of the Church? The Old Testament prophets abound in the possibility: *Behold the Assyrian, the rod of mine anger, and the staff in his hand is mine indignation.* Could it be? There are Christians in Europe who are asking themselves if perhaps it is, and if it wasn't necessary that it come; and if it isn't here to stay and to spread wherever our brothers freeze and starve. . . .[22]

We shall see if a Profane Reformation can be informed by a Church which has either its faith or nothing. We shall see what Christianity can do without Cadillacs.[23]

Could it be that Isaiah's words fit our predicament and that we are witnessing a Profane Reformation in which the atheists are forcing us to implement the Social Gospel?

What is the relation of the thought barrier to the mass media—to the Church? Do lay and religious materials in the mass media tend to strengthen or to break through this barrier? This is, I submit, the central issue of our day for people in our position.

These are hard questions. But we live in times which demand that we ask and answer many hard questions. As in critical detachment we consider the relation of Christianity to popular culture and the mass media, such is our uncomfortable position.

NOTES

[1] "Christ under Communism," *Harper's Magazine* (August, 1960), p. 31.

[2] Paul F. Lazarsfeld and Robert K. Merton, "Mass Communication,

Popular Taste and Organized Social Action," in W. Schramm, ed., *Mass Communications* (Urbana, Ill., 1960), pp. 459-80.

[3] "Madison Avenue's Program Taboos," *Variety,* October 26, 1960.

[4] *Advertising and Society* (London, 1961).

[5] Harold A. Innis, *The Bias of Communication* (Toronto, 1951), p. 85.

[6] Will Herberg, *Protestant-Catholic-Jew* (New York, 1956).

[7] *Ibid.,* p. 86.

[8] *Ibid.,* p. 90.

[9] Quoted *ibid.,* p. 101.

[10] Quoted *ibid.,* p. 102.

[11] *Ibid.,* p. 74

[12] By Everett S. Parker, David W. Barry, and Dallas W. Smythe (New York, 1955).

[13] *The Church and the Mass Media,* Report of a Study Commission of the National Council of Churches (New York, 1960).

[14] *Ibid.,* p. 12.

[15] Gordon C. Zahn, "Social Science and the Theology of War," in W. J. Nagle, ed., *Morality and Modern Warfare* (Baltimore, 1960), pp. 104-125.

[16] "Breaking the Thought Barrier: Psychological Challenges of a Nuclear Age," Lectures 1 and 2, Department of Psychiatry, Johns Hopkins University, Baltimore, March 18 and April 1, 1960.

[17] "Breaking through the Thought Barrier to Survival," address to the Faculty Forum, University YMCA, Champaign, Ill., February 17, 1961.

[18] New York, Church Peace Mission.

[19] See also the article by Paul Oestreicher, who holds similar views: "The Christian in a Communist State," *The Listener* (London), January 5, 1961, pp. 22-23.

[20] Mayer, *op. cit.,* p. 36

[21] *Ibid.,* p. 37

[22] *Ibid.,* p. 30

[23] *Ibid.,* p. 37

Part V

WORLD CHRISTIANITY

11

World Christianity

LESSLIE NEWBIGIN

RESULT OF THE MISSIONARY EXPANSION

THE FACT THAT WE CAN USE A PHRASE LIKE "WORLD CHRISTIANITY" at all with any realism is something new in history. It may be said to be the great new fact of our time in the original sense of the much-quoted and much-misinterpreted words of the late William Temple. For the vastly greater part of its history, the Christian Church has been confined to a small segment of the inhabited earth, and for most of that time it has lived practically in isolation from the greater part of the human race—from the great religious cultures of Asia and Africa—cut off from contact with them by the power of Islam. It is only in relatively recent times that we can in any real sense speak of world Christianity.

Even if we use that phrase, we must remember what a small foothold the Christian religion has in many parts of the world. Sometimes we speak too easily of world Christianity and forget that in many countries the adherents of the Christian faith in all its forms together are but a fraction of 1 per cent of the population. Even the great and justly honored Christian churches of Asia are drawn for the most part from the fringes of Asian culture, and there are relatively very few Christians from among those who are in the central stream of Asian religious culture. Islam remains, as we well know, largely opaque to the penetration of the gospel.

And yet it is true that there is something today which can be called world Christianity. Humanly speaking, it is the result of the great missionary expansion of the last two centuries. That expansion, whatever one's attitude to Christianity may be, is one of the most remarkable facts of human history. One of the oddities of current affairs, perhaps an understandable oddity under the circumstances, is the way in

149

which the event is so constantly ignored or undervalued. It struck me as odd, for instance, in reading the voluminous report of a recent UNESCO conference on education in Africa, to find that, whereas something over 85 per cent of all the school children in Africa are in Christian schools, the report did not, so far as I was able to detect, give even a hint that such a phenomenon as a Christian school exists. The perspective in which we shall be able to see the missionary movement in its real significance is doubtless something for the future rather than the present. For the present, we shall have to accept the fact that secular commentators do not talk much about missions, perhaps because missions have talked too much about themselves.

But to understand the present situation of world Christianity we have to look at more than Christian missions. Christian missions have not operated in isolation. They have been intimately involved in the vast cultural explosion that has carried the ideas, the science, the techniques, the commercial systems, and the economic and political power of Western Europe and North America into every corner of the earth, so that in a few centuries these elements of the culture of Western Europe have become the common property of mankind. In the Western world we often fail to see this movement in its proper proportions because, as the result of the usual error of perspective, we are so much impressed by the internal conflicts within Western culture: the conflict between science and religion, and the conflict between the Communist and the capitalist ideologies. Deep and painful as these conflicts are, from the point of view of world history as a whole they are domestic disputes. However surprising the statement may seem, it must be insisted that in a world perspective it is not these that are the most important fact of our time. The most important fact is that the culture which has become for the first time the single world culture is that which came out of the life of the old Western Christendom; or, to put it in another way, the most significant fact of our time is that the peoples of all nations, even the most remote and primitive, are being drawn into the current of a single world civilization, within which the dominating questions are those that have been raised within the Western Christian tradition and not those that arise out of the other great religious cultures of mankind.

WESTERN CHRISTIAN TRADITION AND WORLD CIVILIZATION

The implications of this fact for our understanding of the modern world and of the Christian task in the modern world are important, as we shall see later. But having emphasized that point, it is now necessary to consider the confused and ambiguous relation which now exists between what we have called the Western Christian tradition and the world civilization of our time. On the one hand, the political power of the Western world is, in the rest of the world, discredited and in retreat. Colonialism is the dirtiest of all possible words in the international political vocabulary. But, on the other hand, the technical know-how of the West is everywhere in demand. We are familiar with the psychological tensions, not to say paradoxes, which this ambivalent situation creates. Those who are actually involved in programs of technical aid are certainly very familiar with it. What is not often noticed is the fact that this interest in Western science and technology, which is universal, is accompanied by an almost total lack of interest in the spiritual roots from which they sprang. In this the West must itself take a large share of the blame, through its own lack of interest in these spiritual roots. The attempt has been made, has it not, to persuade ourselves and the world that modern science is a structure of impersonal fact, existing independently of the personal faith and attitude of the scientific community, as if scientific knowledge and the techniques that flow from it were a sort of a world of fact as compared with religious knowledge, which is a world of personal opinions.

The truth is, of course, that the world of modern science is a vast structure of personal commitment, sustained by the mutual confidence of scientists and by the confidence that the public places in scientists, and rooted ultimately in certain beliefs about the nature of human existence. The rest of the world, however, has taken the hint from the West. It has shown itself uninterested in the spiritual roots of the Western way of life, and of the science and techniques which are now accepted as simply the common property of the world. A distinguished Moslem scholar told me some days ago that in the entire history of Islam there has not been one single scholarly study of Christianity by a Moslem. I think that the same, so far as I know, could be said with regard to Hinduism. It is true, for instance, that the justly famous Hindu philosopher Dr. Radhakrishnan writes a great deal about Christianity, but so far as my reading goes, I find that he uses stones chipped out of Christianity for his own mosaic. I do not know of any place where he attempts, so to say, to understand Christianity from the inside, attempts to put himself in the position of a Christian and understand the world from that standpoint. This is a very striking contrast to the tremendous curiosity of the Christian world about the non-Christian religions. One need not speak of the long history of Christian scholars who have devoted themselves to the study of the non-Christian faiths; to the recovery and translation and publication of the sometimes forgotten scriptures of other faiths; and to the comparative study of these religions. In a very real sense one can say that the renaissance of the non-Christian religions in our time is, in a considerable measure, the fruit of the work of Christian scholars.

What will be the long-term effect of the present generally accepted belief that the science and techniques of the Western world are now simply the common property of mankind and do not require any further sustenance from their original roots? It will surely take time to show. Whether we shall find, in the end, either that this whole scientific world can continue to exist and grow when it is completely severed from the spiritual roots which originally nourished it, or that the great non-Christian cultures will be able to continue to absorb such large doses of scientific ideas derived from another source without ultimately disrupting their own spiritual unity—both of these are points upon which one cannot at this moment say anything more than that time will show.

In the meantime, we have to deal with a single world society, marked by a kind of religious pluralism which Christianity has not known since the Edict of Milan. I want to emphasize both sides of this, the single society and the religious pluralism.

ONE DESTINY FOR ALL MANKIND

On the one hand, in a quite new sense, there is a single human society. Here at The Biblical Seminary, located within a few blocks of the United Nations buildings, it is surely unnecessary to underline that point. There is a whole world, and a growing world, of which the continual meetings in those buildings are only the most illustrious example, in which men and women of all races, all cultures, and all religious faiths are increasingly mingling as complete equals, sharing together a common culture, a common world of ideas, and the consciousness of a common destiny. Mankind is now, so to speak, sharing a single history. Men increasingly feel that there is in a sense now only one destiny for all mankind, that there is no private future for any race or any nation.

This single human society is, as I stated earlier, dominated by issues raised within the Western tradition. If, for instance, one goes to the newly independent countries of Asia and looks at the questions that dominate their political and public life, it is immediately obvious that they are not questions which have arisen out of the ancient precolonial spiritual situation of those countries. Nor has there been anything that could resemble a return to the spiritual condition of the precolonial period. On the contrary, the questions that dominate public life—questions of human rights, of technical development; questions arising from the population explosion, questions posed by the modern forms of Messianism, particularly Marxism—all of these are issues that could not have arisen out of the ancient precolonial pagan religious cultures of Asia. They arise from the impact upon Asia of the society that developed out of the old Western Christendom. The driving power of this single world culture, the thing that gives it its power—so astonishing if you think of it in a historical perspective—to disintegrate such ancient and massive structures as the religious cultures of India and China and Japan, is a secularized form of the Christian faith in the kingdom of God. It is, to put it in other terms, one form or another of the belief that human life stands in the immediate possibility of a new order. The new order may be conceived in various different terms: as the victory of the proletariat, as national liberation, as technical advance, as the achievement of the welfare state with freedom from all human ills, as the victory of the great leader; in one form or another, it is a new world just beyond the horizon which is going to be as different from the present world as day is from night.

It is this faith that gives driving power to the elements of Western culture which are being assimilated precisely by those peoples who are politically in revolt against the West, and which constitute the common civilization of our time. Plainly, this is a secularized form of the biblical faith in the coming of the Kingdom. It is something foreign to the great religious cultures of Asia. It could not have arisen out of them. It has come to them through Western Christendom. It is a striking fact that even while the formerly subject peoples are asserting themselves in the political field against the former colonial powers of the West, they are doing so in the strength of ideas derived from the Western tradition. Such movements as the Hindu Mahasaba in India and the Moslem Brotherhood in Egypt, which have sought to go back to the ancient non-Christian religious cultures to find the ideological basis for their political struggle against the colonial powers, have not been successful in capturing national leadership. This single world civilization which is disintegrating the ancient cultures of mankind and sweeping their peoples into the stream of a single world history, is powered by a variety of secularized versions of the Christian eschatology. And if we know our New Testament, that is exactly what we should expect.

COMPETING RELIGIOUS CONVICTIONS

But this single world civilization is characterized by religious pluralism. We are living in a situation to which Christians have not been accustomed since before the time of Constantine. It is a situation in which not merely different variants of Christianity, and not merely different religions understood as matters of the private life rather than as what controls your entire public life, but different total religious convictions, different dominating ideologies, compete together on equal terms. It is a condition of religious pluralism in which no faith is, so to speak, the established faith, none has the dominant political or cultural power behind it.

This is a new situation. (Perhaps some of the troubles in which churches find themselves are due precisely to a failure to recognize that fact. What one might call a nostalgia for Christendom is a very prevalent ailment among churches around the world.) These different competing religions may be what I have called the new Messianism, the secularized eschatologies of the modern world. They may be the ancient religions of Asia and Islam trying to tackle with their own resources the problems that the modern world brings to their peoples. But there are also concepts threatening both of these types of religion. On the one hand there is the continuing, and I believe growing, attractiveness of one form or other of the Hindu answer to the ultimate problems of human existence, the answer of the Vedanta, which finds ultimate reality by withdrawing from the ever-moving circumference of the wheel of existence into the center where all is still. On the other hand, equally threatening all these competing religious faiths, is the ever imminent and often present sense of emptiness, of meaninglessness, of utter futility which may exist behind a facade of enthusiasm for one or another of the religious alternatives that confront the human race. I have often found in India that those who in their public life are most strident in their repudiation of the claims of Christianity, and most insistent in the claims they make for the continuing validity of one or another of the ancient religions, are at the same time most determined at all costs to get their children into a Christian school; and if one asks the reason, they will answer, "Because it provides some kind of basis for moral values." Behind a great deal of what is said in the name of religion, there does lie, in every part of the world, either that wistful homesickness for the center of the wheel, for the point of rest which is reached by withdrawing from the meaningless movement of the circumference of the wheel; or on the other hand the sense of meaninglessness, the sense of a vacuum at the heart of things, which makes a man realize that he can offer to his own son or daughter no foundation on which to build.

If this is in any sense a true description of the religious situation, how is the Church to respond to it? I want to say that there are, I believe, three conditions that must be fulfilled if the Church is to respond to the challenge of this time.

UNITY IN THE CHRISTIAN MISSION

1. The first is that the Church must become recognizable as a family, in which, in principle, all men of every kind are at home. The necessary implication of a universal gospel is a universal fellowship, and the fact that we now share a universal secular history makes it impossible for us any longer to evade that implication. No one, I suppose, is likely to feel that more acutely than an evangelist in a country like India. One stands in the streets of a big Hindu city, or of a small village, and one holds up Christ as the one Savior of the world, in whom there is neither East nor West, who is neither the Westerner or the Easterner, but simply the Son of Man, the Savior of all mankind. One points to the Cross as the one true crisis of all human history, the one point at which the ultimate issues of human existence—the issues between man and his Maker, and between man and his brother —were finally exposed and settled. And then, through the work of the Holy Spirit, the point comes when the hearer is drawn to ask, "What can I do to become a part of this, to become a partaker in this? What is the fellowship in which I am invited now to enter? Where is it?"

Then comes the embarrassing moment when one has to uncover the truth that this Indian who has come to believe in the one Savior of the world has the opportunity of becoming a Danish Lutheran or a Canadian Baptist or on Australian Anglican or an American Methodist, or possibly even a Scottish United Free Church Continuing! In such a situation one realizes how impossible it is that our churches in their present condition of division could represent to men the one new humanity in Jesus Christ—could be the home in which all mankind, simply as mankind recreated in Christ, reborn through Him, could know themselves to be at home in the Father's house. Every one of these bodies has been shaped, far more than we realize when we are part of them, by the peculiar segment of human history lying behind us in our own country, and in the religious history of the time in which the great separations took place. None of them, as things stand, is a potential home for the whole human race.

The only way in which we can think of the Church's missionary task in the single world of today is in terms of one fellowship in all the earth, whatever the forms of that fellowship may be, and whatever the visible bonds by which that fellowship is acknowledged and preserved. The Church must surely be present to this world of ours as in some sense one family, recognizable in each place you meet it as one family, holding out to all men the secret of peace with God and peace with the brother.

In fact, however, this is not what we show the world. We show a fantastic medley of splintered fragments, divided on every ground of race and tradition and doctrine. We do not, when men meet us, show them the face of the one Savior, but rather a fantastic gallery of caricatures. It is at this point that the significance of the ecumenical movement, as I understand it, lies. Its significance does not lie in the creation of big organizations or impressive programs. Organizations are needed, and programs are needed from time to time and should not be despised. But the significance of this movement is that it provides a place where we can listen to one another, or rather listen to our Lord speaking to us in the unfamiliar accents that we hear from one another, so that we may receive correction from each other and learn from Him through one another where it is that we have misunderstood Him and so distorted His gospel in the face of the world.

Therefore the question at issue in this movement for Christian unity is not that of the size of our churches, but of the meaning of our churchmanship. It is the question whether or not the Church in our day can present to mankind the lineaments of a fellowship recognizable to men of every race and every culture as the household of God, the family of the one Father. Only a Church that has been willing to face the experience of this kind of mutual correction, which can be painful and difficult, will be in a position to commend the gospel to this growingly unified and yet religiously divided world of today.

THE CHRISTIAN MISSION AND WORLD HISTORY

2. The second condition, as I understand it, of effective response to the challenge of this time is a true theological understanding of

what God is doing in the secular world outside the Church. Now, this is a difficult field of discussion. It was one of the points at which real theological debate began at the New Delhi Assembly, but unfortunately the time available to us there was not sufficient to carry it very far. How shall we understand truly the relationship between what God is doing for the salvation of men in Jesus Christ in his Church, in the preaching of His gospel and the administering of His sacraments, and what God is doing in the entire secular history of the world—a world which is not outside of His control, but still subject to His sovereign will?

There is an obvious danger that we identify the work of God so wholly with the program of the Christian Church, to put it crudely, that we have no means of interpreting or understanding the world around us. When that happens, as it does happen, then we get a complete misconception of the nature of the missionary task. We come to think of missions as a kind of program we have to promote, as a cause which is going to collapse if we do not back it up, as something we might conceivably drop if it appears to have been mistaken, a cause which ought to be visibly and increasingly successful in the world. Is it not at this point that we find the nub of many of our difficulties in the missionary movement today? The period that is behind us, the period of the last hundred and fifty years, was from the point of view of Western Christendom a period in which history seemed to be going our way. Things seemed to be developing in the right way, and one could feel that the missionary movement was helping them along. But some other things have happened in recent years. Perhaps the most dramatic from the point of view of missions is what happened in China: the absolute closing down of the single largest piece of missionary endeavor of our time. But there has also been the closing of other doors, the shrinking of Christian influence in many parts of the world. There is the fact, to which many of us have only recently waked up, that with the population explosion going on all around us, even with all our evangelistic advance Christianity is a shrinking minority among the world's people. It does not look as if the Church's mission were the winning cause in quite the way that it could be made to look a decade or two ago. Am I wrong if I suggest that this is where a good many of our difficulties come in?

If so, how do we understand these events? Do we treat world history as if it were just a sort of background, a sort of scenery of no intrinsic importance to God, which does not need to concern us

except when it impinges upon God's work, either to help it along or
to stop it? At this point, I believe, real theological rethinking is
needed. We need to turn to the Bible afresh for an understanding of
the relation of the Church's mission to the secular history of the
world; the relation of what God is doing in the Church to what God
is doing in the world.

If one turns to the great missionary passages of the Old Testament, it is very plain there that Israel is not being called upon to
promote a sort of world movement or program. She is not being
called upon to assist God to cope with the problem of Assyria and
Egypt and Babylon. On the contrary, these great pagan empires
are but the small dust in God's hands. He raises them up and He
casts them down as He will. The role of Israel is to be the witness
and interpreter to the nations of these events—events which would
otherwise be meaningless to them. Israel has been admitted into the
counsels of God and is therefore commissioned to be His witness.
Israel's mission, then, is not something separate from, or over
against, the events of secular history. It is the place at which the
true meaning of these events is known, and at which, therefore, witness is borne to God's purpose in them.

One finds the same thing when one turns to the New Testament. I
want here to speak only briefly of the famous apocalyptic passage in
St. Mark 13. The context, you remember, is the prophecy of the
destruction of the Temple. That sounds like the exact contrary of
what the disciples of the Messiah had a right to expect—like an an-
nulment of the great central prophecy that Mount Zion would be
the place to which all the nations would come to be the peoples of
the living God. The disciples are deeply disturbed and ask for understanding of what is to happen. In reply Jesus gives them an interpretation of the times in which they and we have to live. It is a summons
to understand the events of secular history in the light of His mission.
The chapter shows us five characteristics of these times which we are
called upon to recognize.

First, they are times in which men expect and get messiahs—times,
in other words, in which we can expect messianic movements. "Many
will come in my name, saying, 'I am He!' "—claiming, in other
words, to offer total salvation to mankind. The days are gone when
men expected that life would go on as it had always done; when the
generations rose and fell like the seasonal blossoming and fading of
the flowers, and men counted the years as they did until recently in
the South Indian villages, by means of a cyclical calendar instead of

a linear one, because all events are expected to return to their starting point after the manner of the cycles of the natural world. This is now ended. The coming into the world of Him who is the Alpha and the Omega means a polarization of human affairs. Things can no longer be interpreted in cyclical terms because the question of man's ultimate destiny, the destiny of mankind as such, has been raised.

Pagan religion knows the idea of individual salvation, the idea of the individual taken out of world history into a transhistorical salvation. But this is something different. This is salvation for mankind. This is the vision of an end to which human history as a whole moves. Once that question has been raised, peoples and tribes who have lived for thousands of years in the natural cyclical pattern of existence find themselves drawn irreversibly into the current of a single world history, governed by the question of man's ultimate destiny and total welfare or salvation.

Second, the sign of these times is that they are times of tumult and suffering. Here there is an exact parallel between our Lord's words about His own suffering and His words about the suffering of the world. "The Son of man must suffer . . ." "These things must come to pass." And these two are linked together by the fact that both of these sufferings are filled with hope, because they are the birth pangs of the Kingdom. Therefore he who has entered into the fellowship of Christ's sufferings will enter with hope into the sufferings of the world.

Third, these are days of suffering for the Church. But the Church's sufferings have the special character of witness, *marturia*. "Take heed to yourselves; for they will deliver you up to councils; and you will be beaten in synagogues; and you will stand before governors and kings for my sake. . . . And the gospel must first be preached to all nations." There is a witness to be borne to the whole world concerning God's salvation, a witness to be borne both by preaching and by suffering. This is indeed the purpose of these days, because in Jesus the end of all things has been revealed. He is the Omega to whom the whole alphabet of human history moves, but the fulfillment of all things in Him is delayed in order that all men may have the opportunity to recognize Him and to accept their true destiny. And yet, as we have seen, it is the appearing of the true Messiah which precipitates the appearing of the false messiahs, of those who offer total welfare to mankind on other terms than His. It is only by His actual coming at a certain point in history, and by the actual coming of His gospel to a nation at a certain point in history, that nations are forced out of the cyclical prehistoric pattern of their natural existence and brought face to face with the question: to what end? The witness of the Church is thus the point at which the meaning of the time in which we live comes to light.

Fourth, however, this witness is only in a secondary sense the witness of the Church. Primarily, it is the witness of the Spirit. "It is not you who speak, but the Holy Spirit." That is the steady teaching of the New Testament on the subject of witness. In the days when Christian missions have worked, so to say, down the currents of secular power, they have been tempted to forget this truth and to conceive of their task rather in terms of a cultural program of penetration and training and uplift. We have talked about training up the younger churches, talked in terms for which the New Testament gives us no warrant. The fact that the Christian mission now has to learn to work against the currents of secular power is making many of us rediscover this New Testament truth, that witness is primarily a supernatural event, the work of the Holy Spirit at the point when the Church is *in extremis*, at its point of weakness and foolishness in the eyes of men.

Fifth and finally, these are days in which the world moves through suffering and witness to the ultimate issue, to the exposure of the false saviors and the coming in power of the true Savior, the Son of Man. This means that world history is not the story of a gradual ascent toward a perfect world in which missions are called upon, as it were, to give a bit of a shove on the way up. It is the story of a conflict in which the issues are more and more sharply defined until the final issue. The crises of history, as we call them, are the foreshadowing of the ultimate crisis. In this passage our Lord is looking forward to the particular crisis occasioned by the destruction of Jerusalem by the Roman armies. But behind this particular crisis—not to be identified with it (He warns us against that common error), but behind it, beyond it—lies the ultimate crisis which concerns the manifesting of Christ and Antichrist, the true salvation on God's terms and the bogus offer of salvation on other terms, the offer of total welfare, peace, security, happiness, everything that Big Brother can give us. Thus the lines are drawn through history more and more sharply. Those who followed the Antichrist appear to have things going their way. They see results. Those who follow Christ walk by faith through perplexity, suffering, and contempt. The process of polarization goes on, and he that endures to the end, the same shall be saved.

If that is at all a true interpretation of what the New Testament has to say about the understanding of the secular history to which the Christian mission is the clue, then the rise of these new Messianisms, the power of pagan empires, and the apparent weakness and foolishness of the Church should not cause Christians either surprise or alarm. The Church is not in itself the bearer of the whole substance of God's will for human history. The Church is set in the world as the witness to the work of God the Father, who is bringing men to the point of decison for or against His Son Jesus Christ, in whom He wills to sum up all things. Jesus did not appear among men as the one who shaped and directed the course of world history according to His Father's will, but as the one who, as a Son, accepted the Father's disposition of world history as the form in which His mission was to be accomplished. So also it will be with the Church. There is, therefore, no room for anxiety about the Christian mission. It is in the Father's hands. There is room only for faithfulness.

THE HOLY SPIRIT AND THE CHRISTIAN MISSION

3. The third condition to be fulfilled, I believe, is this. As I have already suggested in speaking about Mark 13, witness in the New Testament is always portrayed as the work of the Spirit. It is not something under human control. It is not something that we can organize or plan. Indeed, it is something which is apt to happen precisely at the point when the Church has no human resources, at the point when the disciple is called before kings and governors and does not know what to say. At that point, it will be given him what to say because it is not he but the Holy Spirit who speaks. The temptation, when we were in the position of power and authority in the world, is to forget that. When the Western Christian nations were in that position, the temptation was to think of the missionary task in terms of a program which we planned and carried through, in which we had our strategy of training and development. Of course, there is a proper place for all that. But this is surely a time when we need to remember the basic meaning of witness in the New Testament. Witness is something the Holy Spirit does, and into which we are caught up. The fact that we have forgotten this has resulted in a kind of distorting of the very concept of mission in the minds of ordinary people. The very word "mission," whether in the context of home mission or foreign mission, has come in the minds of most people—has it not?—to carry the suggestion of a movement of descent, of

pity, of condescension, a movement toward the backward, toward those who need help. Where this word "mission" and "Church" go side by side, am I wrong if I suggest that the word "mission" always has in it the suggestion of something directed towards the backward, the unenlightened, the underprivileged? The result runs right through all the problems we wrestle with in the missionary world: paternalism on the one hand, dependence on the other. One of the reasons why some are unwilling to take the task of missions seriously in the secular context of today is precisely the presence of these overtones in the very word.

In the New Testament the situation is the opposite. The Christian mission does not move from the highly developed countries to the underdeveloped. When St. Paul went from Antioch to Rome, he was not going to one of the backward areas. He was taking the gospel to the powerful, the rich, the educated, those in positions of authority. It was in that situation that the first disciples learned the power of the Spirit in human weakness and foolishness to convict the world of sin, of righteousness, and of judgment—the power of the Spirit to use the weak things of the world to confound the mighty. Forty years ago, when the modern missionary movement was at the zenith of its strength, Roland Allen wrote two books, *Missionary Methods—St. Paul's or Ours* and *The Spontaneous Expansion of the Church*, in which he challenged the whole dominant conception of the missionary task. At the time he wrote not much attention was paid to it, but before he died he prophesied to his son that his writings would come into their own around about the year 1960. It has proved an uncommonly accurate prophecy. In the new situation we face today we are learning to take more seriously what the New Testament says about witness as the work of the Spirit, by which, even in weakness and foolishness, even without great human resources, the supernatural power of the gospel can make itself known victoriously in the face of the powers of this world.

The rise of the movements that have placed their emphasis on the freedom and sovereignty of the Spirit has sometimes been accompanied by a distressing divisiveness, a breaking of Christian fellowship into smaller and smaller groups in the name of spiritual fervor. As Dr. John Mackay has put it, there has been a pitting of ardor against order. But that false dichotomy rests upon an imperfect understanding of the Spirit which separates His work falsely from the work of Christ in His Body, drawing all men to Himself. And perhaps at that point the shape of what I have been trying to say becomes clear. It really adds up to this: that the fulfillment of our missionary task in the new circumstances of this time calls for a theology of mission rooted in the trinitarian understanding of God's nature. This means, first, that we take seriously the fact that the Church in all the world is the one Body of Christ, who through it invites all men of every kind to be knit together in one fellowship. Second, however, it does not mean that the whole purpose of God for history is—so to speak—embodied in the history of the Church. Like the Lord Himself, the Church is called, not to be the ruler of events, but to accept the Father's disposition of events as the form in which its mission is fulfilled, and through which it is to bear witness to all the nations of the true meaning and end of history. And third, this witness is not primarily the witness of men, not something within the power of men to commend. It is the Holy Spirit who bears witness to the Father by His presence in the life of the Church of His Son. And because the Spirit is free and sovereign, He always goes ahead of the Church, calling the Church to follow.

It is, I think, significant that in the earliest centuries of the Church, when the Christian message had to be articulated for the first time in the context of a religiously pluralistic pagan society, it was in terms of the doctrine of God as Father, Son, and Spirit that it was done. In that society, the doctrine of the Trinity was—as Athanasius called it—the *arche,* the starting point from which coherent thinking could begin. Now that the Constantinian era has ended and we are again in a religiously pluralistic world, it may be that we shall have to find in that doctrine the starting point for a coherent and compelling statement of the Christian mission to the world.

12

Christianity and the Challenge of Africa Today

DONALD M'TIMKULU

NO ONE WRITING ABOUT AFRICA TODAY CAN AVOID USING THE PHRASE "changing Africa." It has become as much a part of our vocabulary as the words "darkest Africa" in the days of our grandfathers in the late years of the nineteenth century.

No matter how one tries to avoid the use of a phrase which is in danger of becoming a mere cliché, one cannot truly present the Africa of today without putting right in the center of things this concept of change. For the dominant feature in the life of Africa today is change. While one realizes that everywhere modern man is living in changing times, yet the fundamental difference between life in the West and life in Africa lies in the accelerated tempo of change, which creates tremendous problems for the African as he tries to make his peace with his own history, at the same time shouldering the burden of world history of which he has become a part.

BUILDING AFRICA ANEW

Today as the peoples of Africa rapidly gain their freedom and independence, they are faced with the task of building anew; not on entirely new foundations but on foundations already laid in a cultural and historical past which has owed a great deal to the coming of Christianity.

On the other hand, political freedom has brought in its wake a new awareness of the cultural heritage of the people and a pride in their own past. At the same time, the increasing impact of industry

and technology has brought a widespread acceptance of modern
social values and economic standards of life, so that traditional culture is itself being repatterned, causing not only a split in values but
a state of confusion and uncertainty in the social and moral world of
the African. The nature of change in Africa, therefore, is not only
political, but social, economic, and moral as well. In each of these
spheres the Church faces tremendous challenges, but herein also lie
the greatest opportunities for the growth of Christianity throughout
the continent.

The rise of new nations in Africa is not a threat, but a tremendous
opportunity for the growth of a Christian community which will be
firmly rooted in the soil of Africa—a Christian community not separate or a group apart, but involved in the surging current of new life,
so that it finds itself not outside but within the larger whole of the
national communities. Only in this way can Christians make a meaningful contribution to the life of the new nation-states. For we must
remember always that while the Church is not "of this world" it is
in the world, and must therefore play an important and leading
role in the process of nation-building that is taking place all over
Africa.

In the past this has not always been the case. The Christian has,
by and large, shied off from his political responsibilities. The missionary in many cases tended to encourage this attitude by preaching
what he called "the pure gospel" with its emphasis on personal salvation and otherworldliness, decrying any interest in the fulfillment
of political aspirations as a concern for the things of this world. The
results of this attitude were twofold—both disastrous to the development of Christianity:

1. It tended to keep Christians in comparative isolation: a community apart, living its own life relatively untouched by the tides of
thought washing in and out all around them. This isolation must be
broken if Christianity is to grow in Africa today. Let me borrow
from a friend this very neat analogy to illustrate my point.

In the old days the missionary looked at Africa and found it a very
dirty pond with some very fine-looking fish in it. In his goodness he
decided to build a new pond with crystal-clear water; he proceeded to
remove the fish one by one from the dirty pond to the nice clean pond
in order to give them a better life, and so they prospered in a way. Nowadays we have come to realize that this was the wrong technique. We must
not continue to try to remove the good fish from the dirty pond in
which they live with their fellows, but we should concentrate our efforts

in making clean the water of the dirty pond so that the fish may live a better life there.

In other words the Christian in Africa must recover his sense of national belonging, at the same time keeping what he has gained in his Christian faith and fellowship. Only thus can he make a positive contribution to the new life surging through Africa and ensure that Christian ideals and outlooks become part of that life.

2. As the tide of national consciousness began to flow more strongly, those who felt most keenly about political affairs found themselves more and more estranged from the Church. There was a general feeling, expressed in many ways, that if one was to work for political independence one had to work outside the Church. This attitude was further buttressed by the accusation of those outside the Church who claimed that the Church in any case was an arm of the colonial regime, and therefore could not interest itself in the struggle for liberation of the people. Christianity has even been accused of serving as the vanguard of commercial and imperialist expansion. Some have claimed it was brought to Africa first of all to "soften" the people, so that imperialist powers could take control and subjugate them. This biased interpretation of history, although false as a whole, is not entirely unsupported, as study of some missionary letters will show.

The committed Christian, therefore, has been fighting a rearguard action to counter these views, not only by committing himself more fully to his faith, but also by greater dedication and devotion to the mission of the Church to the world, to the end that all men may believe. For this loyalty to our Lord Christians throughout Africa have suffered much in their personal lives, through ostracism and other social pressures, in some cases even unto death. One need only recall the magnificent stand made by the Christians of Kenya during the Mau Mau disturbances, a witness that has made the Church stronger today than it was before the days of Mau Mau. When one remembers the ensuing acts of heroism, loyalty, and devotion to the faith shown by the Christians of Cameroon and their African pastors in their struggle against terrorists—a struggle that went on for more than three years, in which more than a hundred churches and schools have been destroyed, and the Christians have come back and rebuilt them, in some cases for the second time—in the face of such acts of dedicated witness in Africa, one is amazed at the superficial judgments of some Western observers who claim that Christianity is on the retreat in Africa.

Nonetheless because of the churches' own acts of omission in the past, one must admit that many of the younger and educated people in Africa today have come to feel that the Church is irrelevant to their situation. The Church does not understand their problems, nor is it in sympathy with their strivings. This, it seems to me, is the great danger for Christianity in Africa—that it will become irrelevant and make little impact on the lives of men where they are in the dust and heat of the changing Africa of today.

AFRICAN NATIONALISM

For those of us who are interested in the co-operative effort which is the modern missionary enterprise in Africa—an enterprise that has ceased, and must cease, to be one of working *for* Africans and become in all respects one of working *with* Africans—it is of vital importance that we understand the true nature of African nationalism. For this is at once a product of and a reaction against European colonial dominance. Under the banner of nationalism the African is now asserting his manhood and his right to be treated as a man, just like other men—not to be regarded as different, peculiar, inferior, or even superior to others. He is asserting his right to be treated as a person and not merely as a member of a group branded with the sign of inferiority by its colonial masters. He no longer acquiesces in the standard he thinks was arbitrarily set by the European. He does not seek acceptance into the world community by virtue of having become a "black European"; he insists on being recognized as a man, with all his African-ness.

This is the spirit that is sweeping through Africa. It is the spirit that has supplied the dynamic to all movements for independence, but let us recognize also that it is the dynamic back of that urge for expression of the African personality in art, music, literature, and worship which is simmering throughout Africa today. As such it should be welcomed and encouraged as the opening out of a people's soul. But like all great creative forces it must be channeled into areas where it will do most good, and must especially be saved from pious sentiments and destructive slogans, and be faced with the responsibilities it brings by its very existence.

This is the task that faces the Christian Church in Africa today as it meets the challenge of nationalism. To be able to do this the Christian must himself be firmly grounded in his faith and belief that Jesus Christ is not only the Light of the World, but the Way. In my humble opinion, this can only come about when the Church in Africa becomes truly rooted in the soil; when the faith we preach and the way of life we espouse has become truly a part of ourselves and not something just passed on to us by our missionary fathers. In other words, this task can only be accomplished by a Church that has become truly indigenous to Africa—a Church truly communicating the content of our faith and, in its witness of reconciliation, touching every aspect of the life of the people of Africa.

Let me pause here to clarify a misunderstanding that always arises whenever one talks of an indigenous Church. This has often been interpreted as meaning that the Christian in Africa desires to see a new kind of Christianity which will grow out of African culture, because as a faith it is regarded as foreign. This is a gross misconception.

The essential question is not how to make Christianity indigenous, but how we as Christian Africans can become rooted in the soil. We realize fully that the faith of the Christian, which is centered in the gospel of Jesus Christ, is not indigenous to any one national culture. It has a world dimension. What should become part of the environment therefore is not the gospel, but people who are committed to the claims of that gospel and who want to witness to its truth in that environment. Only when this has been attained shall we have a truly indigenous Church—when we as Christians in Africa no longer merely aim to preserve the forms of Christian worship, the Church organization, and the patterns of theological expression handed down by our missionary fathers, but seek to evaluate their efficacy in communicating the content of our Christian faith in our own situation, and then to adapt them in accordance with the accepted religious traditions of each country and people.

Now this is not a new discovery. From the early days of Christianity the need for such adaptation was recognized, although the Church generally tended to lose sight of it in the confusing era of colonialism, when it seemed to be taken for granted that Christianity was best expressed only in Western forms. Fortunately for the future of the Church, that assumption is now being seriously questioned in many quarters.

In the light of this promising situation Christian leaders are becoming concerned at the influx, since World War II, of many missionaries from new mission agencies who have come in with policies in no way different from those followed by the early missionaries of the nineteenth century. For many of these groups, coming late into the vineyard, the wheels of history have stood still, and they do not seem to realize the mood of modern Africa. I say in Christian charity that we admire their zeal and devotion to the missionary call, but we would wish they might grow more conscious of the burden of history that has created the Africa of the 1960's; otherwise this new zeal may become a further stumbling block to the growth of Christianity in our land.

In discussions about Christianity and the rise of national consciousness in Africa the fact is not often enough stressed that a good deal of what is happening today is the direct result of the emancipating power of the Christian gospel, and that the Church through its teaching and its educational and health programs has been one of the most potent revolutionary forces at work in the continent. It laid the foundations on which others are building today. The Christian gospel kindled in the mind of the African a new sense of human dignity, a new image of African manhood, and a new vision of a human community in which racial differences are completely transcended. It must, therefore, carry through its mission in contemporary Africa.

But this has not been the only revolutionary force. Industry and commerce have come in, not only changing the living habits of people, but causing a great deal of the confusion of values which is so apparent in Africa today. Industry has revolutionized the African traditional pattern of life by introducing such factors as the migratory labor system, a money economy, and an urban way of life, as well as imparting to the African technical skills and know-how by which to manipulate the forces of nature. The moment the African ceased to depend upon nature for his subsistence and began to manipulate it to improve his living—at that moment he entered the modern world, which technological advance is rapidly changing into one world.

So that at one leap, as it were, Africa is undergoing two revolutions. The first has been a change from a "communalistic" society based on a subsistence economy and having a strong sense of cohesion through the solidarity provided by family and kin and by the rule of social custom. From this society the African has moved into an individualistic money economy society with a much quickened tempo of life and a much higher regard for material values, a society which puts upon him the heavy responsibility of choosing between conflicting values without aid of the reassuring voices of kin and the clear injunctions of custom. In this society he is lonely and confused.

Meanwhile, as he crowds into the cities and industrialized areas, he is undergoing the same revolution that faces the modern world as it moves from the industrial into the technological era and even the atomic age. The modern world is itself confused as it seeks to find some sure foundation in this shifting sand of values. The African now, in one swift turn of history, has become contemporary man with all his load of frustrations and the temptations of secularism.

This situation is one of the great challenges to the Church in Africa today—common throughout Africa, as new independent nations tackle the problem of economic uplift for their respective countries, and new cities, new harbors, and great industrial projects mushroom everywhere. The Church alone can provide the answer. For in these urban areas are gathered not only Christians but thousands of non-Christians who are open to evangelization. While there is still need to go out into the small rural villages to seek a few, thousands are now at the very doorstep of the Church, if it will adapt its methods and patterns to the needs of urban populations. Too often we still use the methods and procedures that proved so successful in rural areas, and expect that these will work with the same measure of success in the urban settings.

This cannot be. Even so brief an analysis of the situation as I have made here must indicate the futility of such an approach. The urban man is a man with new needs, new aspirations, new problems that confound him day by day. We must make the gospel relevant to him in the situation where he is. We must try to understand the new society God is building up in Africa, and the new patterns and strategies that will enable us to communicate our faith more effectively in these conditions, to the end that God may be glorified. It may be necessary, for instance, to work out new patterns of the ministry, or new schemes of lay training which would make it possible for the laity to play a more important role in the work of the ministry, "for the edifying of the Body of Christ." One notes with appreciation the work that is being done along these lines by such agencies as the Mindolo Ecumenical Foundation in Northen Rhodesia and the Kenya Christian Council in their Conference Centre at Limuru. One would like to see more of these pioneer outposts in many other parts of Africa shedding their light along the frontiers of Christian mission today.

A NEW KIND OF CHURCH

As Christians we must believe that God is working out His will in these movements in Africa; that He is creating a new kind of world, and creating a new kind of Church for the fulfillment of His purposes. We must try to find out, therefore, under the guidance of His Holy Spirit, what God means to do with this new kind of Church in the new world He is creating in Africa. This must be our continuing task. We believe that when God decided to reconcile disobedient man unto Himself through His Son, He showed us His concern for all the needs of man. We believe also that He did not cease to work, but is still working in our own time, through the Holy Spirit, to reconcile the world to Himself.

In this belief, the Church must go out into the world to witness to God's love for all men. In Africa this will mean not only that we go out in renewed strength to evangelize the continent, but that the Church must play a more active role in the improvement of social conditions, in the growth of a stable home and family life, in the political strivings and aspirations of the people, in providing sound and enlightened leadership, and in the guidance of youth, as well as in laying solid foundations in the faith that upholds the people of God.

In this great task of reconciliation lies the major contribution of the Christian Church in Africa today; but if Christianity is really to make its full witness unequivocal in these times, it must speak with a more prophetic voice and denounce evil, wrong, and injustice even in the high places of this world. It must recover the uncompromising spirit against injustice and wrong that fired the hearts of the prophets of old and enabled them to say, even to King David, "Thou art the man" who has committed this great sin.

The way ahead for Christianity in Africa has many twists and turns which will need careful negotiation, but I do not believe this means we must immediately jump to panic stations. One need not be appalled, for instance, by the fact that in some independent countries of Africa today Christianity is a minority religion. In truth, Christianity has always been a minority religion in Africa. It enjoyed, however, the privileges of a majority religion through the good offices of the colonial powers. This was bound to end, and any shedding of tears over that circumstance would seem to indicate a poor grasp of the facts of history. If Christianity is to flourish in Africa it must stand on its own feet, asking favors of no one and prepared only to manifest in its works and witness the abiding love of God. In such a Church the test of life and growth will not be bigger and bigger statistics, but the quality of life of its members.

So, as we look ahead and see Christianity faced with so many challenges, we are not alarmed, for we have seen this high quality of life among the Christians of Africa, and we believe that in God's grace and under His guidance those challenges will be made into opportunities for the spread of His kingdom to His honor and glory.

13

The Vocation of the Christian Apologist:

A STUDY OF SCHLEIERMACHER'S *REDEN*

JAROSLAV PELIKAN

THIS IS A TALE OF TWO CITIES, OF ATHENS AND JERUSALEM, AND of an effort to establish meaningful communication between them. Can Protestant theology speak to the world of thought and action sketched out in the preceding chapters of this symposium—a world engaged in a power struggle, a world in which science and psychiatry have now managed to meet many of the needs previously supplied by the Christian faith, a world where the techniques of communication seem to swamp or even to displace the preaching of the Word of God, a world throughout which the various religions, Judaism, and other forms of Christian obedience have put Protestantism on the defensive? For despite all the brave slogans about relevance, the sacredness of the secular, the modesty of an evangelical theology, and an answering theology, present-day Protestant thought is poorly equipped to meet the questions and issues of such a world. It would all be very simple if one could merely cast the Word of God into that world as a stone is cast into a pool, and ask that the Holy Spirit speak miraculously to those whose concerns this symposium describes. But can Protestant theology take these concerns seriously enough to address them without losing its ability to say something that is recognizably Christian and even distinctively Protestant? Or must Protestant theology choose between the two cities, Athens and Jerusalem, confining itself to the language of Zion regardless of what a modern Athens may say or think?

It is, I take it, my task in this series, as a historian of the Church and of its theology, to provide some historical perspective on Protestant theology and to look for some resources in the theological tradition of Protestantism that will explain the tale of the two cities and answer the questions I have just raised. Can the Protestant Jerusalem produce spokesmen to the Athens of world revolution and still remain Jerusalem? What is the apostolic vocation of the apologist who speaks to Athens? The Epistle to the Ephesians informs us that the ascended Lord has given gifts to his Church; "and his gifts were that some should be apostles, some prophets, some evangelists, some pastors and teachers . . ." Where does the apologist fit into this catalogue of gifts and offices? To answer that question—which is, of course, merely another way of putting the question of Athens and Jerusalem—this essay will examine the apologetic first fruits of one of the most important Protestant theologians since the Reformation, the discourses *On Religion* of Friedrich Daniel Ernst Schleiermacher.[1]* What was his vocation as a Christian apologist? Was he an apostle, an evangelist, a prophet, a priest, a betrayer? In the case of this apologist—and perhaps of all apologists[2]—the answer to that question would appear to be Yes. Perhaps the question of "Christianity and world revolution" will come into clearer view in the light of the vocation of the Christian apologist.[3]

THE APOLOGIST AS APOSTLE

The vocation of the apologist is characterized by a sense of mission. It is concerned with "the cultured among [religion's] despisers," it speaks *ad gentes* or *contra gentiles* or *ad nationes*. Thus it partakes of the vocation of the apostle as one who has been sent and commissioned by the resurrected Lord.[4] The apologist knows himself to be one who has received a charge from Another, and his apologetic assignment is in response and in fidelity to that charge. The nature of this charge may vary considerably within the limits of such fidelity, but one useful criterion for studying the vocation of any apologist is the question of what credentials he offers. In Schleiermacher's apologetics two sets of credentials appear, each of which helps to illumine the vocation of the apologist according to the *Reden*.

At the very beginning of his appeal Schleiermacher presented one set of apostolic credentials, his certified membership in the class of those "who are experts [in religion], not only according to their own profession, but by recognition from the state and from the people."[5] What would qualify him as an apostle according to these credentials would be his professional standing as a clergyman, attested to by the

* The notes for this article will be found on pp. 186-89.

responsible spokesmen of society. But through most of the *Reden* this attestation was absent. When Schleiermacher did return to it, in the fourth address, he put himself on the side of his audience by decrying the close alliance of Church and state, which certified as clergy many men who had not caught the spark of true religion. There were "many among the leaders of the church who understand nothing of religion, but who nevertheless, as servants of the state, are in a position to earn great official merit."[6] It seems, then, that his preliminary appeal to the accreditation of the clergy by the state did not represent the basic credentials that Schleiermacher wanted to present to his hearers.

In the same breath with these credentials the apologist declared the grounds on which he really wanted to be heard, when he spoke of being "divinely swayed by an irresistible necessity within me . . . compelled to speak."[7] At the beginning of the third address he likened this necessity to the creative urge that rises within the artist or musician, and he returned to this analogy in the fourth address.[8] From the lyrical, almost dithyrambic prose of these passages it is evident that for the apologist himself this constituted the *impulsus scribendi* about which Protestant orthodoxy had been so well informed.[9] He was responding to an impelling urge from within; this was his vocation, more than any mission from without. Those who would like to dismiss this as subjectivism should remember the summary of the contrast and the affinity between these two sets of credentials in the apostolic declaration (I Cor. 9:16-17): "If I preach the gospel, that gives me no ground for boasting. For necessity is laid upon me. Woe to me if I do not preach the gospel! For if I do this of my own will, I have a reward; but if not of my own will, I am entrusted with a commission" nonetheless.

For the purposes of this inquiry into the vocation of a Christian apologist, the significant feature of Schleiermacher's response to this inner necessity is that the Athens to which he was speaking understood and revered such stirrings of the soul in the creative genius, even as it scorned the use of diplomas or pedigrees (and therefore of proof of ordination) to certify the poet or the wise man. The *Gebildeten* to whom he addressed the *Reden* shared with him the conviction that an autonomous certification of the poet or wise man qualified him as no heteronomous validation of his education or lineage or orders could. By affirming this conviction Schleiermacher was attempting to show that the logic of the appeal from heteronomy to autonomy would support a further appeal from autonomy to theonomy. Thus the cultured were "however unintentionally, the rescuers and cherishers of religion,"[10] and Schleiermacher saw his apostolic mission in the discovery and documentation of their implicit piety.

Interpreted superficially, this undertaking might lend support to the question of the vocation of the Christian apologist with the pseudo-apostolate described in 2 Cor. 11:12-15.[11] It seems to be a surrender of the objective warrant of the apostolic ministry to the free-floating subjectivity of a holoscopic Romanticism. If it is, and if the ministry of the Christian gospel needs such an objective warrant to be faithful to its apostolic vocation, then the vocation of the Christian apologist is indeed apostasy. But the ministry of Augustine and Chrysostom would suggest that the presentation of subjective credentials has always been a legitimate strategy in the announcement of the Christian message to the despisers—as well as to the devout.[12] Indeed, the inclusion of Paul among the apostles represented an admission that such subjective credentials might have validity.[13] As for Schleiermacher himself, it can be argued that his "subjectivism," especially as it evolved into the theses of *The Christian Faith*, came to grasp the deeper implications of the vocation of the apostle as perhaps no theology since the Reformation had done.[14] And therefore it may well be that Schleiermacher's vocation as an apologist made him understand the vocation of the apostle more sensitively and therefore more faithfully.

THE APOLOGIST AS EVANGELIST

The term "evangelist" as used here partakes of both meanings of the word:[15] one who describes the meaning and message of Jesus Christ, as Matthew, Mark, Luke, and John did; and one who appeals to the unconverted to accept the meaning and message of Jesus Christ, as latter-day evangelists do. To assess the work of Schleiermacher the apologist, it is necessary to examine his message and to identify the appeal that he addressed to the cultured among the despisers of religion.

"The sum total of religion," Schleiermacher wrote, "is to feel that, in its highest unity, all that moves us in feeling is one; to feel that anything single and particular is possible only by means of this unity; to feel, that is to say, that our being and living is a being and living in and through God."[16] This was his evangel in the *Reden*, as he described to his readers what it meant to contemplate "the eternal existence of all finite things, in and through the Infinite, and of all temporal things in and through the Eternal."[17] Throughout the second address he formulated his message in language almost reminiscent of physiology, speaking of "surrendering" and of "taking up into the inner unity of [one's] life and being" as, in a way, the metabolism of the religious life.[18] In the name of such a conception of religion he gave an account that was at once empirical (in that he dealt with positive religion rather than with natural religion[19]) and interpretive (in that he held no brief for the specific forms in which positive religion has appeared during history.[20]).

A stress upon the positive religions set Schleiermacher off from most of the apologists of the century that was just coming to a close when he wrote the *Reden;* it also made him an important figure in the early phase of the scientific study of the history of religions that was about to begin.[21] Most of the apologists of the eighteenth century had reduced the message of religion to God and immortality,[22] with the possible addition of freedom; an older contemporary of Schleiermacher's had disposed of these issues two decades earlier in *The Critique of Pure Reason.* During the seventeenth century the apologists had concerned themselves with miracles, revelation, inspiration, and prophecies.[23] These issues had been producing "systems, commentaries, and apologies"[24] during the sixteenth and seventeenth centuries, for in various combinations and with various concessions they had been identified as the content of religion. Now Schleiermacher was appealing to a higher court than reason, to *Gefühl.*[25] But the brief that he presented was not merely reason or feeling, but history.[26]

The spirit furnishes the chief nourishment for our piety, and history immediately and especially is for religion the richest source. History is of value for religion not because it hastens or controls in any way the progress of humanity in its development, but because it is the greatest and most general revelation of the deepest and holiest. In this sense, however, religion begins and ends with history.[27]

The message of religion, its evangel, must therefore always be a history as "the greatest and most general revelation." But that which was thus revealed was not general religion per se, just as the revelatory history was not just any history. The history that constituted the message was specific, but by means of it one could know the universal meaning of religion. Hence a preoccupation with "general religion" blinded the cultured despisers to the meaning of religious history; on the other hand, a preoccupation with the minutiae of religious history blinded the orthodox to the deepest meanings of the history, because they confused these minutiae with "the fundamental intuition of the religion."[28]

The message of this evangelist, therefore, was a sacred history, through which his hearers could learn the meaning of religion. What was the relation of this sacred history to the Christian evangel? The answer to that question may become clearer from an examination of Schleiermacher's performance in the second vocation of the evangelist as one who appeals and invites. As could be expected from his definition of religion, Schleiermacher would not insult his audience by trotting out the hackneyed proofs for the credibility of religion and the superiority of Christianity. Nor would he "recommend it merely as an accessory"[29] for keeping society moral. The history of such proofs supported the inner aversion both of the apologist and of his audience to this form of evangelism. If the apologist as evangelist was to make a bid for the loyalty of his readers, it had to be on other grounds.

One argument by which Schleiermacher appealed to the cultured despisers was the genetic. This is at least partly what he had in mind when he said in the peroration to the *Reden* that his readers were "rooted with [their] whole knowing, doing, and being" in religion, specifically in Christianity.[30] The genetic argument seemed to have particular force for him when he considered the preoccupation of both Rationalism and Romanticism with moral issues. This preoccupation had given his readers a sense for teleology which they mistakenly attributed to their ethics. Actually, Schleiermacher argued, such a teleology was a "torn off fragment" of religion rather than of morality.[31] It could not have come into being without religion; and Schleiermacher, whose own mature ethic was to be rooted in his doctrine of the Church, seems to have meant that this fragment could not be sustained without religion either.[32]

Nevertheless, Schleiermacher's own ideas about the role of history in religion prevented any undue reliance upon the genetic argument. A more prominent appeal in his *Reden* was the esthetic.[33] One of the most powerful passages in the *Reden* is that in which Schleiermacher challenged the Romantics in his audience to consider the fuller implications of their fine-grained esthetic sense, and thus from "the sight of a great and sublime work of art" to be "met by such a beam of your own sun and turned to religion."[34] From this esthetic realm came one of the metaphors in which the apologist cast his most basic appeal, an appeal that eventually transcended the esthetic. "A man's special calling," he declared, "is the melody of his life, and it remains a simple, meager series of notes unless religion, with its endlessly rich variety, accompany it with all notes, and raise the simple song to a full-voiced, glorious harmony."[35] This would seem to be the most comprehensive of all his evangelistic appeals, for here he promised that the singular and individual perceptions which each man could identify as his own unique vocation were not negated but fulfilled by the coming of religion. On this ground both the genetic and the esthetic evangel could make sense.

THE APOLOGIST AS PROPHET

If the apologist is to be heard, he must be able to speak the language of his hearers. But if he is to be worth hearing, he must differentiate himself sufficiently from his setting to stand over against it and to address it. The biblical office of the prophet illustrated this duality. The prophet was a much more deeply rooted member of the total life of Israel, including its political and cultic life, than the biblical scholarship of the nineteenth century acknowledged.[36] At the same time, his commission from God obliged him to speak out against the people, also against the political and cultic life of Israel. Carrying out a prophetic office within his vocation as a Christian apologist, Schleiermacher had to direct his prophetic denunciation at two distinguishable (though not separable) entities, the organized Church and the secular culture.

As has already been pointed out, Schleiermacher had deep misgivings about the organized Church, which reciprocated them. This meant, first of all, the detestable enormities of the papal Church. "Modern Rome, godless but consistent, hurls anathemas and ejects heretics. Ancient Rome, truly pious and religious in a high style, was hospitable to every god."[37] Eastern Orthodoxy, he believed, was practically "defunct"[38]; for "all depth is lost in the mechanism of antiquated usages and liturgical forms."[39] Anglicanism likewise was dead; "they know nothing of religion, except that they all preach devotion to ancient usages and defend its institutions."[40] And so on through Christendom, as he summarized in one *ceterum censeo*: "Who would venture to say that all, that even the majority, that even the foremost and the most notable of those who for many a day have ruled the great ecclesiastical assembly, have been accomplished in religion or even members of the true Church?"[41]

Nor were there merely the fulminations of an intellectual against the ecclesiastical activists. Some of the sharpest prophetic points were aimed at the intellectuals of the Church, "who believe that the salvation of the world and the light of wisdom are to be found in a new vesture of formulas or in a new arrangement of ingenious proofs."[42] Religion, he said, "is as far removed, by its whole nature, from all that is systematic as philosophy is naturally disposed to it"—this from the man who was to write the most important systematic theology since the *Institutes*. Even a cursory study of the *Glaubenslehre* will reveal how seriously Schleiermacher continued to take this Protestant principle even and especially when he undertook the composition of a dogmatics.[43] As the *Sendschreiben an Lücke* made evident,[44] he applied to himself the principle he had voiced in the *Reden*.

[The theologian] is not only to be an inspired man and a teacher, but in humility he is to present himself also for universal testing. Nor shall anything be spared, not even what is most loved and dear; nor shall anything be indolently put aside, not even what is most generally acknowledged. Though it may be praised from without as something holy and may be set up before the world as the essence of religion, from within it must be subjected to a severe and repeated test.[45]

Because the prophet subjected himself and his Church to a severe and repeated test, he had the right to speak a prophetic word to his culture as well. Schleiermacher the apologist exercised that right to the limit. A quick catalogue of the vices he denounced will document both his power of observation and his courage. He saw the frustration of the do-gooders, who "wish to work on humanity . . . [and] have an ideal of the individual to which no one corresponds."[46] In devastating language he described the precious spirits who "dart off into the great, glorious world to get for themselves little impressions: how they inspect the delicate markings and tints of flowers, or gaze at the magic play of colors in the glowing evening sky, and how they admire the songs of the birds on a beautiful countryside."[47] With exquisite scorn he attacked the utilitarians, who had to be practical even about art and who used religion as an "occasion to win some few young people for caution and economy in the use of their powers and for the noble art of strengthening life."[48] These and other vices the prophetic apologist traced at least in part to the illiteracy about religion, any religion, that characterized the otherwise learned and sophisticated culture to which he was speaking.[49] In the power of his prophetic proclamation, the apologist both identified himself with this culture and found the distance he needed to stand over against it and to address it.

THE APOLOGIST AS PRIEST

The *bête noire* of the prophet is the priest. They have more in common than either of them would care to admit, and Schleiermacher's dogmatics brilliantly expounded the Christian intuition that saw prophet and priest converge in Christ—but only there.[50] Of the two, it is clear that the priest stands in greater danger of capitulating to his culture. Because his is a ministry of mediation, the priest tends to substitute both/and for either/or. How an apologist understands his priestly ministry of mediation, therefore, is a useful guide to understanding his vocation.

As a man I speak to you of the sacred mysteries of mankind according to my view, of what was within me when with youthful enthusiasm I sought the unknown, of what since then I have thought and experienced, of the innermost springs of my being which shall forever remain for me the highest.[51]

In this celebrated strophe at the beginning of the *Reden* Schleiermacher announced his priestly commission to initiate his readers into the sacred mysteries. Later he spoke again of "sacred mysteries discovered and solemnized, which are not mere insignificant symbols but, rightly considered, are natural indications of a certain kind of consciousness and of certain feelings."[52] Repeatedly he described his apologetic vocation as that of mediating between religion and *die Gebildeten unter ihren Verächtern*. That was indeed the vocation of the seers and saints, who mediated "between your limited way of thinking and the eternal laws of the world."[53] It seems that Schleiermacher the apologist saw himself as a priest inducting the mystes into the holy place, but acknowledged that others or Another had to act as high priest.[54]

Some such distinction between priest and high priest would seem necessary to treat fairly and accurately the role of Christendom as a mediator between mankind and the sacred mysteries of mankind. This was the role that Schleiermacher envisaged for the empirical Church, standing as it did between the world and the true Church. It was to be, he said, "a mediating institution whereby to come into a certain contact with [the true Church], as it were an atmosphere, both as a medium for purification and to attract new material."[55] Here he anticipated the reinterpretation of the priesthood of believers that he was to formulate in the *Glaubenslehre:*

> Christendom as a whole, as the human race already united to the Redeemer, stands to the rest of humanity in the relation in which the priests stood to the laity. For it is only in so far as there exists a real vital fellowship with Christ at least in one part of the race that there is also a relationship between him and the rest.[56]

It would therefore be slanderous to represent this apologist as a self-anointed priest who usurped a mediatorial vocation between the Church and the world. His awareness of the spots and wrinkles in empirical Christendom did sometimes outweigh his institutional loyalty; but outweighing both was his conviction that through the mediation of empirical Christendom, with all its spots and wrinkles, it was nevertheless possible for men to be reconciled with the Infinite. Accompanying this realism about the Church visible, however, was a sense of being set apart from the common masses, and therefore also from the Church. Consideration of the apologist's vocation as priest must raise the question whether the apologist's identification with his culture has also allied him with a special caste in that culture more closely than he is allied with the Church. In other words, apologetics must deal with the problem called accommodationism in the history of missions.[57]

There is much evidence to support the contention that the apologist who wrote the *Reden* felt himself a member of such a caste. He was proud that his speech did not betray his ministerial office—"betray" in the sense of "tip off"![58] He could contrast "the people" with "all who want to be considered cultured."[59] He spoke of "our party."[60] The conventional religionists "do not despise religion, and they are not to be called cultured. But they destroy religion as much as they can. . . . They are still the dominating party, and you and we are but a very few."[61] He was sometimes so snobbish and condescending as to be priggish in his treatment of "the commonest forms of humanity, ever returning in a thousand copies."[62] When he spoke of "descending among persons limited to one earthly aim and effort. . . . a steward of religion among unbelievers, a missionary among savages . . . . an Orpheus or Amphion. . . . a priestly figure,"[63] he was speaking both as a priest of the sacred mysteries of Christ and as a Romantic mystagogue.

Apparently Schleiermacher sensed the danger in this confusion.

Therefore in the very next paragraph he took pains to clarify his affinity for, but also his differentiation from, the cultured Romantics. A study of the situation at the end of the eighteenth century suggests that both Athens and Jerusalem needed such mediation, for all its risks. The essays in this volume compel us to draw the same conclusion, for all its risks, about our time.

THE APOLOGIST AS DISCIPLE

The evangelist calls others as one who has himself been called. Similarly, the disciple teaches others as one who has himself been taught. A theological evaluation of the vocation of the Christian apologist must pay attention, therefore, not only to what and how he teaches, but also to how he interprets his having been taught. Hence the vocation of the apologist must be interpreted within the framework of the relation between master and disciple.[64]

The language in which Schleiermacher described the dependence of disciple upon master in the *Reden* stressed the maieutic and temporary role of the master. In religion, "if anywhere, this tutelage is only a passing state. Hereafter, each man shall see with his own eyes, and shall produce some contribution to the treasures of religion. . . . You are right in despising the wretched echoes who derive their religion entirely from another."[65] Perhaps the most significant statement of his view came in the third address. "Of course there is in religion a mastership and a discipleship. But this attachment is no blind imitation. It is not the master that makes disciples, but he is their master because of their choice."[66] A later note appended to this passage was an effort to square it with the biblical view of election as enunciated in places like John 15:16.[67] Yet Schleiermacher could not extricate himself from the implications of his position on the meaning of discipleship. "It is most preposterous," he said, "to wish to limit any pupil to a single master."[68] He was even willing to posit a Platonic doctrine of anamnesis in support of this view of disciple and master.[69]

From some of these passages it might appear that Schleiermacher, like Kierkegaard and Augustine, was operating with a qualitative distinction between human teachers and Christ as Teacher.[70] Then discipleship to Christ would be different in kind from discipleship to any other master. Whether or not this was his later and more mature position,[71] it seems clear that he intended no such distinction here in the *Reden*. In fact, each time he referred to Christ he immediately explained that he was not making this distinction. Speaking of "one of the greatest heroes of religion" whose observation of the lilies of the field had given him serenity, Schleiermacher immediately went on to say: "How much more should we gain [insight and serenity], we who have been permitted by a richer age to go deeper!"[72] In the most extensive witness to Christ anywhere in the *Reden*,[73] the same warning appeared: "Yet he never maintained that he was the only mediator, the only one in whom his idea had actualized itself. All who attach themselves to him and who form his Church should also be mediators with him and through him."[74] This seems to show that the general axioms regarding master and disciple quoted earlier applied also to the relation between Christ and the Christian.

Yet it would be an oversimplification to leave the problem of discipleship here. There was one more element in Schleiermacher's handling of the problem that qualified and deepened his view of it. This was his recognition of the subtle connection between discipleship and individuality. His polemic was directed against both an individualistic and a slavish distortion of that connection. In one of the most penetrating discussions in the *Reden* he set out to show that when several persons refer their personal religion to the same relation and call this relation the source of their devotion, this does not necessarily mean that they have surrendered their individuality to one another or to the source.[75] "Thus understood," he said a little later, "the church is properly called the common mother of us all."[76] Discipleship meant the recovery of authentic selfhood in relation to other disciples. It meant also the growth of the disciple from the status of servant to the status of brother and friend in relation to Christ the Master.[77] This theory of discipleship would be a surrender of Christian vocation if the New Testament and the tradition of the Church did not urge a "non-Christocentric Christology" upon theologians. But since they do, this definition of the disciple may not be treason after all, but the obedience of the son who refused and then repented (Matt. 21:28-32).

THE APOLOGIST AS BETRAYER

Anyone who seeks to define the vocation of the Christian apologist to the cultured despisers would do well to remember that the first of the disciples to approach the *Verächter* was the *Verräter*, Judas Iscariot.[78] Discipleship always has the potential of becoming treason; and the more profound the discipleship, the deeper this potential would seem to be. All the disciples fled when the enemies smote the shepherd, but it was the man of the rock who came back to deny him.

Schleiermacher has been accused of compounded treason; as he pointed out years later, it was difficult to understand how he could have been guilty of these mutually contradictory betrayals at the same time.[79] He has repeatedly been accused of betraying the cause of the institutional Church to its Romantic critics. His opponents charged him with betraying theology to the speculations of "the holy, rejected Spinoza"[80] and "the divine Plato."[81] Some readers saw his willingness to put the Bible on the plane of "every later utterance of the whole church, and therefore of the Divine Spirit"[82] as a betrayal of Protestantism to Roman Catholicism. The Romantics, meanwhile, felt betrayed by his curious stubbornness about remaining a theologian, a clergyman, and, of all things, a preacher, when some of the best minds of the time were moving from theology to history and philosophy.[83]

But the fundamental betrayal of which the author of the *Reden* has been accused is the betrayal of Christian revelation to the *Gefühl* of the natural man. Revelation became "every original and new communication of the universe to man."[84] Grace was equated with "interchange between the entrance of the world into man, through intuition and feeling, and the outgoing of man into the world, through action and culture."[85] The Christian message speaks about a point in time; but (to stay with the mathematical metaphor) "the whole circumference of religion is infinite, and is not to be comprehended under one form, but only under the sum total of all forms."[86] The doctrine of the Incarnation is a way of speaking about a particular man and a particular event under Pontius Pilate, but Schleiermacher could say at the beginning of his last address: "I would, as it were, conduct you to the God that has become flesh. . . . I would have you discover religion in the religions."[87] And if none of these religions could provide a man with a spiritual home, he was not to feel restrained "from developing a religion suitable to his own nature and his own religious sense."[88]

From the other essays in this volume it is evident that a Christian apologist intent upon betrayal will not lack for opportunities amid the world revolution of our time. As the magisterial researches of Geffcken made clear, treason to revelation is a continuing danger of the apologist.[89] The author of the *Reden* did not escape the danger of betraying Jerusalem to Athens. If he had, he would not have been faithful to his vocation. But did he fall victim to the danger? Perhaps the most sagacious answer to that question has come from a theologian noted for his fundamental opposition both to apologetics and to the theology of Schleiermacher.

It will not do to lodge a complaint against Schleiermacher that, because in every conflict he always accepted the opinion of the culture and denied the opinion of traditional Christianity, he consciously betrayed Christianity to the learning and the cultural consciousness of his time. But if one is to avoid this complaint—and avoid it we must—then there is no alternative but the recognition that as an apologist for Christianity he truly played upon it as a virtuoso plays upon his violin, [selecting] those tones and melodies that would sound, if not pleasant, then at least acceptable to his hearers. Schleiermacher speaks not as a responsible servant, but, in true virtuoso fashion, as a free master of this material.[90]

NOTES

[1] *Über die Religion: Reden an die Gebildeten unter ihren Verächtern* was first published, anonymously, in 1799; a second and revised edition appeared in 1806; a third, with further revisions, came out in 1821. These three editions have been collated in the standard critical edition: Friedrich Schleiermacher, *Reden über die Religion*, G. Ch. Bernhard Pünjer, ed., (Braunschweig, 1879). The standard English translation is *On Religion: Speeches to Its Cultured Despisers*, John Oman, trans., with introduction by Rudolf Otto (New York: Harper Torchbooks, 1958); it is based upon the text of 1821, without any indication of changes from the earlier editions. In my footnotes I shall refer to the Pünjer volume as *Reden*, with a superscript numeral to indicate the edition; I shall follow this with a reference to the Torchbook edition in parentheses (ET). Wherever possible, I have adhered to the Oman translation, altering it only for the sake of accuracy or clarity.

[2] Cf. Paul Tillich, "The Two Types of Philosophy of Religion," *Theology of Culture* (New York, 1959), pp. 10-29.

[3] In an earlier and more elementary form, some of this material has appeared under the title "Kerygma and Culture" in the journal *Discourse*, II (1959), 131-44.

[4] Cf. Adolf Harnack, *The Mission and Expansion of Christianity in the First Three Centuries*, James Moffatt, trans., with introduction by Jaroslav Pelikan (New York, 1962), pp. 319-68.

[5] *Reden*[1], p. 3 (ET 2). See Wilhelm Dilthey, *Leben Schleiermachers*, I, Hermann Mulert, ed. (Berlin and Leipzig, 1922), 407-19.

[6] *Reden*[3], p. 206 (ET 170).

[7] *Reden*[2], pp. 2-3 (ET 2).

[8] Reden[1], p. 148 (ET 119); p. 184 (ET 151). See the brief but helpful

comments of Paul Seifert, *Die Theologie des jungen Schleiermacher* (Gütersloh, 1960), pp. 50-53.

[9] Cf. the passages collected in Heinrich Schmid, *The Doctrinal Theology of the Evangelical Lutheran Church*, Charles A. Hay and Henry E. Jacobs, trans. (Minneapolis, 1961), pp. 43-45.

[10] *Reden*[1], p. 174 (ET 141).

[11] Cf. Irenaeus, *Adversus Haereses*, III, 5, 1, in F. Sagnard, ed., *Irénée de Lyon contre les hérésies* (Paris, 1952), p. 121.

[12] See the comments of Chrysostomus Baur, *John Chrysostom and His Time*, Sr. M. Gonzaga, trans., I (Westminster, Md., 1959), 206-58.

[13] Cf. John Knox, *The Early Church and the Coming Great Church* (New York and Nashville, 1955), pp. 97-100.

[14] Friedrich Schleiermacher, *Der christliche Glaube nach den Grundsätzen der evangelischen Kirche im Zusammenhange dargestellt*, Martin Redeker, ed. (7th ed.; Berlin, 1960), I, 74-112.

[15] Cf. *The Oxford English Dictionary*, III, "E," (Oxford, 1933), 329.

[16] *Reden*[2], p. 60 (ET 49-50).

[17] *Reden*[2], p. 47 (ET 36).

[18] *Reden*[2], p. 72 (ET 58).

[19] *Reden*[1], pp. 243-44 (ET 214); cf. Otto Ritschl, "Das Verhältnis von Empirie und Spekulation in Schleiermachers Reden über die Religion," in *Schleiermachers Stellung zum Christentum in seinen Reden über die Religion* (Gotha, 1888), pp. 29-44.

[20] *Reden*[1], p. 274 (ET 237).

[21] Therefore Albrecht Ritschl could even speak of "the general science of religion [*die allgemeine Religionswissenschaft*], which was established by Schleiermacher's *Reden.*" *Schleiermachers Reden über die Religion und ihre Nachwirkungen auf die evangelische Kirche Deutschlands* (Bonn, 1874), p. 62.

[22] *Reden*[1], pp. 120-33 (ET 92-101); p. 12 (ET 9).

[23] *Reden*[1], pp. 115-17 (ET 88-90); cf. Basil Willey, *The Seventeenth Century Background* (New York, 1953).

[24] *Reden*[1], p. 43 (ET 33).

[25] Anton Hammer, *Die erkenntnistheoretische Bedeutung des gefühlmässigen Erfassens bei Schleiermacher* (Freiburg, 1934), is an attempt to gauge the epistemological role of *Gefühl* and to distinguish it from mere feeling-as-emotion. A similar attempt, which, though it concentrates upon the *Glaubenslehre,* is relevant also to the *Reden,* is F. Siegmund-Schultze, *Schleiermachers Psychologie in ihrer Bedeutung für die Glaubenslehre* (Tübingen, 1913), pp. 131-210.

[26] Hermann Süskind, *Christentum und Geschichte bei Schleiermacher*, I (Tübingen, 1911).

[27] *Reden*[2], pp. 102-103 (ET 80).

[28] *Reden*[1], p. 274 (ET 237).

[29] *Reden*[1], p. 28 (ET 21).

[30] *Reden*[1], p. 300 (ET 267).

[31] *Reden*[1], p. 107 (ET 83).

[32] The whole development has been put into a new light by the dissertation of Holger Samson, *Die Kirche als Grundbegriff der theologischen Ethik Schleiermachers* (Zürich, 1958).

[33] In my *From Luther to Kierkegaard* (St. Louis, 1950), pp. 109-12, my interpretation of Schleiermacher was deeply influenced by Emil Brunner, and therefore I made the esthetic element less ambiguous than it in fact is, at least in Schleiermacher's mature system.

[34] *Reden*[2], p. 171 (ET 138-39).

[35] *Reden*[2] p. 114 (ET 87). The first edition had "virtuosity" instead of "special calling."

[36] Cf. Norman W. Porteous, "The Prophets and the Problem of Continuity" in Bernhard W. Anderson and Walter Harrelson, eds., *Israel's Prophetic Heritage*, Essays in honor of James Muilenburg (New York, 1962), pp. 11-25.

[37] *Reden*[1], p. 68 (ET 55).

[38] *Reden*[3], p. 304 (ET 272).

[39] *Reden*[3], p. 30 (ET 23).

[40] *Reden*[2], p. 13 (ET 10).

[41] *Reden*[2], p. 199 (ET 164); here again the first edition had "virtuosos" for "accomplished in religion."

[42] *Reden*[3], p. 23 (ET 17).

[43] Cf. *Der christliche Glaube*, I, 148-54 (Thesis 27).

[44] *Schleiermachers Sendschreiben über seine Glaubenslehre an Lücke*, Hermann Mulert, ed. (Giessen, 1908).

[45] *Reden*[1], p. 281 (ET 244).

[46] *Reden*[1], p. 95 (ET 73).

[47] *Reden*[2], p. 85 (ET 65).

[48] *Reden*[3], p. 162 (ET 131).

[49] *Reden*[2], p. 16 (ET 12-13).

[50] *Der christliche Glaube*, II, 105-36 (Theses 102-104).

[51] *Reden*[1], p. 4 (ET 3).

[52] *Reden*[1], p. 185 (ET 152).

[53] *Reden*[2], pp. 96-97 (ET 74).

[54] *Reden*[1], p. 10 (ET 7).

[55] *Reden*[1], p. 207 (ET 171).

[56] *Der christliche Glaube*, II, 135-36.

[57] See, for example, Kenneth Scott Latourette, *A History of the Expansion of Christianity*, III, *Three Centuries of Advance* (New York, 1939), 349-55.

[58] *Reden*[1], p. 3 (ET 2).

[59] *Reden*[2], p. 92 (ET 70).

[60] *Reden*[1], p. 165 (ET 134).

[61] *Reden*[1], p. 163 (ET 131-32).

[62] *Reden*[1], p. 97 (ET 75).

[63] *Reden*[3], p. 190 (ET 156).

[64] For my understanding of the subtlety of this relation I am indebted to the essays of my late colleague Joachim Wach, *Meister und Jünger: Zwei religionsgeschichtliche Betrachtungen* (Tübingen, 1925).

[65] *Reden*[3], p. 118 (ET 91).

[66] *Reden*[1], p. 152 (ET 123).

[67] *Reden*[3], p. 176 (ET 143).

[68] *Reden*[1], p. 208 (ET 172).

[69] *Reden*[2], p. 56 (ET 44).

[70] Cf. Augustine, *The Teacher* (*De magistro*), XI, 36-38, Joseph M. Colleran, ed. and trans. (Westminster, Md., 1950), pp. 175-77; Reidar Thomte, *Kierkegaard's Philosophy of Religion* (Princeton, N. J., 1948), pp. 200-203.

[71] In a recent dissertation at Princeton Theological Seminary, *Schleiermacher's Theological Method with Special Attention to His Production of Church Dogmatics* (Ann Arbor, 1962), Terrence Nelson Tice has argued for the Christocentricity of Schleiermacher's thought, setting himself against much recent criticism.

[72] *Reden*[2], p. 91 (ET 70).

[73] *Reden*[1], pp. 281-87 (ET 245-50).

[74] *Reden*[2], p. 285 (ET 248).

[75] *Reden*[1], p. 259 (ET 225).

[76] *Reden*[2], p. 261 (ET 227).

[77] *Reden*[3], p. 176 (ET 143).

[78] Cf. the excursus of Karl Barth, *Church Dogmatics*, II-2, G. W. Bromiley and T. F. Torrance, eds. (Edinburgh, 1957), 458-506.

[79] Cf. the catalogue of these accusations, *Sendschreiben an Lücke*, p. 9.

[80] *Reden*[1], p. 52 (ET 40).

[81] *Reden*[1], p. 172 (ET 139).

[82] *Reden*[2], p. 286 (ET 249).

[83] Cf. Karl Barth, *Protestant Thought: From Rousseau to Ritschl*, Brian Cozens, tr., with introduction by Jaroslav Pelikan (New York, 1959), p. 311.

[84] *Reden*[1], p. 116 (ET 89).

[85] *Reden*[2], p. 117 (ET 90).

[86] *Reden*[2], p. 65 (ET 54).

[87] *Reden*[1], p. 239 (ET 211).

[88] *Reden*[3], p. 258 (ET 224).

[89] Johannes Geffcken, *Zwei griechische Apologeten* (Leipzig and Berlin, 1907).

[90] Barth, *Protestant Thought*, p. 327 (translation my own).

14

The New Challenge
before the Younger Churches

RICHARD SHAULL

WE HAVE BEEN HEARING FOR SOME TIME THAT THE MODERN MIS-
sionary enterprise has come to the end of an era. The younger churches
have also come to the end of an era, and this fact constitutes the
greatest challenge facing the Christian Church in its world mission
today. Such an affirmation does not imply standing in judgment on
these churches. I am convinced, not only that the older churches have
arrived at the same point, but also that the unsolved problem in the
mother churches, and limitations and mistakes in the work of the
Western missionaries, lie at the roots of the crisis the younger churches
face today.

We have arrived at a moment when this challenge must be taken
with the utmost seriousness. It sets before us both the danger of the
breakdown of these churches and an opportunity for new advance.
Which of these paths any church will follow may depend upon the
seriousness and openness with which its leaders analyze the problems
before them and strive to meet them. After a great many years of
contact, direct and indirect, with the churches of Asia, Africa, and
Latin America, it is clear that this ending of an era is a rather general phenomenon. The reader is urged to keep this in mind. The following study, however, will be limited to the specific example this
writer knows best.

THE PROTESTANT MOVEMENT OF BRAZIL

Any crisis in the life of a church is complex because many factors
are involved. In Brazil, two of these should receive special attention:

1. The Christian churches in Brazil suddenly find themselves in a new world which they are hardly prepared to understand or to meet. The shock of this is especially hard for those Protestant churches which began their work one hundred years ago, because the problem has arisen for them only very recently. By a strange irony of Providence, the type of Anglo-Saxon Protestantism which the missionaries brought to Brazil a century ago was able to meet the longings of the Brazilian soul and the needs of a new nation in a time of intellectual and social ferment in a way which Roman Catholicism had completely failed to do.

To a people religious by nature and tradition, but dissatisfied and confused, Protestantism brought a warm evangelical faith centering in a personal experience of Jesus Christ. Through the preaching of the Word, hymn singing, and Bible study the rich emotional life of the Brazilian soul was touched and transformed. The deep joy of Christian faith became a reality in the midst of problems and sufferings. Men and women were challenged to take a decision for Jesus Christ which led to the total redirection of their lives and to radical moral transformation. Bandits were converted; rural folk found new life in the midst of their monotonous existence; and atheist intellectuals were overwhelmed by the truth of the gospel. A new type of spirituality and of human existence developed which met the deepest needs of a people and exercised a strange attraction over those among whom the Protestants lived. It was this rich, joyful, and quite unfanatical spiritual life that has impressed those who came from other parts of the world and entered into a close relationship with Protestant communities in diverse parts of the country.

The Protestant Church brought a new dimension and depth to community life on the plantations and in the smaller towns and cities. In these areas stable natural communities existed in the nineteenth century, but they did not necessarily represent much richness or depth of human relationship. Roman Catholicism was a strong force for social unity but it was not able to bring a transformation in these relationships. With the establishment of the Protestant congregations, this change became a reality. Those who came to know the radical renewal of the gospel discovered that they belonged to each other in Jesus Christ. Thus a new type of human relationship developed in which plantation owners or their sons in the cities and the ex-slaves were brothers in Christ; they participated in a community of shared responsibility and engaged together in the work of evangelism. Here again a quality of life developed which was amazingly relevant to the human situation and constituted a powerful witness to the gospel in each local community.

The Protestant movement was able to relate itself in an unusually creative way to the new forces stirring in Brazilian life at the end of the nineteenth century. The Brazil of that period has often been referred to as a sleeping giant awakening from his slumber—it was becoming aware of itself and its potentialities and seeking the foundations for a new way of life. Protestantism met this hope in a most relevant way. It provided not only a new ideal, but also the power to make it a reality by transforming the whole life of the individual convert and his family. The gospel provided a new sense of more integrity, a new seriousness of life and work. Children were nurtured on this, and every effort was made, often at great sacrifice, to provide them with an education. The local congregation became a school in democracy and in responsibility which existed nowhere else in Brazilian life. The intellectuals who had felt the impact of new ideas of democracy and freedom were easily led to send their children to Protestant schools and to support Protestant causes; many were soon converted. An unusual number of outstanding families in São Paulo and elsewhere were converted to Protestant Christianity in the early decades, and the number of leaders of national life who studied in Protestant schools as children and were profoundly influenced by them is even more impressive.*

Brazilian Protestantism, which discovered how to relate itself so creatively to the world of a former time, is now feeling the first rude shock that comes from awareness that conditions have changed and that it has practically no idea of how to relate itself to the new world taking shape around it. Those who have been brought to this discovery are gradually becoming conscious of the nature of this new world from which they cannot retreat; many others realize that something has gone wrong, but draw back on the threshold of the new day because they are afraid of its implications or feel unprepared to deal with them.

The tremendous strides in technological and industrial development have led to the rapid growth of large cities, population expansion, and mass internal migrations. As a result the situation in which Protestant spiritual, ethical, and community life was nurtured is rapidly becoming a thing of the past. Possibilities in almost all areas of life are accompanied by new threats of human disintegration. The whole

* Condensed from a chapter by the author in Hyla Stuntz Converse, ed., *Raise a Signal* (New York: Friendship Press, 1961), pp. 111-14.

structure of community life that existed earlier in village and town has given place to the confused and isolated individual and the masses. A dynamic society has taken the place of a relatively static order and has made almost all patterns of church institutional life and missionary expansion quite obsolete.

The more concerned and sensitive among the Brazilian youth are no longer attached primarily to the ideas of liberty and democracy and the patterns of responsible living in a middle-class society with which Anglo-Saxon Protestantism has been identified. The emancipation of the masses, the elimination of social injustice, and national development occupy the center of their thought. Thus they are concerned about ideas and movements which will make it possible to change the basic structures of social, economic, and political life. Their deepest emotional experience and their sense of participation in life come from their identification with the masses and their involvement in groups engaged in this struggle—that is, in revolution. Here is a whole new and exciting world in which the Marxist may be at home, but the Protestant, by and large, is not. The evangelical community has shown an unusual ability to take on the mores of a bourgeois society and to leave undisturbed and uninvolved many of the younger generation who are interested mainly in getting ahead in the world. As a result, we are known for our lack of concern for social justice and our lack of sensitivity to human need. In general, those very institutions which in an earlier period put the Church in a frontier position, in contact with the most creative forces of its day, have now identified it both with the more conservative classes and with North America. At a time when new enthusiasm for education leads to literacy campaigns among the masses and the desire for democratization of educational opportunity, our schools have become more and more restricted to the upper classes in order to exist at all, and tend to absorb such a large proportion of our resources in time, energy, and funds that we are hardly free to be much concerned about the educational challenges facing us in the new world.

The new world is also creating its own radically new mentality. Rapid social change has cut the new generation loose from the traditions of the past, while many of them are impressed with the emptiness and artificiality of the world their parents have passed on to them. This has brought them to have a profound distrust of their elders and to reject almost all the inherited patterns in Church and society.

The spread of science and technology has brought new ways of understanding reality and new ideas of what is important. A secular mentality is more and more dominant, which has not the slightest interest in the Church as an institution with power and prestige in society and which tends to consider unimportant and irrelevant the concerns felt by our traditional Protestantism as religious or spiritual. Most of the students with whom I have had contact in the last year who best represent this mentality simply have not the slightest interest in these matters, for religion seems to them to have no relationship whatsoever to the major issues of human life and destiny as they are facing them today.

In the course of a few years, the old world in which Protestantism was at home has gone, and a strange new world has suddenly broken around us. We are not the only ones to be perplexed by it. By and large, the Roman Catholic Church, still so closely tied to the Constantinian era and the *corpus christianum*, is even more perplexed by the course of events. Only the Pentecostals and the Spiritists seem to go blithely ahead, because they have discovered how to reach the uprooted masses in the large cities on the most elemental level of experience on which they function. Whether they will be able to deal creatively with the new world in its full impact in the future is quite another matter.

2. In this new world, the crisis of Brazilian Protestantism is basically the crisis caused by the breakdown of pietism.

In daring to venture into this area, it is with the full recognition that I am treading on holy ground. It was precisely this pietism that made the development of Protestantism in Brazil possible. Pietism was the source of its vitality as well as its rapid growth. It was pietism that made possible such a creative relationship of Protestantism with the Brazilian situation in the past, and provided the deep and meaningful religious experience, the rich community life, and the strong evangelistic passion that have been the strength of Protestantism in this country over decades. It is only natural that when we raise questions at this point, the older generation, still sustained and nourished by it, is easily upset. They rightly fear that its collapse might leave the Church with nothing to take its place; they are right in insisting that Protestantism cannot go forward without a vitality of spiritual life and power such as pietism produced.

But, in full recognition of all this, one is forced to conclude that no other single factor is so responsible for our present crisis as the breakdown of the pietistic heritage. It represents an oversimplification of the realities of Christian faith and life which now has disastrous consequences. It presupposes the existence of certain structures of theology and liturgy, of Christian community and of life, but does not give them a central place in its oversimplified understanding of the gospel. As the churches that grew out of this tradition developed, they were unable to deal creatively with these issues, and in the world in which they now find themselves the problem takes on new and almost overwhelming dimensions.

Moreover, pietism comes very close to being heretical at one point; in its understanding of the relationship of Jesus Christ and of the Christian to the world. It represents one of the first serious attempts of the Church to meet the challenge of modern secularization. But it was a mistaken attempt, which resulted in fleeing precisely from the place where God is at work, from the concrete situation in the world in which the whole structure of Christian life and community must take form. The result of this has been a profound crisis which now begins to manifest itself in several major areas of Christian life and witness.

THE MODERN CRISIS

The early missionaries, in their attitude toward theology, were very much in the pietistic tradition. The Calvinists saw theology as important in order to have a correct definition of the gospel, yet revealed very little excitement about its significance in confronting the human situation or ordering the life and structures of the Church. Some Baptists and Methodists showed this same interest in theology; most of them completely ignored it. In both cases the end result was the same: the missionaries were unable to equip the Church with a vital theology. This has affected many areas of Church life. Practically no theological literature of any significance has appeared within a century. Without constant theological renewal, many elements—some of central importance in the gospel—tend to be neglected. To date, very little has happened which would reveal a creative relationship of evangelical Christianity to the major intellectual and human problems of the nation.

Now, with a new world developing around us in which people in and out of the Church are trying to get their bearings, no word has yet been heard from Protestantism. The laymen of the younger generation, caught in this situation, demand something of their pastors which they are often unprepared to give; this in turn creates new ten-

sions and insecurity. At this moment, many signs of theological renewal are beginning to appear among laymen and ministers which
offer new possibilities for the future. But such renewal can come only
as we are able to go beyond the limitations of our pietistic heritage.

For some of the early missionaries, at least, worship and the sacraments received serious attention. In the sermons and articles of Ashbel
Green Simonton, the first Presbyterian missionary, the sacraments
occupy a central place. But pietism was not prepared to sustain this
concern. Gradually the sacraments received less attention, while the
growth of revivalism shattered the classical structures of worship.
The whole order of service was built around bringing people to an
emotional experience and a decision for Christ. As the fires of revival
gradually cooled, a vacuum developed which all too often was filled
by a sermon or by a stereotyped but theologically meaningless order
of worship. It is hardly surprising that at this point there is general
malaise throughout the Protestant churches—an attitude of revolt
among many young people, who simply refuse to attend church services regularly; and at the same time a profound longing for meaningful form of worship as indispensible for human life in the midst of
so many forces of disintegration.

Lacking any clearly formulated doctrine of the nature and structure
of the Church, pietism left it unprepared to meet the challenge to renewal of congregational life in the new world. The same type of congregational life that made community real in the small towns and
rural areas of a former day is quite ineffective in the new society. Now
what is demanded is the creation of adequate structures of human
relationships in communities where practically none exist. For this
we are unprepared.

The missionaries brought to Brazil patterns of Church life and
organization which had their limitations even in the milieu from which
they came. Transported into an alien culture without serious re-examination and renewal, they tended to encourage the development of
unauthentic patterns of ministry and authority, of ecclesiastical organization and Church life in general, which seriously hinder the building up of the Church. Worst of all, the pietistic tendency to flee from
the world has led to the development of congregational life in terms
of a program of religious activities which are, at best, marginal to the
real life of men in the world, and often almost totally irrelevant. The
more the good churchman becomes involved in the life and work of
the Church, the less is he free to be a Christian in the world. As a
growing number of students have discovered, their full participation

in this sort of congregational life leads them to a deep sense of alienation from the centers of life in the world in which they are convinced God is at work.

THE PATTERN OF CHRISTIAN LIFE

Those who are living on the threshold of a new world developing around them are amazed by the possibilities of new life it opens up; at the same time they are almost overwhelmed by the threats of human disintegration which are also present. This provides the Christian Church with a moment in which it has an extraordinary opportunity to proclaim and live the new life that Jesus Christ offers to the world. For this, also, pietism is quite unprepared. Its traditional response has been that of providing an emotional experience and a set of negative rules to guide conduct. When human life is falling apart, this type of emotional religious experience may make the situation even worse, while the rules prescribed have become a burden too heavy to be borne and are quite unrelated to the deeper human problems young people face today. What is required of us is nothing less than the total restructuring of human life in Christ.

At this point a word should be said about the situation of the Roman Catholic Church. It does not face the problem created by pietism, but it is equally unable to deal with the new world of which I have been speaking. Its pre-Reformation piety has long since revealed its lack of transforming power. Its program and church structure are even more out of contact with the real world than those of Protestantism, and its hierarchical structure makes it less free to meet the challenges of a rapidly changing society. In the history of this nation, at those few moments when there existed a real possibility of creative relationship between the Roman Church and Brazilian reality, Rome has drawn back and brought the Church into line at the cost of cutting its contact with the human situation.

At the same time, we cannot ignore the fact that, within its rigid structures, the Roman Church has emphasized certain elements which are absolutely essential in the preservation of Christian faith, and which the pietistic heritage is in danger of losing: theology, liturgy, sacrament, and the sense of Christian responsibility in the world, which now expresses itself principally in the groups of lay Catholic Action. The Reformation of the sixteenth century raised fundamental questions about the legitimacy of the forms that Roman Catholicism gave to each of these elements—questions which need to be raised in

Latin America today. But any type of Protestantism which has lost any of these elements is ill prepared to fulfill its mission in its encounter with Roman Catholicism.

It is not surprising, then, that we find a general and widespread unrest in the Church today. Many young people lose interest in the Church and leave it. Evangelistic expansion is slowing down except in the rural areas, where the old patterns of society still persist. A growing number of laymen and ministers are becoming more and more aware of the crisis we confront and are attempting to meet it in a variety of ways.

It is natural that some should react by seeing in the type of concern here expressed a dangerous virus which must be isolated and overcome so that business can go ahead as usual. Caught in the structures of a world that is passing away, they can deal with the present only in the degree that it conforms to the past. They seek refuge in a greater emphasis on authority in the Church and its ministry, which in the end makes it even more difficult for the Church to deal with the new world around it.

Another effort, which flourished some ten years ago and still lingers on in some quarters, attempted to solve the problems through revivalism and was encouraged and carried on primarily by imported evangelists. If the analysis of the situation I have made is correct, this can only lead to futility. In fact, the failure of these movements to make any lasting contribution, in spite of the intense efforts of many involved, is an indirect confirmation of what I have been saying. Only to the degree that we discover radically new forms of Christian community and Christian life in the world can we hope for the depth of revitalization these movements would like to achieve. The temporary success of even the best of these evangelists tends to blind our eyes to the real isues and thus delay our search for adequate solutions.

Thus the conviction is becoming more and more widespread that we have come to the end of an era, and that only by radical renewal of all the structures of the Church's life can we go ahead. Not everyone has succeeded in articulating this conviction. There are quite a variety of ways of understanding both the nature of the problem and the point at which our efforts at renewal should be concentrated. It is much easier to analyze the problem than to know how to meet it, and the uncertainty and frustration this produces are not easy to live with. But we are gradually led to the conclusion that what is demanded of the Church today is a revolution as radical as that which occurred in the sixteenth century, and that we are called to live and wait on the frontiers where God is bringing this renewal to pass.

Having arrived at this point, I would very much like to stop, for it is most difficult and dangerous to attempt to say anything more. Each of the younger churches is a living organism, striving to discover the most adequate expression for its life and witness in the concrete environment in which it is set. As those who form part of that culture strive to find their way, new forms are being given to the Christian community. The most important thing to bear in mind, at least when we speak of the Church in Brazil, is that this basic Christian community exists throughout the country. It is composed of men and women who know that Jesus Christ is their Lord and Savior and who are totally committed to His service. They may not yet have a clear understanding of what is demanded of them in the new era they are entering, but the foundation has been laid. In this, those who went before were faithful and fulfilled their mission. It is the task of the new generation to continue their work by giving adequate form to this life and witness of the Christian community in the new world.

What form this renewal must take, we do not know. Our experience of recent years has shown us that it is very easy to formulate an impressive theory of what should be done and how we should do it, but the reality with which we deal in Church and world is so complex that it soon shatters or at least reveals the limitations of the best of our theories. Small groups are struggling with the problem on diverse frontiers, yet they have very little to show in terms of results. Rather than discuss what they are trying to do, they would much prefer simply to invite others to be involved with them.

NEW DEVELOPMENTS OF HOPE

Yet, recognizing all this, there are still a few things that can be said at this time. Speaking as one from the outside who has been given the privilege of sharing in some ventures of this type, I would like to indicate certain directions in which we are being led and what is happening at the points of our involvement.

The most significant thing is the relationship between biblical and theological study and our experience of involvement in the world. As such study has taken place in the context of involvement, it has given new orientation to our efforts; at the same time, our theological understanding has been renewed and confirmed by our experience in the concrete situation in the world. Because it has happened this way, we are very skeptical about the value of stating here, in a more or less academic way, certain theological conclusions to which we have come, or what they seem to mean in terms of the renewal of the life of the Church. For those who are in close contact with recent biblical and theological studies, these conclusions will have nothing revolutionary about them—so long as they are seen as academic propositions. When, however, we take them as the basis for the reconstruction of Christian life and the Christian community in the world, they become indeed disturbing, exciting, and revolutionary realities which open up new possibilities of understanding and action.

1. God renews human life in the very center of man's struggles in the world and in history. As shown above, our whole pietistic heritage led us in quite the opposite direction. Our experience of Christ's presence and saving power tended to express itself in a special spiritual or religious sphere which became further and further removed from the crucial issues of the world in which we live. The local congregation, likewise, developed a program of activities which drew the believer out of this world.

In this situation, the biblical understanding of the place where the Triune God is at work comes with revolutionary consequences. It is precisely at this point that the Old Testament caused such a radical about-face in religious concern. The prophets were interested in the questions of everyday existence and politics, for these were the areas in which God's work in the world raised crucial questions for human existence; they were the areas in which man's relationship to God and to his neighbor were spelled out in terms of obedience or disobedience. As Ronald Gregor Smith has said, "All the incidents and situations which compose the raw material of the biblical writings arise out of the common experience of men in society—experiences of love and hate, of loyalty and betrayal, of greed and self-sacrifice, of guilt and restitution, of patriotism and treachery."* The New Testament does not change this. Rather it sets before us the Word made flesh, the Son of God who became incarnate, taking upon himself the totality of the human situation, and whose life, death, and resurrection affected the destiny of man and of history. Thus Christian faith directs our attention to the social, economic, and political situation in which we live— to the life of man within the concrete orders of the world. This is the place where God has chosen to work out man's salvation and where the Good News of the gospel is received and lived.

2. God renews man's life in the particularity of his social existence. We live our lives as members of a particular nation, class, and cul-

---

* *The New Man* (New York, 1956), p. 16.

ture. The new life that Christ offers must take form within these orders. In recent years a number of studies have been made of the biblical concept of *nation* which are extremely illuminating at this point. They show us how central this concept is in the Old Testament, where it refers to all the expressions of the particularity of man's social existence. God's blessing is for the nations; it is with them that He deals. Abraham was chosen so that in him all nations might be blessed. St. Paul recalls this promise—noting that the Scriptures "preached the gospel beforehand to Abraham"—and sees its fulfillment in the redemption of Christ, wrought in order that "in Christ Jesus the blessing of Abraham might come upon the Gentiles" (Gal. 3:8, 14).

Let us not confuse our understanding of this by falling back into the old debate about an individual versus a social gospel—a discussion which is completely alien to the whole biblical understanding. What is here implied is that God gives his saving grace to man in the context of the class, race, group, and culture to which he belongs. He does not work in a vacuum. Rather, as the gospel spreads among a people, it takes the total cultural and psychological heritage of that people—temperament, emotions, ways of thinking and of being—and transforms all, giving a new shape and direction to it. The Christian community that comes into existence in any place is thus the new man in Christ as it takes form among a particular group or class of people. For pastors or missionaries to come into any particular group from the outside is a very dangerous business, except as they become totally involved in the human situation there, understand that the Christian congregation must give expression to God's work among that people, and work in the openness of the Holy Spirit toward the goal this implies.

3. The presence and power of the Triune God in the renewal of human life is most evident on the frontiers of change where the old order is passing away and a new order is coming into being in the world.

The God we know in the Bible is on the move. He has a purpose for human life and acts to carry it forward. As men are always building up structures of life which are contrary to this purpose, God's judgment accompanies His mercy; he must tear down in order to open the way for the renewal of life. "See, I have set you this day over nations and over kingdoms, to pluck up and to break down, to destroy and to overthrow, to build and to plant" (Jer. 1:10). The kingdom of God has come into the world in Jesus Christ. Its coming means both judgment upon the old orders of human existence and the constant presence, within them, of the new order by which they are being transformed.

Thus the constant pressure of God's judgment and mercy creates a dynamic situation in the world. Where human life is breaking down—that is, where the emptiness and unauthenticity of our existence is being laid bare—there the Christian community discovers the most creative possibilities for human renewal. Where God's judgment is most severe on our social, economic, and political order, there the Christian community is witness to the new possibilities of ordering human life in all these spheres. We must therefore conclude that the Christian congregation is called to come into being not merely in the world, in the particularity of man's social existence, but also on the frontiers of change, in every moment and in every generation. It need not struggle desperately to preserve the obsolete patterns of its own life or the world of the past; rather, it is free to accept the frontier on which God has placed it and rejoice in the miracles of His work there. At the same time, it is not tempted simply to accept the new uncritically, for the new may be as much an instrument of man's revolt against God as the old. What it is free to do, however, is precisely this: to be present at the point where the struggle between Jesus Christ and the demonic forces is taking place, and there be the instrument and first fruits of the renewal of life which God's redemptive work opens before the world.

Quite a number of small groups of Christians in Brazil today suddenly find themselves in this very situation. They did not exactly plan it this way, but it happened, and with it has come a new understanding of the gospel and its relevance for the modern world. In many cases, the first shock of this discovery has been accompanied by an awareness that the life and program of the local congregation—most of those things that absorb our time and energy—are almost totally irrelevant. We have found ourselves in somewhat the same position as the farmer who, when asked by a stranger how to go to a certain town, made several attempts to explain, got more and more mixed up, and finally said, "Mister, if you are going to that town, this is the wrong place to start from." Many have concluded that, when the Christian community is willing to take the leap of faith into the very center of the concrete human situation of the world today and become involved in it, the Holy Spirit will give it the new forms by which human life in Christ will be renewed and by which it can thus live and witness to Him. It is still too early to have any clear idea of what these forms will be, but one thing is clear: there can be no turning back.

In this situation, the life and witness of the worker-priests in France have taken on new significance for us. They went into the factories originally with the simple intention of getting to know that milieu and discovering how best to evangelize the workers. They discovered that they and the Church were living in a new world in which the old forms of priesthood, congregational life, and witness were no longer relevant. They also discovered that in this new world, where the workers had long since abandoned the Church and Christianity as irrelevant, the gospel had meaning and power and would create new forms for the Christian community. It was this double discovery that carried them forward in a course of action which eventually led to their suppression. This discovery also so overwhelmed them that they could not turn back even in the face of the decision of the Vatican. It may well be that today, in Brazil and elsewhere, the Church is being confronted by the same question. The possibility of finding the pathway of renewal may depend, to no small degree, upon the way in which the Church responds to the challenge thus presented to it.

I should like to illustrate all this by one concrete example: that of several small groups of Christian university students and young professionals with whom I have had the privilege of being closely related in recent months. These students are aware that they are living in the new world I have described, and they are intrigued by it. They also have deep Christian convictions and commitment, although they have been increasingly dissatisfied with the traditional patterns of congregational life, and some of them have practically stopped going to church. In one way or another they have become tremendously involved in the world, at the point where things are happening today in Brazil. This means that they are participating actively in student politics and in other student organizations, in which the focus is on the struggle to change the basic structures of social, economic, and political life in the direction of greater justice. In this involvement they have discovered their relationship and solidarity with the peasants and industrial workers; they have also entered into a new type of relationship with their fellow students and have become more aware of the forces of disintegration at work in their lives, and of the desperate search in which students are engaged for authentic existence.

The students who have become thus involved have done so as members of the Student Christian Movement, which has gone with them into this experience and provided some sort of Christian community life for them. It is within these nuclei that a new vision of the form of

the Church in the new world has begun to take shape, for they have
discovered that what they used to search for desperately in the Church
has now come to them as a gift which they are called to receive and
make real in their midst.

The type of religious experience that pietism offered to former generations did not materialize for them, and this left them in a vacuum of
doubt and uncertainty. Now they have discovered that the Christ who
is supremely present in the affairs of men and women in the world, in
the midst of those who are hungry and exploited, makes His presence
real in the life of those who are involved with Him and His suffering
for the world. As they participate in Jesus' concern for the neighbor
and His relationship with others, they discover the secret not only of
human existence but also of a living relationship with Christ Himself.
Students formerly disturbed about the relevance of the gospel for the
human situation today have awakened to the fact that academic discussion of relevance got them nowhere, but when they became seriously involved with Christ and with neighbor at the points where
God's activity in the world was most manifest, such discussions were
quite unnecessary. For years, in our student movement, we have been
engaged in a study of how to go about evangelism among students—
how to get to the students and talk to them about the gospel. What
these students now realize is that they are involved with their colleagues in issues raised by the coming of Christ. Thus every conversation that takes place is essentially a conversation about the gospel, and
evangelism becomes the natural center of all human relationships.

What is most important of all, we are gradually becoming aware
that in this new context Jesus Christ is offering us the possibility of a
new form of human existence, a new life in community. That is indeed
the Good News in the face of the forces of disintegration of our time.
As we have been forced to face some very serious problems of members of our own group, we have been given at least a foretaste of what
happens as life is rebuilt around Christ and as the realities of forgiveness and healing liberate and reintegrate human personality. We have
been given a new experience of the depth and joy in human relationships among those who have been freed by Christ to lose themselves
in service to their neighbor and find, in Him, the possibility of meaning
and security in an empty and insecure world.

We are also beginning to understand that this possibility can be ours
only to the degree that the traditional means of grace are available and
received in this community. The very elements of our traditional congregational life, which had lost almost all meaning for these students,

are now being recognized as the very food by which this new life is daily nourished and sustained. Bible study and prayer, worship and sacrament, pastoral care and life in community: these are the means of grace which must now become the indispensible support of our life in the world. But they become means of grace for us only as they are at our disposal in the very center of the world in which we are involved, in the precarious Christian community which the Holy Spirit is calling into existence there. This implies that they must be given an entirely new form as the patterns of congregational life in the new world in which we live, a form which we have not yet found.

Let me conclude with two brief observations.

1. These students realize that this recovery of Christian life and witness also thrusts them into dangerous contact with Communism. In Brazil at this moment it cannot be otherwise. This is where God's judgment confronts us; this constitutes the major and most decisive encounter in which our Christian obedience will be determined. Here we see why Communism represents the major Christian heresy of our time, at least in the underdeveloped countries. It is Marxism that affirms that the decisive things are really happening in the center of the life of the world—that is, in the economic and political struggles of our time. It is Marxism that insists most strongly that people can find life only as they identify themselves with the situation of the masses, and with their life and struggles. And Marxism is the most dynamic affirmation in recent times, in a perverted way, of the fact that where God is most fully at work is on the frontiers of change; and this affirmation is made at a moment in which churches seem almost to have forgotten it. The fact that Communism shows little enthusiasm for those who want to be on the frontiers of change in a Communist society does not necessarily weaken its influence in countries where changes are urgently demanded, and where the Marxist is the one most concerned in bringing them about. To retreat from this encounter will be fatal for us. But to be exposed to this heresy without being unduly influenced or overwhelmed by it is not easy. This is especially true in the present situation in Brazil, when the suffering of the masses is so great and the demands for change so strong; when Marxism seems the only force capable of bringing about these changes in the direction of social justice; when Communism can appear as a utopian hope— rather than what it really is, after it has been firmly established in power and the first wave of revolutionary enthusiasm has passed. Our pastoral responsibility is to be present with these young people on this frontier, where all our human limitations are laid bare and we learn

again what it means to live by faith and to trust only in the power of God.

2. We come now to a final word about the implications of all this for ecumenical relations and especially for the missionary enterprise. As churches we are related to each other in the recognition that we have serious mutual problems and must search together for answers. Our missionary responsibility toward the younger churches can no longer continue uncritically in the traditional patterns, for we may do many good things that will, in the end, make the situation of the younger churches worse, rather than help them to become more dynamic instruments of mission in their countries. To continue to think in terms of going out to do the same things in the same old way, whether in evangelism, audio-visual work, education, or exchange of ecumenical personnel, is no longer to act responsibly.

We are called today to discover how to work together in our search for renewal at the center of the world's life, and to offer in all humility the gifts God has given to our particular Church to the service of our task. For us as North Americans this makes demands upon those who would go abroad which we still comprehend only vaguely, and for which we are almost totally unprepared. For example, in going to Brazil, are we willing to face seriously demands such as participating as students in situations similar to those mentioned above—even engaging in revolution and trying to discover how to receive the gift of life which God offers? Are we willing to pay the price of this venture? Let us not answer this too quickly. But if we are able to accept the challenge, we may have before us one of the most creative opportunities of participation in the mission of the Church and in its renewal that has arisen in recent Christian history.

Part VI

_____

A THEOLOGY

FOR THE NUCLEAR AGE

15

A Theology of Repentance

JOSEPH HAROUTUNIAN

POWER AND PIETY IN THE NUCLEAR AGE

THE NUCLEAR AGE IMPINGES UPON THE PUBLIC MIND MAINLY IN terms of flight into space and atomic warfare. Flight into space represents a new age of power and expectation of glorious things to come, while the threat of atomic warfare has produced a new age of dread and an expectation of universal death and destruction. Thus we are torn between hope and despair, and despair is the greater of the two. When we see atomic power in the context of world-wide struggles for power and the overwhelming complexity of the problems raised by nations and peoples on the move, it is hard not to become panicky with the feeling that we are being driven by forces beyond our control, toward we know not what obscure and surprising destiny. Hence the nuclear age has become for us above all an age of anxiety.

But anxiety is not the only significant modification of the human spirit today. As suggested above, the age of anxiety is also the age of power. The holocaust we fear would be the work of a new power in human hands—a power approximating that once attributed to divine beings. The power of life and death over men and nations, the power to all but destroy the earth, is very special. It is the power of a god, of a being who is spirit and not flesh. It is like omnipotence and evokes ultimate concern—which, according to Paul Tillich, is the essence of religion. In a new way we hear again the words of the serpent to our first parents: *eritis sicut dii*. What we are witnessing today is a new, almost irresistible temptation to deny our finitude as human beings, a denial that appears justified by the very fact of atomic power. Even while we live in the dread of annihilation, we also live with a feeling that not even the sky sets a limit to our powers and possibilities. Man today is out for mastery, autonomy, and infinity.

We know that this new power which at once exalts us and crushes our spirit is neither a gift nor an accident. It is the hard-won prize we owe to a breathtaking increase in man's knowledge of the nature of things. It is the outcome of our science and technology, both of which are incredibly clever human accomplishments. Of course, science has always been a matter of human knowledge and ingenuity. But much science in the past has been a process of observing nature with the help of simple and relatively crude instruments; its outcome in power has been rather moderate. Today, science is a highly complicated and sophisticated manipulation of things, and its yield of power is immense. It uses not natural objects, but artifacts produced in ways and under conditions found nowhere on earth or in heaven. Its instruments are machine-made, its machines are made by other machines, which are made in turn by others. The powers it uses are generated by whirring dynamos and transmitted by systems of rotation which have only the remotest connection with the motions of natural bodies. Natural causes and effects are replaced by new interactions, and even time and space have acquired new rhythms and qualities. Science and technology have given us a world in which nature is largely replaced by artifacts, things born by things made, things given and found by things invented and perfected by men.

This new world is the setting of our public life and even of our private affairs. It is not necessary to list all the machines and gadgets and goods that largely occupy our spaces and our times and create and sustain our way of life. We need only to consider what life would be like without our cars and airplanes, our TV-sets and washing machines, our lighting and heating systems, and the infinity of things in our department stores, drugstores, hardware stores, and groceries. And we are told that, unless we are destroyed by our bombs, marvels are coming in this nuclear age beyond all expectation or imagining. In short, not only the scientist and the engineer, but also the common man today lives and moves and has his being in a man-made world of power and production vastly different from the natural environment and its vicissitudes that formed the mind and the soul of his forebears.

It is inevitable that the nuclear age should greatly reduce the natural piety that was deeply and pervasively woven into the cultures of the past. Men who use natural objects as raw—very raw—materials for the production of their artifacts cannot be expected to have toward them the sense of kinship that was integral to the piety of our fathers. People who eat and drink without regard to seed-time and harvest-time, who keep warm and cool without regard to summer and winter, who go about their business without a thought of day and night, who provide for themselves a myriad of goods without help or hindrance from nature—such people can hardly be expected to live by the traditional sense of "absolute dependence" which is at the heart of natural piety.

The nuclear age evokes, not a piety of dependence and creaturely finitude, but a spirit of mastery and of methodical calculation. Authentic piety today is a matter of curiosity and competence and perseverance and faith in the "experimental method"; of truth and integrity in the sense of "calling a spade a spade." To put it rather crudely, knowledge and power come not by prayer to a Power behind nature, but by science and technique and organization; not by the worship of nature's God, but by a godlike redisposition of reality. Natural piety today is more or less an avocation, practised through leftover habits of thought and feeling rather than through any sense of kinship with, or dependence upon, nature.

It is true that contemporary knowledge of atoms and stars deepens rather than removes the mysteries around us. The man of science to-day may be astonished and mystified by the marvels revealed by his "transformer-rectifier high-voltage apparatus," or by the new techniques available for the investigation of the universe at large. There is mystery enough in the new science for any one's taste. But the wonder it induces is esthetic and intellectual and quite apart from the mixture of wonder and trepidation in "natural religion." In any case, man today is out to explore the universe, not to accept it. He achieves his ends not by propitiating his God but by perfecting his instruments. The omnipotent God of natural religion is being replaced by the omnipotent man of the nuclear age. This being so, religion is not likely to profit from the marvels and mysteries of contemporary science.

It may be argued by the traditionalists that in spite of man's present-day knowledge and power, his finitude is and will remain impregnable; that, whatever he may accomplish, he is still subject to sickness, physical catastrophe, and finally death itself. He is dust and returns to dust. However great his power, his life is but for a moment, like the grass of the field, and comes to an end "like a sigh." It may be pointed out that the man of the atom is rather a fool in his economics and politics and ethics; that he may know much about his atom, but knows little enough about himself. One may insist on asking how it comes about that this new god is so incompetent in his affairs as to live his days in a state of frightful anxiety.

Such observations may be valid, but they are no longer conducive to piety or belief in God. The man of the nuclear age knows that he is mortal; but he is impressed by his power rather than by his mortality. He is not unduly troubled, in spite of all religious and existentialist exhortations, by the prospect of his own demise. Power is what he has, and the life after death is what he at best doubts. He celebrates his power and learns not to deplore his finitude. Having the power of a god, he is in no mood to seek another god to save him from his mortality. His power is his life and he does not seek another. As for his imperfections and frustrations, he does not care to exaggerate them; and he certainly will not, with his science and power, give up hope for a paradise on earth. In short, the man of the nuclear age is not a man of natural piety, and the God of natural religion does not fit into his way of life.

The world picture of the nuclear age does not include God. The cultivated man today finds no God in his reactor, and he finds none through his telescope. God is not among the rushing electrons and He is not visible in outer space. This should be no surprise, since nobody has ever seen Him. The difficulty with belief in God today is that the piety that quickened and sustained it lacks the seriousness of living concern. The traditional preoccupations of natural religion with God, evil, and immortality have lost both urgency and rationality to those who belong heart and mind to this power age. Even if there were a God, we would hardly know what to do with Him. Supreme Being, First Cause, Unmoved Mover, and even the Ground and Power of Being have become rather pretentious but altogether harmless ghosts. Modern man may talk and even argue about them. But when it comes to practical life with all its absorbing problems and prospects, he bows them out of the scene of action. In short: natural theology is not for the nuclear age.

NATURAL THEOLOGY AND CHRISTIAN THEOLOGY

If the above review has any truth at all, it calls for a reconsideration of the traditional synthesis between natural theology and Christian theology. To begin with, it has not been and is not now unquestioned that the God of natural religion is the God of the Christian faith. It has not been and is not now unquestionable that the living God of the Bible is "the God of the philosophers," or that the Trinity is

Necessary and Infinite Being. The more or less tidy superimpositions of the Christian faith upon natural religion, or of Christology upon natural theology, have long been debated, especially in Protestant circles. The arguments about Christianity and religion, revelation and reason, grace and nature, indicate a permanent ambiguity in the Christian mind with respect to faith and piety. There are ancient distinctions between "true and false religion," between faith and idolatry, between theology and mythology, which indicate a perennial awareness of a contradiction between gospel and religion. The Church has recognized more or less clearly that Jesus Christ represents a revolution in the knowledge and service of God, and that the Christian faith requires the conversion of *homo religiosus*. In short, the symbiosis of Christian faith and natural piety has been less than happy, and the living God of Scripture has long been at odds with the God of "universal religion."

It would seem that the decline of natural piety in the nuclear age constrains the Christian thinker to reopen the question as to whether "God the Father, Son, and Holy Spirit" is one of the names of God otherwise commonly known as the Power behind the universe. Is it true that the Christian knows God first as the Maker and Ruler of the cosmos, and afterward as God and Father of our Lord Jesus Christ? Do we know God through nature or the physical world first, and through the man Jesus and his Church secondly? Where do we turn first for our knowledge of God: to Jesus and his people, or to reactors and the things revealed by them? The old debate between revealed and natural theology should perhaps now become a debate between humanistic and scientific theology; between theology that takes its clue from Jesus and theology that takes its clue from atoms and stars.

It may well be objected at this point that to turn first to Jesus Christ at this time is to turn aside from science and thus not to solve the problem of science and theism, but to shelve it. It may be said that, since we live in the nuclear age, to make Christology rather than cosmology the key to the knowledge of God is to be intellectually irresponsible and irrelevant; that this is to practise a double-talk and double-thought which are wrong as well as futile. And it may be that in the long run and ultimately it cannot be done.

But we are not engaged in constructing an ultimate theology. I do not deny, but rather affirm, that a Christian as thinker must respond properly to culture and therefore to the science of his day. This is a matter of the ongoing intellectual responsibility of the Christian theologian. Our question is whether a Christian who sets out to think about God may begin with something other than Jesus Christ and his Church or people. May he begin with atoms and stars rather than with the life he has in the company of his fellow men? Maybe this question should not be settled too readily in favor of the new science. One should remember that the living God of the Bible is the Lord and God of Abraham, Isaac, and Jacob; the God of Israel and of its prophets, priests, and kings; the God of Jesus and his Church; the God of nations, tongues, and peoples. When the Church fixed its mind and soul upon Jesus of Nazareth, of the seed of David—upon His Person and His work as the revelation of the living God—it committed itself to faith in a God who not only created man in His own image but also constrained him to know God and serve Him by life together with his fellow man.

The Bible is a book about, first, God's ways with men, and secondly, His ways with the world at large. In the Bible, physical process is inseparable from human history, and together they are subject to His wisdom as well as power. God's covenant overarches both nature and history, and His people neither exist nor know Him apart from it. The Bible does not permit us to seek to know God with the aid of atoms and stars before He meets us in the communion of Christ with His Church and in the communion of His people one with another.

The preoccupation of the nuclear age with atoms and space presents a new temptation to neglect our humanity as fellow men. This might well be called the lopsided age, in danger of toppling over because of sheer imbalance. Men have become extremely clever and competent with machines, and equally simple and incompetent when it comes to social life. There is no proportion between our mastery over things and our fruition in dealings with one another. We have much "truth" from our laboratories, but little from our associations; much goods from our factories, but little good from our fellowship; much that pleases our bodies, but little that satisfies our souls. We are losing our grip upon humanity and learning a new contempt for ourselves and our fellows. In the Babylon of the nuclear age men are being pushed aside, pushed around, and pushed under. They are being used and abused all around us. They are being subordinated to systems of machines and power, and denied the integrity and fulfillment of "intelligent creation." Even their death and destruction is nowadays contemplated with a frigidity which is in itself horrible. In short, the priority given in our time to physics and engineering over our life together is a massive violation of humanity that promises neither truth nor good for the nuclear age.

THE URGENT TASK OF CHRISTIAN THEOLOGY

What, then, is a Christian theologian to do first? Is he to look into reactors and telescopes, hoping that he may find the God of natural religion? Is he to argue "from science to God," to a generation that has the power to play God—to build and to destroy? Is he not rather to remind this same generation, many of whom bear the name "Christian," that Jesus Christ, this fellow man, is the Truth, the Way, and the Life, and that there is a truth of decisive consequence for us fellow men, which appears by our faithfulness one to another. The Christian faith is that Jesus is the Son of God; and that means, in this connection, that we are not to look elsewhere rather than to Him for our knowledge of God. This in turn means that our first business is not with our dynamos but with our fellow men, not with the moon but with the earth and its peoples. The Christian faith is a celebration of Jesus Christ and His Church. The Christian theologian is committed to this faith and to the humanism that inevitably follows from it. Therefore he is committed to the priority of Jesus Christ, as God's self-disclosure, before any other thing in heaven or on earth, including atoms and stars.

For such integrity in theology, which our intellectual situation demands of us, we need a new single-mindedness. In a new way and with a new vigor we need to try to think as Christians whose business is with Jesus Christ. To begin with, we may well have to distinguish between natural religion and the Christian faith. The two do not coincide. There is a "sense of absolute dependence" which goes with alienation from the life we have with our fellow men in this world and not with consent to it or joy in it. There is a belief in God the Creator and Providence which expresses not so much pleasure in life as misery in it, and in its anxiety turns a man not toward his neighbor but away from him. There is a love of God which is cold in love of man, a trust in God which seeks its own and not the things of others, and a knowledge of God which cares little for God's covenant of mercy and peace with His people. The God of such religion is a supernatural Power available to restive creatures, but not the living God of a people who rejoice in His faithfulness. It is His business to save men from evil; but righteousness is to Him an afterthought and a means to another good. This is the Power behind the universe sought after by natural religion, once through nature and now, presumably, through the machines of our science.

But there is another God, of Moses and Israel, of Jesus and His Church. His is not the power of the cosmic God, but the grace of the God and Father of the Lord Jesus. With Him the covenant of love comes first, because love is His life with His people, and the life itself of His people. He is the God who loves sinners and gave His Son for their redemption. He promises no happiness without communion, no freedom except in justification, no health without sanctification, and no peace without reconciliation. It is not the business of this God to prevent any and every evil, to protect us from any and every suffering, and to promote our good as seems good to our eyes. It is rather to give us freely the grace to overcome evil with good, to have joy in suffering, and to live in the peace of righteousness by hope. He does not promise or give any life, in this world or in any other, except the life of His kingdom, which subsists by His love in Christ Jesus among His people.

The knowledge of this God is by His turning to us in mercy and judgment. It is by Christ's receiving those who have rejected Him, by His honoring those who have despised Him, by His recognition of those who have ignored Him. It is correspondingly by our turning to Christ, which is repentance. This repentance is re-entry into communion, the positing again of one's neighbor and oneself as fellow men who are brothers of Jesus Christ. It is a reconciliation of those who have fallen out, a justification of the fellow man, a sanctification of the soul and the person. Repentance is the stirring of a new life in fellow men "dead in sin," and with it the emergence of a new mind without which there is no knowledge of God.

Christian doctrine—every Christian doctrine—being a modification of the doctrine of God, is properly believed, understood, and received by repentance. Especially, a man cannot say one solitary thing about the living God properly, without repentance. Take two of the best known of God's names: Creator and Father. One might say "Creator" and mean Maker, Artisan, First Cause, and so forth, by arguing about and from things in the physical world. One might say that things must have a Maker, or that cause and effect imply a First Cause, or that contingent beings point to an Ultimate Being. One might debate the language and logic of such inferences and take sides for or against them. One might do these things, as has been frequently done, without repentance; that is, without turning to Christ and His people. A man would thus "know" God but ignore his neighbor. He would express and confirm his "sense of absolute dependence," but remain independent of his brother. He would be grateful to God, but for himself and not for his neighbor. He would hope in God, but leave out his brother both in the hoping and in the thing hoped for. And if he loved God, he might well do it without loving his neighbor as himself. In short, faith in God the Creator as Maker and as Determiner of destiny, by the use of any of the traditional arguments for the existence of God, in so far as these express the logic of natural piety, has as such no connection with repentance and therefore with faith in the living God.

Faith in God according to the Christian mind, on the other hand, is inseparable from repentance. This is so because the Creator of the Christian faith is the living God who is not known as Creator or by any other name, except as the Lord God of Moses and Jesus, God of the Covenant, and the faithful God. But covenant means fellow men, and God who covenants is the Creator of fellow men. God reveals himself as the Creator in Christ's communion with His people and in the people's communion one with another. We know ourselves as creatures, in all our concrete finitude and dependence, by communion; and it is in communion that we call the living God our Creator.

The same argument holds for the other name of God: the Father. There are ways of saying "father" without repentance. We may even say "Father" in order not to repent. We may say it and mean that God is "perfectly good"; and by good we may mean that He protects from all evil and fills us with all good things. In this temper of mind, we may doubt and debate everything about our ideas of God, but we will not doubt or debate His goodness—that is, His will against evil and suffering, and for His children's unmixed happiness. It is obvious that such a belief in the fatherhood of God requires from us neither change of mind nor change of spirit. A man may have to be credulous, but he does not need to repent in order to believe in the Father of natural religion.

But who is God the Father of the Christian faith? Is He not the Father of the Son, our Brother, who died for our sin and rose again for a new life in His Church? This is the living God who is not known as the Father apart from forgiveness of sin and our adoption into the household of God. The Father is the Father of a family, and it is as members of Jesus' family that we know God as our Father. Without family there is no father, no matter how good a person called "father" may be. Natural religion seeks a "father God," but not a family of God. Therefore it knows neither the living God nor His family. Hence, in Christ Jesus, God has revealed Himself as the Father of the family of mankind.

We should look more closely into the family as reconstituted by Jesus Christ. What is a family? Certainly it is a social unit formed by marriage and procreation. Certainly in the family the father usually provides, the mother feeds and clothes, and the children are provided for, fed, and clothed. Certainly the family usually eat together, sleep in the same house, and benefit from the common economy of the household. But when all this is said, and more, it still has to be added that the members of the family may speak to each other, may care one for another, may love one another. The family is a seat of human freedom and responsibility. It calls for recognition and respect and justice. It is the place where fellow men exist as fellow men, in almost sheer dependence one upon another; and it is in the family that selfishness is at its most devastating and deadly. If in the family we know love in all its power and excellence, we also know there indifference in all its perfidy and work of despair. One hardly knows sin without the family, whose members violate one another and turn its primal joy into sorrow. The Bible, which has taught us to say "Our Father," has also taught us that we are a family of sinners, of violators who are at all times to approach both God and neighbor in repentance. Indeed, God provides. But He provides for sinners. And so it is that He is the Father.

The same is true of the other names of God, especially of his so-called natural attributes, such as His infinity and His power. Let us consider first His infinity. There are ways of speaking of it which are irrelevant to repentance. We might think: a mountain is finite; the sun is finite; a cluster of nebulae is finite; but God is infinite. The space occupied by everything is finite; and as against all things, the space occupied by God is infinite. Even overlooking the recent criticisms of the notion of space involved in such a statement, there are of course well-known difficulties with it. If God occupies infinite space, how then is the space He occupies related to the spaces of the universe and of the things in it? If He is outside them, and therefore beside them, how then is He infinite? If he contains them, how then need He be more than the sum of them all? And what if space itself be boundless? How then is there an infinite space of God? Or, is space itself God? And so on.

If we say that God is not spatial as things are spatial, the question is, how then is He spatial? We have no way of putting content into the notion of a space unlike our own. *Via negativa* ends in sheer negation. If we say that we use the word infinite analogically—that is, that God's space is both like and unlike our space, then the question is, how is it like any other space? And this question is hard to answer. If we speak of God's space using our own space as a symbol or metaphor, we hardly know what we are speaking of. Besides, symbolic utterance may be closer to religion than literal language, but it is not therefore an expression of the faith that goes with repentance. Any idea of God's space and infinity arrived at independently of His Word in Christ Jesus is incongruous with our knowledge of the living God.

God is infinite as Creator and Redeemer; as both together. He is infinite not as occupying the space of the physicists, but as the Creator of the space of His people in communion with Him and one with another. As communion differs from existence in general, so the space of communion differs from the space of the distribution of things in our cosmos. There is a space of fellow men which goes with their life together, as there are spaces of things which correspond with their motions among themselves. We may speak of space in both instances, because fellow men exist in their communion no less than things do in their interactions. But we may not confuse the two spaces. So also we may speak of God's space, and with it of His infinity, provided we do not confuse God either with fellow men or with things. God has His space, or rather *is* His space, as the Creator of His people who exist in communion under covenant. He is spatial as God and Creator, for He *is* as the Creator. He is spatial as the living God who is gracious and sustains His people against sin and all the things of sin. He is infinite as Creator and Redeemer, while we are finite as fellow men and sinners. Since God has His own space as the Creator and is not finite as a fellow man, He is infinite as the "God of grace and glory," as "God and Father of our Lord Jesus Christ." In short, God who is infinitely gracious is infinite in His space. He, and He alone, is the living God who is infinite.

The original space is the space of God's self-revelation as Creator and Redeemer; and that space is infinite. Next comes the space of our communion as God's people; and this space is finite. Then comes, in the order of knowledge, the space of things or of the universe at large; and this third space is possibly both finite and unbounded.

Let us now consider God's power and how we are to understand it in our power age. Natural religion is a celebration of God's supernatural power, or His power over physical nature. All the things

that happen in heaven and on earth with the changing seasons, bringing man weal and woe, are said to be the works of God the Omnipotent First Cause. Men who have suffered grievously from nature's
inclemencies, to be finally met by physical death, have turned beyond
nature to nature's God and by worship and entreaty sought redress
and a happy life. They have believed in an Ultimate Reality infinitely
good and infinitely powerful who alone could deliver them from
evil and keep them from it. Thus the power of God has been no less
precious to natural piety than His fatherly goodness.

Belief in such a God has produced its own insoluble problem in a
world where evil, and evils, perennially strike dumb terror into the
human soul. It has never been easy to reconcile the notion of God's
sheer goodness with that of His omnipotence. No ingenuity of the
natural mind has been, or is, capable of understanding the ways of
the God of natural theology.

Moreover, men overcome physical evil today not by petition but by
science. They reduce evils and increase goods by seeking out "second
causes," not by seeking out the First Cause. Physics, chemistry, biology, medicine, manufacture, and engineering—these are the sources
of human well-being today, and not supernatural power. Power in
the power age is from generators made by man, and not from the
Supreme Being of the religion of nature. It operates not in nature but
in a world of artifacts which, by way of our cities, is man's proper
environment. In this age, the Power of natural religion is a fatuity.
It apparently does nothing of any consequence, and men do not take
it seriously any more.

Be all this as it may, it requires neither faith nor repentance, neither
reconciliation nor love, to believe in the supernatural power of natural
religion. Whatever religious men may speak of by saying "power,"
they do not speak of the Cross and Resurrection of Jesus Christ, or of
the forgiveness of sin and the new life in the Church. But in the
Christian faith the power of God is known in the man Jesus, in His
freedom and love as a fellow man, by which the reconciliation and reunion of His people strangely occurs in faith and hope. For us Christians who by God's grace know the misery and hopelessness of mutual
violation, the prime miracle is Jesus Christ, who never ceases to evoke
our wonder and praise. The second miracle is that we do praise Him
among His people, by a renewal of our dignity as human beings and
of our integrity as fellow men. The power of God to us is the power
of God's Spirit, by whom sinners learn to forgive one another, and
there is joy and peace among them. This is the power of God without

which all other power, whether of man or of nature, is vanity, because it is the power by which we exist as fellow men in our cities and in our world at large. We know of no power of the living God apart from our life as God's people in communion. But since we exist as fellow men by communion, the first taste we have of God's own omnipotence is by His communion with us in Christ Jesus and His Church. If we are not impressed by this omnipotence, we are given no other which we may intelligently believe and freely enjoy. But it does take faith and repentance, a new being and a new mind, to see the omnipotence of God in Moses and Israel, in Jesus and His people.

The natural man is impressed by the powers of nature, and he is hardly our contemporary. The man of the city is impressed by the power of his engines, and these threaten to destroy him. The man of faith is impressed by the power of Jesus Christ in the Church. He goes rather limping between faith and religion on the one hand and between faith and autonomy on the other. But the nuclear age, in which the very existence of man is at stake, does not permit such graceless footwork. It is time to stop and follow after the Son of God and the Son of Man, so that He may lead His people to life and peace in the communion of saints.

CHRISTIAN THEOLOGY IN AN AGE OF ABSURDITY

The nuclear age has been called the age of power, the age of science, the space age, the age of anxiety. But it has not been called the age of humanity. This is the age of absurdity, in which nearly absolute power in man's hands is matched by his nearly absolute incapacity for fruition. The more methodical and ingenious science becomes, the more senseless and clumsy our politics. The more breathtaking our knowledge of atoms and stars, the less we know how to live in peace. The more the engineers succeed with our machines, the more we fail with one another. We are proficient in manipulation but deficient in love, and without love there is no humanity. The fact seems to be that love and manipulation are two different things, and one is no substitute for the other. In this age of manipulative science, manipulative economy, manipulative politics, and manipulative ethics even love is turned into manipulation, which is absurd and therefore deadly. It is one thing to commune with people, quite another to construct machines; one thing to love as a fellow man, quite another to experiment as a scientist. To confuse the method of science with the freedom of love is to practice an obscurantism beside which the darkness of the savage mind is sunrise. Man and his machines belong to two different orders of being. Christ and the dynamo cannot be subsumed under the same species of entity. If Jesus is the Son of God, then the dynamo is not even an angel of God. The living God is the God of communion, not of manipulation.

Since this age of absurdity is the outcome of the dominance of our machines over people, and since machines are creations of physical science, a theologian has to think twice before he sets out to reconstruct natural theology according to present-day knowledge of atoms and stars. The God of Einstein's science is no more likely to be the Lord than were those of Newton's and Darwin's science. A God who is the Mathematician thinking out the cosmos, or a Magician in charge of the bizarre movements within the atom, or the Generator of hydrogen atoms in the stellar spaces, may resemble the God of the Christian faith no better than did the celestial mechanic and the *élan vital*. The very existence of such gods has been debated and denied on very good grounds. In the nuclear age, when natural piety is reduced to a sense of curiosity or at best wonder, the God of science may find few worshipers indeed. Few pietists in our time are likely to study scientific theology, and fewer people are likely to be impressed by either their logic or their speculations. In any case, and to begin with, the living God is the Creator of fellow men, and the Lord God of Israel is heard and known in the common life of His people. When His covenant with the Church is neglected, He is denied and idols take His place in the minds and hearts of the people. One primary task of Christian theology in the nuclear age is to be a clear and persistent warning against the idolatry of knowledge and power set above the communion of fellow men. It must be ready for a sharp and sustained opposition to any "knowledge of God" that excludes the forgiveness of sin, and any worship of God that is not also obedience to the commandment, "You shall love your neighbor as yourself." This is not simply a matter of theology. It is also a matter of ethics, and ethics is for fellow men a matter of life and death.

There is no way from the individual theorist to the living God. Science itself, with all its knowledge and power, is a social enterprise. Our would-be solitary spectator neither exists nor knows, except as a fellow man. He does not do anything as a human being except as a fellow man. In this day of scientific institutes and organizations it should be rather painfully clear that every thinker is heavily indebted to his fellow men and every builder to his fellow workmen. It is fellow men who pursue science and investigate their universe, and it is they who ask the question of God. Since natural piety is on the decline, the very quest for God arises in our communion, and without it we neither seek nor find Him. If there be a way from science to God, the starting point for us Christians must be the Church of Jesus Christ.

Repentance, *metanoia*, today means in part a radical change in perspective, which shall enable us to see all things as fellow men. The reality of the world, the objectivity of the world, the knowability of the world, presuppose the reality, objectivity, and knowability of our fellow men, without whom we ourselves do not exist. The primary "other" is Jesus Christ, who presents us to our God and our neighbor and our world. Original ignorance, original perversity, is the pretension that we know the world, and with it God, without our life together. For this reason we may believe and understand that, if we have no God, it is because we deny that we are neighbors. This is what the Incarnation means; for there God became man in order that man might know God. This is what the mission of Jesus means; for this man was the revelation of God's grace, and therefore of God Himself. This also is what the Church means; for there the Spirit of God bears witness to the living God, as forgiven sinners forgive one another to the glory of God the Father, Son, and Holy Spirit. Thus it is that God Himself has sought us and found us, and thus it is that He would be known by us.

Nevertheless, Christian humanism today has to be a serious and informed response to the mind of the nuclear age. There is no "eternal gospel" that can be preached while we cultivate an invincible indifference to and ignorance of the spirit of our time. Certainly no theology that is not worked out in our situation will help us to hear and understand the Word of God in the Church. The theologian who thinks in this age is obligated to learn what he can of its mind. He must understand, as it were from the inside, the method of science and scientific thought. Science, and the technology that goes with it, may well be a profound and perchance radical modification of the human spirit. The theologian today is confronted with a "post-modern" man who needs a gospel appropriate to his condition—to his triumphs and troubles, his temptation, his sin and bondage, his hope and despair. The theologian may not remain aloof to all this. He needs to know it in his mind and soul, and to theologize for a Church which, willy-nilly, exists in the nuclear age and must hear the Word of God in it.

Still, little will be gained by way of some new modernism. Our first business is not to reconcile religion with science, but to set before the post-modern man the reconciliation that is in Christ Jesus in the

Church. It is not to seek, anxiously, new arguments for "belief in God, freedom, and immortality," but to remain faithful to Jesus Christ and His people. The *faux pas* of the age is that it tries to live and have peace by the power of things and not by the love of fellow men. Men see deeply and widely into things, but they are blind to their brothers. Like their machines, they see a great deal and calculate well. But they do not hear the human voice and cannot tell it from wind. In all this there is a terrible untruth and bad faith. We have nothing we have not received by way of our neighbor. It is therefore impiety, perversity, and plain wrongdoing, to seek life and good in running our machines rather than in the communion of our fellow men. This is the turning away that makes ours an age of darkness, and there can be no light except by turning again.

It does not take much insight to know how hard it is for man with his nuclear power to turn to his brother. His machine is his means of escape from his brother. Power in one's own hand is a substitute for the love for which one must always depend upon another. Even though power is no substitute for grace, and the end of it is death rather than life, it does promise limitless good and its lure is very hard to resist—so that it is easier for a camel to go through a needle's eye than for a master of the atom and of space to live as a fellow man.

There is need for a new piety of awe and faithfulness in the presence of Jesus Christ: for a human rather than a natural piety, evoked not by power but by love, not by goods but by communion; a piety that fears infidelity before it fears evil, and hopes for forgiveness before it hopes for peace and plenty; a piety of gratitude and dependence in the Church, and of freedom and joy among God's people under the covenant of grace. But such piety is a gift of the living God in the Church and can be practised only in repentance. For this reason, as I have tried to explain, theology for the nuclear age must above all be a theology of repentance, in that age of science which is also the era of power.

16

The God of the Bible
Versus Naturalism

CARL F. H. HENRY

IN THE SUMMER OF 1961 *The American Scholar* CARRIED A
stimulating essay on "The Evasions of Modern Theology." Rabbi
Samuel Sandmel characterizes the manner of modern theology as perceptive and poetic, clever and cute—terms, he says, that are "necessary for appraising the works of even such men as Reinhold Niebuhr,
Martin Buber, Paul Tillich, Karl Barth and Rudolf Bultmann." However, the substance of modern theology, he complains, seldom has
lasting satisfaction. It is neither relevant to the modern plight nor does
it confront contemporary thinkers in any significant way. "I want the
theologian to enlighten me on what I should think and what I should
do," he states. "I want him to grapple with Darwin, and Freud, and
Marx, and atomic power, in the public arena where I can look on—
and this I do not find him disposed to do. I still read the theologians.
But more and more I find startlingly little substance or relevancy."

Such a judgment on recent theology should disturb us deeply. The
Christian doctrine of God, after all, has held clear relevance for the
spirit of every successive period of Western thought. Not only has
the fire of its meaning withered the shallow roots of man-centered
utopian expectations; it has also illuminated times of dark despair
with bright promise and hope. What about today? Does the Christian
doctrine of God burn with inescapable heat into the fiber of modern
thought and action?

The issue is not whether unbelieving critics still argue against the
God of the Bible. From age to age they have hurled their competing
ideologies against one aspect and then another of the Christian view

225

of God. Take for convenience' sake that remarkable Westminster Catechism definition, "God is a Spirit, infinite, eternal and unchangeable, in his being, wisdom, power, holiness, justice, goodness, and truth." Not only one, but each term readily calls to mind some great theological-philosophical struggle waged over the nature of God. In the history of Western thought one familiar attribute after another has become a battlefield where lively skirmishes marked the conflict between sacred and secular views of ultimate reality. Each time the Westminster definition comes to a comma, one senses how much is at stake in properly delineating the divine perfections over against their secular and speculative dismissal as arbitrary and irrelevant.

Is God really *Spirit*—immaterial, invisible reality? Materialists said no. Their material alternatives—stuff—ultimates of one sort or another (in ancient times "indeterminate matter," in modern times "neutral entities" or "space-time" and so on)—took their place one by one in the horror chamber of false gods, until at last dialectical materialism openly went anti-God.

Is God really *infinite*? John Stuart Mill in the nineteenth century and Edgar S. Brightman in the twentieth worshiped a finite deity. But the tide of philosophy soon passed them by on the premise that a finite God is no God at all.

Is God really *eternal* and *unchanging*? No, said those who revered evolutionism as divine and meshed all reality into the time process. Since Darwin, however, the alternatives have sharpened. Either one makes evolution a secret god, as do the Marxists in dialectical materialism, and thereby rejects unchanging morality, eternal truth, and everything fixed and final. Or one exempts from change and decay such realities as truth and right, and thus acknowledges an eternal mind and morality.

In our own time the crisis of theology runs far deeper than in all previous centuries of Western thought. No longer is Christianity engaged simply in a life-and-death struggle against conflicting philosophies of the nature of the supernatural world. Rather, the coalition of spiritual ignorance and disinterest in doctrine with materialistic secularism, naturalistic philosophy, and Communist social theory now requires theological decision by the Western world at every significant level of thought and life. No longer does the debate concern only this or that activity of God, or this or that attribute of God. It reverberates, rather, through the whole province of theology. The debate requires not merely choosing between gods; it demands decision for or against the supernatural as such, for or against deity, however defined. At stake is a choice between the God of the Bible and human nihilism.

MAN-MADE GODS

Because our generation has lost so much of its Christian heritage, theology's most important problem, namely, the precise definition of God, seems to many people an impractical and esoteric pursuit. While modern man zestfully explores outer space, he seems quite content to live in a spiritual kindergarten and to play in a moral wilderness.

The spiritual shallowness that characterizes modern secular man now reveals but few traces of doctrine once supplied by the Christian faith. His deliberate spirit of detachment from the theological heritage of the Bible has sealed off more and more of the deep historic foundations of inherited beliefs. The loss of his belief in God as World-Ruler —hence of the divine governance of the world—has been matched by a lost sense of the divine control of natural processes. To lose God as mankind's Judge and Redeemer has both silenced holy condemnation of the primary evil that saturates the world and darkens our own hearts, and also orphaned a wayward race in its dreamland of secular rescue and progress. In his desire to control the universe man repeatedly puts himself in God's place, but the idea of God's Son as substitute in man's place he dismisses as incredible nonsense. The loss of God the Peacemaker, moreover, leaves a vacuum that promptly attracts many secular substitutes. Among them are leagues of pagan nations whose own need of healing disqualifies them from ministering to each other's distress. Such spiritual decline has prepared the way for assorted totalitarian tyrants. Claiming to be the great I AM, these self-styled deliverers promise to release mankind from earthly bondage and redirect history into some new course. These spurious claims become popular as secular man surrenders awareness of God's predestinating purpose and original and basic divine intention in creation. Harassed and foundering, he gives full devotion to evolutionary emergence, economic determinism, and other false explanations of life.

But even greater troubles lie ahead for those who bypass full knowledge of the one true God. Impoverished notions of deity that no longer express the inherent glory of God soon take shape; they represent merely some nebulous and assumed divine relationship to man and the world and make no real effort to realize the multiplicity of divine perfections in their biblical fullness. The fading conviction of the Lord's glory quickly becomes just some indefinable awareness of divinity, a shadowy mass of abstractions. God hovers about as Eternal Wisdom, First Cause, Omnipresent Will, Infinite Power, and so on. The resulting image has no true likeness whatever to the biblical revelation of the living God. But secular philosophers and scientists often expound these confused concepts of God with proud piety. Given to speculation and postulation, they ignore the divine triunity and God's predestinating will, justice, and mercy as only marginal mysteries; they overlook man's predicament in sin and evade his need of saving grace. Particularly misunderstood in the vague pronouncements about "the riddle of ultimate reality" is the fact that to delete the divine perfections is actually to deny both the fullness of God's being and the sovereignty of His revelation. Scientism also frequently invents and enthrones its own pseudo-divinities—all incapable, however, of creation, covenant, prophecy, promise, incarnation, atonement, or resurrection. On such a basis, secular man finds it easy to glory in his conquest of nature or to extol man himself as the highest of all known beings. This lack of belief in the living God and failure to expound His scripturally revealed purposes have led to what may be called the fatal paralysis of today's higher learning. For all its sophisticated delight in modern civilization, this age has regressed to a subtle form of polytheism. No serious scholar, of course, would deliberately champion a plurality of gods in the ancient pagan sense. A visit to many American universities, however—even to some divinity schools —will reveal that many influential teachers sharply disagree over the definition of ultimate reality and actually cultivate faith in an assortment of deities. Such pantheons of divinities on our campuses escape death by ridicule only because limited study schedules expose students to no more than four or five competing God-concepts in a single semester. Were we to line up all the views of deity promulgated on some large campuses, we would soon discover that many more ultimate principles or gods govern our neopagan world than ever functioned in the world of ancient polytheism. Not the absence of gods, but rather the acceptance of a plurality of conflicting divinities in the name of academic openmindedness, defines the modern dilemma.

This commitment to false gods goes even deeper. Not only does modern man fashion his own deities; he also retains a sense of dedication to what he calls the divine. While he may disallow the biblical concept of God, his Christian heritage perpetuates a desire for personal relationship. This feeling he transfers to postulated divinities. Civilized man therefore not only nurtures false deities, but also stresses the need to obey and to honor them. It is man's own ideals that both create and reflect whatever he considers such divine patterns of being. Even in high academic circles, moreover, secular man looks to these postulated divine powers for all sorts of benefits. Through such modern secular faiths he covenants even with Hitlers and Khrushchevs instead of confessing his disobedience to the One God who truly commands us and covenants with us. He prefers man's perishable, transient words to an unalterable Word of divine revelation; he prefers alliances with tyrants to reconciliation with God, union with men of bad faith to union with the God who has sworn to be faithful.

Whatever sincere motivations the pseudo-gods may sustain in man, whatever deep reverence they may promote, whatever ardent zeal they may inspire, we must consider these powers not as friend but as foe. These man-made gods remind us of their makers; like the Greco-Roman nobility of old, they masquerade in a righteousness of self-divinity and self-sufficiency. They mirror man's unyielding pride and his natural incapacity for mercy. Because their very exaltation is a lie, these pseudo-gods are incapable of self-humiliation. They do not become "God in our stead" because, apart from sovereign grace, fallen man's imagination cannot comprehend true humility.

Our age is passionately devoted to such causes of togetherness as the United Nations, NATO, SEATO, the Arab League; to labor unions, even church union movements and ecumenical assemblies. It seems remarkably disinterested, however, in that priority-holding alliance of the New Testament, namely, man's union with Christ. The tyranny to which Western minds now often submit results from fusing and confusing spiritual ideals with secular or man-made programs whose main interest in Jesus Christ is simply exploiting the propaganda value of His name.

SECULAR VIEWS OF THE SUPERNATURAL

In recent centuries secular rather than biblical ideas of the supernatural have often been supported by influential churchmen within the Christian community as well as by unaffiliated scholars. Supposedly Christian thinkers thus have joined in the modern attack upon the biblical revelation of the Creator and His creation. This ecclesiastical revolt against the traditional view of God has taken may forms. Scholars have attached specific limitations to God's being; or they have compromised His independence of the universe; or they have stipulated in advance the necessary course of His actions. They have thereby curtailed the primary creative freedom of God, on the one hand, and have postulated man's boundless freedom on the other. We have already noted the inner relationship between such limitation of God and the assertion of man's self-determination. Once man claims the prerogative of legislating the acts of deity and no longer lets God fix the limits of human possibility, and the creature inevitably exalts himself above his Creator.

Modern attempts, like that of the late Shailer Mathews, to explain the concept of God as King of the universe as a mere oblique postulation from man's experience of earthly rulers in Old Testament times were perverse misinterpretations of theological truth. Speculations which thus rested faith in God's lordship on mere human analogies were inadequate to portray the absolute and infinite marks of the sovereign Lord, namely, creation *ex nihilo*, preservation of the universe, and power over man's destiny both in life and in death, including the future resurrection and judgment. The construction of such arbitrary views has a wholly natural or normal explanation, however. The appropriateness of designating God as Lord became less and less compatible with modern democratic egalitarian idealism. Emphasis on man's freedom and indeterminateness required a humanistic theology that dethroned God as sovereign ruler of the universe. Only when man's self-deceived spirit truly confesses that God is Lord, that He alone holds sway over man's body and soul, in life or in death—only then does man's enslaved condition and need for the sovereign Creator's liberating and redeeming work become fully apparent.

Superimposing speculative ideas on the historic view, liberal thought dressed the Christian God in trappings borrowed from secular divinities. Some theologians did not hesitate to depict God's power as finite. As for wrath, they said, either dissociate it from God's nature or deploy it in the service of divine love. God's grace, moreover, became a matter of man's subjective attitude rather than an objective reality that resolves personal guilt. Gone was the supernatural deliverer out of Egypt, the giver of the Law, the God of Israel, the hope of the prophets, the God of Sinai and Zion, the God who speaks and acts for Himself. Liberal theologians proclaimed their reconstructed deity to be the more obviously "real" God because philosophical method presumably supplied more persuasive ideas about ultimate reality than did the "device" of special divine revelation. Consequently the exposition of God's nature fell decisively under the well-turned adjectives of the worldly-wise philosophers of religion. Modernist scholars came to caricature the idea of special divine revelation; for them divine disclosure meant simply progressive insight. God's self-revelation of His absolute and infinite lordship they arbitrarily set aside. They deflected any encroachment of divine revelation by first of all referring every question about the nature and knowability of God to the modernistic consciousness. That is, the possibility of knowing God they rested not on God's self-revelation, but rather on the tolerance of modernist presuppositions. After deflating every "thus saith the Lord" to a "thus saith the prophet" or "thus saith the apostle," these thinkers then stuffed their own words and pronouncements into the vacuum they had created by peremptorily dismissing the Word of God. Divine disclosure and declaration were changed to human interrogation. "Yea, hath God said . . . ?" The authority of Holy Scripture was appealed to only to dissolve it, and isolated passages were divested of their meaning in context in order to support some erroneous notion of divinity. Thus in the professed household of faith a mortal attack was inflicted upon the Christian revelation of God. In place of the revealed God appeared the reconstituted God.

Nor did liberal theology substitute for the violated Christian doctrine only one new concept of God. Rather, it replaced the biblical doctrine by a score of alternative and competitive concepts. Their variableness and impermanence have never been more apparent than in the modern aftermath of the revolt against the Christian revelation of the Creator-Redeemer God. Eventually both the weight of self-contradiction and the counterwitness of the Bible disqualified this cacophony of independent voices. Some divinity scholars were forced to ever greater suppression of God's witness in order to reinforce their own. While they presumed to speak for Jesus Christ, they actually withstood His witness. But even when speculative gods differed sharply from the biblical God, the fear of idolatry was nowhere expressed. In this confusion and disagreement over dogma, many liberals saved face by the only course that seemed open to them: they demoted the significance of theological doctrine and made spiritual obedience the sole principle of Christian faith. The essence of Christian experience was defined as volitional trust, no matter how conflicting the intellectual definitions of the religious object of that trust might be.

NEO-ORTHODOXY

Against the arbitrary restriction of God to the world-process with its tags of immanence and pantheism one could expect a radical reaction sooner or later. And indeed the whole movement from Kierkegaard through Barth to Bultmann has for its credo the transcendence, freedom, and otherness of God. The demand for existential obedience, the newly emphasized "virtue" of naked faith, the dialectical insistence on "paradox," and the ecumenical emphasis on Christian togetherness canceled much of the widening uneasiness over doctrinal differences. That existential or dialectical theologizing as much as theological rationalism might do battle against the living God was scarcely suspected.

In place of the voiceless God now emerges the stuttering God, a self-disclosing divinity whose disability could only reinforce man's uncertainty concerning the nature and work of Deity. Within the motif of transcendence the existential-dialectical thinkers diverged from each other upon very different paths. We mention as examples only Gogarten's espousal and Barth's rejection of existentialism, and Bultmann's rejection of redemptive history. All agree in declaring God's utter freedom over against man. What is more, they do so in a reactionary rather than strictly biblical way; that is, they exaggerate, they overstate the transcendence of God in relation to His created universe. This overassertion of God's freedom therefore involves new difficulties for contemporary theology. Among its vexing problems are the image of God in man; the form and content of general revelation; the relation of revelation to reason, to history, and to nature. Inevitable, of course, is the question how Jesus of Nazareth and His teaching are to be defined in respect to divine disclosure. It is no surprise that the exciting but tedious effort to adjust such tensions within existential and/or dialectical premises should eventually face shipwreck through obstacles not wholly different from those on which modernism foundered. In the one theology, the shallows of immanence, in the other, the overpowering forces of transcendence, loosed the exposition of divine freedom from its proper scriptural controls.

The "theologian of revelation" was able to arm himself with many of the tenets of biblical theology. What he professed to "hear" in the encounter with God, however, was in its main features merely an echo of prophetic-apostolic revelation. Even when he denied the priority of this echo he gained respect as a biblical theologian for a season because what he professed to hear afresh coincided with the prophetic-apostolic witness. But his new-found prestige was short-lived; theological competitors who appealed to the same revelational encounter professed to hear the novel and bizarre. The theology of the Word of God has its Barth and Brunner, but also its Tillich and

Bultmann. It should surprise few students of the theological scene therefore that alert observers find little permanent substance and relevance in much that grips Protestant passions in the crisis of contemporary thought. Since no theologian of contemporary confrontation can claim a monopoly on spiritual encounters, even a theology of revelation may range itself against the self-revealing God.

Neo-orthodoxy pointed a rebuking finger at prideful modernism for conceiling the fact that God speaks! But how can neo-orthodoxy defend as piety its own rejection of revealed concepts and words which the biblical writers repeatedly and unhesitatingly attribute to His speaking? In neither theological situation was the deciding principle really the protection of divine or of human freedom. Twentieth-century interpreters simply considered themselves better qualified than the original recipients of God's revelation to define the manner and content of His communication to the ancient prophets and apostles. It was therefore an inadequate doctrine of the inspiration and authority of Scripture that betrayed twentieth-century theology into unworthy, unstable, and unauthorized views of the Christian God.

GOD AND REASON

We noted earlier the complaint that much contemporary theology lacks substance and relevance, and it has been stressed that the prime task of theology is the precise exposition of the nature of God. I have commented on the fact that in our time secularism no longer aims its attacks at this or that divine activity or attribute, but now lunges against every facet of the Christian doctrine of God. We see that secular modern man has sealed off most of the biblical revelation of God, and his substitutes are so many and so diverse as to constitute a pattern of modern polytheism more confusing than that of the ancient pagan world. Within the Church itself modernism contributed to this decline by its rejection of special revelation and its flirtation with many concepts of God. We have seen that, whereas modernism exaggerates the immanence of God, neo-orthodoxy exaggerates divine transcendence in a reactionary manner; and the neo-orthodox recovery of special revelation is vulnerable through its failure to exhibit the rationality and objectivity of divine revelation. Now it is time to emphasize that the aspect of the doctrine of God most neglected today—in an age of widening irrationalism—is that of the intellectual attributes of God, and such theological neglect not only does an injustice to the content of the Christian religion, but lends an inexcusable advantage to non-Christian world-life views.

If some one shaft of radiance above many others in the Christian doctrine of God can challenge the swift-falling darkness of our times, it is the biblical reinforcement of the place of reason. It would be easy to mistake such a comment for mere rationalism that banishes the fact and necessity of a transcendent revelation of God, ignores the depravity of the human will, foregoes the need of supernatural grace, and fails to find the center of the Christian religion in the person and work of Jesus Christ, God's only Son. Such rationalism was precisely the error of modern idealistic philosophy, an error so pernicious that it neglected the realities of special revelation and redemption. No such deviation is intended. We affirm the self-revealing God to be rational, the eternal source and ground of truth. We affirm that the Logos is integral to the Godhead, that God reveals Himself rationally, that is, in intelligible propositions. We affirm that the inspired Scriptures authoritatively record divinely revealed truth about God and His purposes, that the Holy Spirit uses this truth to persuade and to convict. We affirm that the Christian message seeks from man in the world not only a response of will and feeling, but also the assent of his intellect. Strangely enough, Protestantism now abandons this balanced proclamation of the Christian religion to the evangelicals, and reproaches fundamentalist Christianity for rationalism. Actually, of course, evangelicalism is thus but continuing the historic Protestant promulgation of the gospel. Proclamation of the intellectual attributes of God and warning to the fast-fading twentieth century about its neglect of God's rationality and truth are urgently needed. By its emphasis on rational revelation, biblical religion promotes respect for the intelligibility of reality and experience. The cardinal importance of this fact is self-evident if Christianity is to compete with secular views of life and history in the public arena, rather than simply in the private realm of feeling and decision.

A theology for the nuclear age concerns more than the atoms as such, for the world of the atom now involves to an unprecedented degree the crucially related concerns of human worth, survival, and destiny. If modern theology is to be relevant by grappling with "Darwin, and Freud, and Marx, and atomic power," then this requirement can be met only by comprehensively relating God's being and purpose to all existence and human decision. To proclaim a view of men and things controlled by the biblical disclosure of divine decision and deed is one thing; to shape an up-to-the-minute view of divinity fitted to the perpetually-in-process-of-revision theories of the world and man is quite another. Most lacking—and something that many contemporary theologians have stifled—is just such a comprehensive exposition of the Christian revelation. If one's belief about God means anything, it should bear decisively on one's view of creation, reconciliation, and redemption. If Christian dogmatics blur this relationship, then the doctrine of God veers from its biblical orbit and falls into the gravitational sphere of secular assumptions. Such limited propulsion of scriptural teaching soon loses one aspect or another of doctrine concerning man's origin, nature, renewal, and destiny. Sound theology must expound the whole truth about God's nature and work; it must maintain the centrality of His self-revelation in anthropology and soteriology, ecclesiology and eschatology. If, therefore, we really seek to heal the doctrinal disorders of the Christian community and to cleanse the Church's thought-life of secular speculations, only a recovery of the reality and nature of the specially revealed God, and a fresh grasp of His divine will and way, can achieve this purification.

In the world of culture and of thought, irrationalism today strikes like a venomous serpent. It augurs not merely "man at the end of his tether," as H. G. Wells put it, but "verities without validity" and "mind without meaning." The irrationalistic reaction of Western speculative philosophy against Hegelian rationalism first captured the mentality of European Protestantism through the theological influence of Søren Kierkegaard. Later, in the early decades of the twentieth century, influential Protestant theologians (Barth, Brunner, and Bultmann among them) and philosophers of religion (Niebuhr and Tillich) espoused the so-called "dialectical" theology with its distinctive premise that ultimate reality, the "real" world, confronts the human mind in logically irreconcilable terms. This dogma to supersede all other dogmas became the secret idol of Protestant intellectuals in flight from the rational God. By resorting to the divine Logos without benefit of logic they deepened even more the retreat of reason from religious experience. The Apostle Paul's somber verdict on the errant Gentiles of the first century was that (as classically translated in the familiar King James Version) they had changed "the truth of God into a lie" (Rom. 1:25). Twentieth-century theologians instead have changed the truth of God into a paradox.

The so-called post-modern mind is biased against an objectively ordered world of nature, against the intellectual integration of man's total experience, against the exposition of a rational world-life view. This revolt against rationality and its alternative resignation to ultimate unpattern stem directly from a distrust of reason. The human species cannot permanently espouse the abrogation of reason, however. To do so implies man's self-suicide; to live deliberately in a context of rational and moral chaos and noncomformity is to deny his available rescue from unregeneracy. To remain forever on holiday from fixed rational and moral truths is not peculiarly modern, but it is abnormal and lunatic. What separates this beatnik mood from the manic-depressive is simply the difference between deliberate and involuntary commitment to the irrational and incoherent.

Only a "conventional plot" with the rational maker of an intelligible universe and man fashioned in his Creator's rational-moral image can restore order, meaning, and value to the life of post-Christian man. For if the Logos in fact creates and constitutes a rational universe, if the divine Word absolutely originates what He articulates, and normatively articulates what He originates, then the ontological significance of both reason and goodness is vindicated.

The empirical orientation of contemporary philosophy's scientific, mathematical, and logical concepts exposes them to inevitable revision. Moreover, unless justified by higher criteria, they are also doomed to obsolescence. For beyond the empirical applicability of logic the thinking inquirer must face such deeper questions as the rational status of the objects of our experience, and the unity of knowledge that underlies the scientific search for some comprehensive explanatory principle. Even the post-modern mind is inevitably driven back, therefore, to the one persistent problem, namely, to discover the primary relationship between logic and mind and reality. Does meaning have a supernatural basis? Is human experience logically structured on the fact that man bears the *imago Dei* by creation? Why can the universe be conceptually experienced? How shall we account for the deductive element in science? And what is the relationship between human thought and an independently real world? Such re-evaluation of recent theories of knowledge involves the necessity for re-examining the biblical view of truth and meaning.

Doubt that the real world can be rationally grasped, together with the scientific tendency to limit this real world to phenomenal experience, has distressing consequences not confined to the modern philosophy of science. In the world's great struggle between barbarian reliance on force and the more civilized reliance on persuasion, such irrationalism bequeaths an almost insuperable advantage to the Communist world. For while the Communists rely on revolution and force to gain their ends, they reinforce this militaristic strategy with the rationale of dialectical materialism as the comprehensive canopy for all life's needs and experiences. Communist dogma therefore appeals to man's reason, an appeal the neo-orthodox theologians, like many modernist theologians before them, have outlawed. According to Edwin A. Burtt in *Man Seeks the Divine,* the Christian missionary's banner cry, "Ours is the saving truth, and the only saving truth," now rallies Communists to faith in economic determinism and in ultimate victory of the proletariat. The point is this: to depreciate reason in presenting the Christian faith creates a vacuum which Communism not only gladly occupies, but occupies to the strategic disadvantage of supernatural apologetics. Pagan philosophies that attack the objectivity of rational and moral distinctions and subvert truth and morality to promote their own goals can be met only by a truly coherent and consistent world-life view that rests on biblical premises.

In reviving the doctrine of divine revelation, recent theology, unfortunately, has failed to espouse and vindicate rational revelation. Theology may properly warn us against bisecting the one divine revelation by exaggerated concentration on either general or special disclosure. And it is always timely to hear anew the Bible's witness to the unique redemption in Jesus Christ. It is also necessary to kindle fresh fires of Christian experience in a backslidden Church. But theologians dare not neglect the rational attributes of God; they dare not detach the holy prophets' and apostles' "thus saith the Lord" from thought and language; they dare not divorce the Christ they worship from Jesus of Nazareth; they dare not equivocate over the inspiration and authority of the Bible. To do so not only opposes the witness of Scripture, but in this tragic death-hour of civilization also evades modern culture's deepest question. Among today's countless problems, the same timeless query consistently pushes for attention: "What is truth?" If God is truth, theologians have ever less and less time to say so once again. If they do, they will move from oblique dialogue to death-dealing denial of Darwin, Freud, and Marx, and beyond this to the only life-giving alternative. In every age, including our nuclear age, only God in Christ is able to reconcile the world unto Himself.

Format by Katharine Sitterly
Set in Linotype Times Roman
Composed, printed and bound by The Haddon Craftsmen, Inc.
HARPER & ROW, PUBLISHERS, INCORPORATED